TELL ME
A STORY

ALSO BY CASSANDRA KING CONROY

The Same Sweet Girls' Guide to Life
Moonrise
Queen of Broken Hearts
The Same Sweet Girls
The Sunday Wife
Making Waves

TELL ME A STORY

My Life with Pat Conroy

CASSANDRA KING CONROY

WILLIAM MORROW
An Imprint of HarperCollinsPublishers

HarperCollins books may be purchased for educational, business, or sales promotional use. For information, please email the Special Markets Department at SPsales@harpercollins.com.

A hardcover edition of this book was published by William Morrow, an imprint of HarperCollins Publishers.

FIRST WILLIAM MORROW PAPERBACK EDITION PUBLISHED 2020.

Designed by William Ruoto

Library of Congress Cataloging-in-Publication Data has been applied for.

ISBN 978-0-06-294340-8

23 24 25 26 27 LBC 7 6 5 4 3

To Patrick

TELL ME
A STORY

PROLOGUE

I don't remember driving home, but I must have. My car, which had been in the hospital parking lot for most of the day, was now in the garage. It was January, but I wasn't cold as I walked from my car to the front door. Or maybe I was. I have no memory of going from car to house either. It had been a horrific day that started with an ambulance taking my husband, half delirious with pain, to our local hospital, and it had ended with a devastating diagnosis. Now, I was back in the safety of our house.

But not for long. I had come home to pack our suitcases for another ambulance drive. This one would be taking my husband to Atlanta, five hours away, even though a winter storm was heading that way as well. It'd be a race to see who got there first, the ambulance or the snow. Later I'd learn that the storm easily won.

But I wasn't thinking of snow and the hazardous drive, except somewhere in a corner of my mind. I was trying hard not to think anything at all. If I stopped long enough to think, I wasn't sure what would happen. I could lose it, fall to pieces. That rarely happened to me, but this was different. I'd always been stoic to a fault.

Stiff upper lip and all that crap. Never let them see you sweat. I had a tendency to push the pain down so far that the surface remained calm and collected. Thankfully, I was numb as I entered the house in the late afternoon light of a winter sun. The shock of my husband's diagnosis had hit me hard, like a splat of cold water that takes your breath away. It shouldn't have. I should've seen it coming. Maybe I knew all along but wouldn't let myself acknowledge it, but it didn't feel that way. It felt like I'd been blindsided, slammed by the proverbial Mack truck.

The ER doctor had been kind. He was from New York originally, he told us, and was still adjusting to the South. Our family doctor, with the fabulous Dickensian name Lucius Laffitte, had arrived soon after his office hours. Dr. Laffitte's familiar presence immediately comforted me, or would have, if comfort had been possible. It wasn't as if I hadn't known why the ER doctor had ordered the MRI. Earlier that week, my husband's CAT scan had shown something suspicious in the area of the pancreas. "Pancreatitis?" I'd asked the gastro doctor. My voice must've held a hopeful desperation that he'd heard too many times in his profession. He had not been able to reassure me, though he'd tried, avoiding eye contact.

Both the ER doctor and Dr. Laffitte had been on the phone since getting the results of the MRI. It had been the ER doctor who had delivered the bad news as our grim-faced doctor stood by his side. There was a growth on the pancreas, along with numerous spots on the liver. "A growth?" I echoed in disbelief. The gastro doctor had mentioned it only as a possibility, the worst-case scenario.

"What's a pancreas?" my husband, Pat, asked. A large man with shoulders the width of the bed his IV was hooked up to, he and the bed took up most of the space in the crowded ER cubicle. His question wasn't facetious; it was just Pat. He took little interest in matters of health. Or rather, he'd only developed an interest in the past few years, after a scare had forced a major lifestyle change. For three years, he'd been living healthier than any of us ever thought he could be. He'd stopped drinking, was eating well, exercising every day, losing weight, and looking bright-eyed and happy. And now this. The irony was too much to take in. Later Pat told the doctors that healthy living would kill you quicker than anything.

As doctors are prone to do, the ER guy began to sketch on a pad, reducing our fears to a stick figure with strange little squiggles here and there. Pat and I listened intently as the next gruesome procedure, a biopsy, was laid out. Dr. Laffitte left to begin the calls. Beaufort Memorial, where we were, didn't do liver biopsies. Even if they did, there were no rooms here. It was January, and everyone in South Carolina was apparently in the hospital. No beds were available in nearby Charleston at the university medical complex either. At least we had a cubicle here, we were told. In Charleston, patients were lined up on cots in the hallways of the ER. Although Pat was too ill to be sent home, we'd spent most of the day taking up space now needed for other emergencies. It was a bad time to be sick.

After what seemed like forever, an ambulance was lined up to transport Pat to Emory Hospital in Atlanta. His youngest daughter worked there and had arranged everything after my frantic call for help. As all things Conroy tend to be, the whole drama quickly turned into a comedy of errors. A rare snowstorm was approaching Atlanta fast. The South dealt with snow by closing everything down, even major highways. No local ambulance drivers would go to Atlanta with snow coming. Plus it was late afternoon, with the unwelcome prospect of driving in the dark if something wasn't done soon.

Suddenly a bearded giant of an ambulance driver showed up with a stretcher about half the size of the ER bed that Pat had been on for hours. Grinning broadly, he told us he had just moved here from Michigan and wasn't afraid of a little snow. Southerners were nuts, he added, and I wanted to hug his neck for such an astute observation. When I left the hospital to get our suitcases, I knew Pat would be in good hands.

Or at least he should be with the capable-looking ambulance driver. The friends of ours whom I'd left with Pat were another matter altogether. Bernie, and then another friend, Mina, had arrived about the same time after I'd called family and friends to report what was going on. Both of them were shaky with apprehension but trying to put up a good front. They were a study in contrasts. Mina, a lithe but muscular Japanese woman, was Pat's personal trainer, and Bernie, a stocky little Jewish guy, his best friend since high school. Mina was stern and serious and business-like while Bernie had been, and remained at age seventy, the class clown.

Poor Pat, I thought as Bernie came bustling in cracking jokes, determined to make him laugh. And even as sick as Pat was, it worked. His mood lightened as though the words *liver biopsy* and *mass on pancreas* had never been spoken. Mina pushed me firmly out the door and told me to go home and get the suitcase. Mister Pat, as she called him in her broken English, would be fine until I got back. She could massage his shoulders and make him feel better. It was going to be all right, Miss Cassandra. I was not to worry. Worry was very bad for you.

At home, my numbness carried me through the packing. It was hard to imagine snow as I stared blankly into the chest of drawers where our sweaters were. I didn't even own a coat; the winters were so mild in the Lowcountry. Shawls or light wraps were sufficient. Pat had a jacket, thankfully, hanging in the downstairs closet. I couldn't remember what he'd worn when the ambulance came that morning. Did he even have on shoes? I couldn't remember anything. I'd catch myself standing with a piece of clothing in my hand, staring into space, then have to literally shake myself to get back to the task at hand. I have no idea what I packed.

I carried our two overnight bags downstairs and set them by the door. Then I wondered if I'd packed enough. Surely we'd be home in a day or two! But the weather was supposed to change, and if we ended up staying longer we'd need different clothes. I'd heard folks at the hospital talking about it. First the freak snowstorm, then in a couple of days the weather would be almost seventy. On top of everything else, global warming was sending us a message to ignore at our own peril.

I stood by the front door with my hand on the doorknob to have what felt like one last look at the house that Pat and I loved so fiercely. In April, it'd be four years since we moved into this cozy home perched on a bluff overlooking a tidal creek. Our lives had been so peaceful since then, despite the usual troubles that all of us face as we make our way through the perilous journey of life. Within the span of three years, I'd lost both my father and my youngest sister, who had also been my dearest friend. I couldn't bear to lose anyone else. The thought terrified me, and I turned quickly to go. Neither could I stand to be away from Pat for more than a minute. It was crazy, as though my being there would change the outcome of anything, but I couldn't help myself. I'd only been gone a few minutes but was panicky at the thought that they might take him away before I got back to the hospital.

When my gaze swept by the kitchen, I dropped my hand from the doorknob. It hit me that neither of us had eaten anything all day. That wouldn't do. I wasn't hungry but felt weak and in need of something to keep me going. Since Christmas Pat hadn't been able to hold down anything except smoothies. But he'd need something for the five-hour ambulance drive, and I had a small thermos that'd be just the thing. I'd make him a smoothie before I left.

The kitchen was our domain, mine and Pat's. In our eighteen years of marriage, we'd navigated it together until we'd settled into a routine that suited us both. I did the everyday cooking, and Pat was brought in for special occasions. It was too exhausting otherwise. He had an exuberant personality and larger-than-life presence; unsurprisingly, he prepared meals in much the same way. We could've fed half of Beaufort with the dishes he fixed—large robust stews, huge platters of pasta that he'd learned to cook when he lived in Italy, salad greens tossed in a bowl the size of a washtub. I'd been flummoxed not to find any small bowls or containers in his house when I first moved in, until I realized that Pat had no need for them.

I threw yogurt, frozen berries, protein powder, and a banana in the thermos then whipped it to mush with a hand blender. The smoothie done, I opened the fridge to see what to take for myself. Only when I uncovered a pot did I remember. Had it only been yesterday that I'd made chicken and dumplings in an effort to tempt Pat's failing appetite? After the harrowing events of the day, I'd totally forgotten. Although one of my and Pat's favorite dishes, my chicken and dumplings were such a pain to fix that we rarely had them. But God, were they good! Without bothering with a fork, I fished out several dumplings with my fingers and ate them cold. Figuring that'd keep me going the rest of the day, I closed the fridge and grabbed the thermos.

At the door I set the thermos down next to my purse and suitcases to make one last bathroom run before leaving for Atlanta. I wouldn't be allowed to ride in the ambulance and would need to put the pedal to the metal to follow it, they'd told me. En route to the bathroom I couldn't resist pausing by the wide expanse of glass doors in the back of our living room. Just beyond the bluff, sunbeams sparkled on the wide, slow-moving creek like a scattering of crushed diamonds, and my breath caught at the sight. Late afternoon, leading into sunset, was our favorite time here. Pat and I would stand together in reverent silence to watch the movements and changing colors of the creek. Often, he would reach for my hand.

With that thought, I staggered backward and reached blindly for the sofa. I didn't make it. Instead I found myself slumped on the floor, rocking back and forth with both hands over my face. I heard a godawful wail, like that of a wounded animal, and it took me a minute to know it was coming from me. With no one to witness my pain, no reason to hold it in, I curled up on the floor and cried loud, gasping sobs until there were no tears left.

I have no idea how long I lay there, dazed and spent, until I pulled myself together. Despair had caught me by surprise, but it wouldn't happen again. After several deep breaths I got up, wiped my eyes, and walked away. More than anything I wanted to go back to *before*. I wanted to be sitting on the sofa with Pat as we watched the sunset. I wanted us to fix dinner together while we talked about our day, and how our writing had gone. At the door, I picked up my stuff and went outside without looking back.

CHAPTER 1

START AT THE BEGINNING

It began one cold evening in February 1995, when I met the famed author Pat Conroy at a party in Birmingham, Alabama. He was at the height of success for a writer; after dominating the bestseller list for months, his blockbuster 1986 novel, *The Prince of Tides*, had been made into a movie with Barbra Streisand and Nick Nolte in 1991, nominated in seven categories at the 1992 Oscars.

If I'd arrived at the party a few minutes later, Pat and I would've missed each other altogether. Later, we'd claim that fate brought us together, because of the near misses and coincidences of the way it happened. Pat had flown in that afternoon from New York, where he'd been working on the final rewrites of his upcoming book, *Beach Music*. He'd come to Birmingham to receive an award at a literary conference. He hadn't wanted to interrupt his editing, had tried to get out of making the trip, but his publicist wouldn't let him cancel. Tickets had been sold, the program printed.

While Pat Conroy had reached the summit all writers dream

of, I was just getting started. My first novel, several years in the making, was coming out soon. Exactly how soon I wasn't sure; I'd signed the contract with a small press three years previously and the book was finally a reality. I was living in Montevallo, Alabama, at the time, a college town thirty-some miles south of Birmingham, where I taught composition and worked in the writing center at the college.

Like Pat, I wasn't exactly looking forward to the party, but for entirely different reasons. I'd always been shy and ill at ease at social occasions, cocktail parties in particular. Standing around making small talk with strangers felt forced and awkward to me. That fateful evening I had two parties on my calendar, both in Birmingham. The first one was a dressy, formal affair, which I especially dreaded. At least the second, a meet and greet to welcome the visiting writers at the Southern Voices Literary Conference, should be more relaxed.

At the appointed time I picked up one of my closest friends, Loretta Cobb, for the drive to Birmingham. Loretta and I were not only friends but also colleagues since she directed the writing center where I worked. The two of us went way back, having gone to college together and remaining close ever since. Her husband, Bill Cobb, had been my mentor and writing professor. As one of the presenters at the literary conference, he was already in Birmingham and would be meeting up with us at the second party.

Loretta opened the car door and crawled in with curlers in her hair and a makeup bag in hand. *At least she's dressed*, I thought with a smile. Notoriously time challenged, Loretta always completed her toilette en route to a destination, even when she was the one driving. She and I had known each other so long we were familiar with and tolerant of each other's idiosyncrasies. Good thing, since both of us had plenty. "I like your outfit, girlfriend," I said in greeting.

"I've had it forever," she said dismissively as she buckled up. Southern women always deflected a compliment. It's expected.

"Timing's everything tonight," I reminded her as we pulled out of the driveway. "Don't forget—if we linger too long at the first party, we'll miss the second one." We'd been over this several times; unlike me, Loretta loved parties and was excited about having two on the same night. From past experience, I knew that getting her away from one and to the other would be a challenge. She enjoyed meeting new people and had a well-deserved reputation as a great hostess and conversationalist.

During the half-hour drive to Birmingham, Loretta put on her face and did her hair as we chatted about the difference in the upcoming events. The first party was a large, fancy shindig being held for a good friend and former classmate of ours who'd been made partner of a prestigious law firm. Although Loretta and I were honored to be included in the celebration, we weren't likely to know anyone there except our friend. Hers wasn't a crowd we ran with. The hostess's home address revealed that we'd be in high cotton, which intrigued Loretta but filled me with dread. Birmingham society did high cotton well.

The second event would be more familiar territory for us. There, we'd be with others like us: English teachers, librarians, writers, patrons of the arts. The party was being held at the head librarian's house in an upscale but less swanky part of town. Loretta forced me to admit I was excited at the prospect of meeting the writers from the literary conference's impressive lineup that year. In anticipation, I'd put some books in the car in case I got a chance to get them signed. It seemed impossible that this time next year, I'd be attending the festival as one of the presenters, with my own book to be signed. With a first book, it's unimaginable that anyone would ever ask for a signature.

When we finally located the grand house of the first party, perched high atop Birmingham's Red Mountain, my heart sank. Slowed by heavy traffic on our way, we'd arrived later than planned and the place was packed. We ended up parking several blocks away, and I stopped Loretta as she opened the passenger door, all dolled up now and looking glamorous. "Loretta? Let's just tell her we came, okay?" I pleaded. "So many people are here she'll never know the difference."

But Loretta was having none of it. Ignoring me, she leapt out of the car and tripped merrily down the dark road to the brightly lit mansion in the distance. With a sigh, I picked up my evening bag and followed. I'd taken care with my appearance, as had Loretta, but I felt sure we'd be underdressed. (We were, in sharp contrast to the other guests.) Both of us favored a bohemian-casual look. A snapshot from that night shows Loretta in a fuchsia Bali-Hai number; me in a sparkly sweater with black pants tucked into heavy, lace-up boots.

As I'd feared, the party, though as splendid and elegant as expected, was an introvert's nightmare. The well-heeled crowd of lawyers stood shoulder to shoulder, shouting to be heard over the clamor and jostling one another to get to the bar. Although I desperately needed a drink, I was more interested in finding the buffet table. When our friend called to invite us, she'd said it was being done by Birmingham's top caterer and not to miss the food. Loretta and I had skipped lunch in anticipation, but we couldn't get anywhere near the dining room. Instead we joined the line for the bar, in the hopes that the mob at the buffet would've cleared out by the time we got our glass of wine.

After a long wait at the bar, we were unceremoniously pushed out of the way by the crowd, our hard-earned pinot grigio sloshing in our hands. As I'd predicted, we knew no one there except the guest of honor, the new law partner who was nowhere to be seen. Shouting at each other over the crowd noise, Loretta and I decided to find our friend before trying the buffet again. Once we made our way to the back of the house, the guest of honor was easy to spot because she was so tall and stately. Although swamped by well-wishers, she stepped out to hug us and seemed genuinely pleased that we'd come. Then she shooed us away, so we wouldn't miss the fabulous spread in the adjoining room.

We didn't make it, mainly because we were too intimidated to elbow our way in like everyone else did. Middle-aged schoolmarms, Loretta and I already stood out like a pair of wrens in a parade of peacocks; I didn't want to create a ruckus by shoving and pushing our way to the trough. "I'm outta here," I hissed at Loretta as we surveyed the crammed dining room. I had yet to catch sight of the table.

"But I'm starving," Loretta whined. "I did without lunch for this."

If she'd get her arse moving, I responded, we could get to the other party before all the food was gone.

As we expected, the other soiree could not have been more different. After the claustrophobic crush of lawyers, Loretta and I breathed a sigh of relief to be back among our own. Here, we were overdressed but knew no one would notice. Even in party attire, writers rarely make the best-dressed list. Also the event was on a much smaller scale, with only fifty or so folks. But we were running late so it was good news, bad news: no elbowing through a crowd, but the party was winding down. We'd missed a lot of it.

Chance meetings, missed connections, wrong turns—none of us knows when our fate awaits us or how many obstacles stand in the pathway. Only later would I look back and marvel at the way things unfolded that night, but at the time, Loretta and I were just relieved to be there. We met several of the guests as they exited the librarian's front door while we were entering. Once inside, Loretta scurried over to tell her husband we'd arrived, and I cornered one of the librarians to ask about the writer I most wanted to meet, one I'd admired for years.

"I'd love to meet Pat Conroy," I told the librarian after we'd hugged, the southern way of greeting even the slightest acquaintance. "It'd be great to tell my students about him." I went on to explain to her how I used examples of his gorgeous prose style in handouts for my freshman classes.

The librarian frowned. "Aw, shoot, honey—you just missed him. You know his dad, the Great Santini?"

I didn't, of course, but knew who she was referring to. The newspaper article about Pat's appearance at the literary festival reported that his father, nicknamed "the Great Santini" as a fighter pilot in the Marines, would be there as well. Pat's autobiographical novel, *The Great Santini*, had exposed his father's abusive nature and the damage his family had suffered as a result. The book had been made into an Oscar-winning movie in 1979, starring Robert Duvall in the title role and Blythe Danner as Pat's mother.

The librarian continued. "The Great Santini got tired and Pat had to take him back to the hotel. I'm really sorry you didn't get a chance to meet Pat! He's *so* nice and friendly. Everyone on the library staff has fallen in love with him."

Disappointed, I asked about a couple of other writers I'd hoped to meet only to be told that they, too, had gone. (Over the years, I've forgotten who they were.) "But there are plenty of other folks here, so go mingle and enjoy yourself," the librarian told me before hurrying off to continue her hostessing duties.

I stood alone for a few minutes and looked around the spacious living room where folks huddled in groups, laughing and talking among themselves. Thankfully, Loretta and I had entered late without our tardiness being noticed or questioned. On my way to the refreshment table I'd spotted in the distance, I paused to greet a couple of friends. Then, taking care not to make eye contact with anyone else, I made a beeline for the table while I had the chance. No one was there, and plenty of food was left. Since I'd had nothing to eat since breakfast I was beginning to feel light-headed.

Out of the corner of my eye I saw that while I'd dawdled, Loretta had fixed herself a plate and stood with Bill at the other end of the dining room. Fortunately they weren't looking my way, so I could grab something before joining them. She and Bill were talking with Jake, a bookseller I'd known for a long time, and a man whom I didn't know. Broad-shouldered, with ruddy cheeks and a wreath of white hair, the man looked vaguely familiar, but I was too preoccupied with my imminent starvation to wonder why. In rumpled, baggy khakis and a red plaid shirt, the stranger was sloppily dressed even for a writer, so I figured him to be a presenter's spouse who'd been dragged along.

With their backs to me, Loretta's group was in a lively conversation, and I checked furtively to make sure no one else was in the vicinity. Forgoing a plate, I started grabbing and gobbling like a starved mongrel—cheese, crackers, fruit, olives—while occasionally glancing over my shoulder to make sure my gluttony went unobserved.

I'd just crammed a whole chocolate-covered strawberry into my mouth when I saw to my dismay that my friends were leading the stranger toward me. Mouth full of strawberry, I was unable to say a word when they introduced us. To this day, I can't settle the debate over who actually made the introductions, as each of my friends takes credit for it. Jake will swear to his dying day that he did, as do Bill and Loretta, so I figure all three of them must've spoken at once. All I remember for sure is this: when Loretta said "Hey, girlfriend, I found Pat Conroy for you," I choked, swallowed, and coughed before blurting out, "Oh, God Almighty!"

Pat threw his head back and laughed a big, hearty laugh. "Not quite, but close enough."

"But . . . you can't be Pat Conroy," I cried, flustered. "When I asked about you, they told me that you'd gone to take your father to the hotel."

Pat shrugged. "Yeah, I was walking out the door when the hostess stopped me. She found someone else to take Dad because she wanted me to make an announcement for her."

Fate, Pat would later say. That's how close we came to missing each other.

Nervous now that I was in the presence of the writer I'd most wanted to meet—one I considered to be among the greatest living writers of our time—I began babbling like an idiot. Even when I saw that Bill, Loretta, and Jake were cringing on my behalf, I couldn't stop myself. For some reason I felt compelled to explain to Pat about the crowded buffet at the other party, and why he'd caught me pigging out. Taking pity on me, Pat motioned toward the table. "I haven't eaten tonight either. Why don't you show me what's good here?" With a nod toward the others, he added, "Y'all excuse us a minute, okay?"

It was the perfect icebreaker. Since I'd already sampled everything, I pointed him toward several things that I'd enjoyed (though truthfully, I'd been too hungry to pay much attention to what I was eating). Pat got into it, though. I wouldn't know until *Beach Music* came out what a foodie he was. He gave each thing I pointed to careful consideration, and he'd give me a thumbs-up and reach for another when something pleased him. The first conversation I had with Pat Conroy wasn't about Proust or Faulkner, or even the other writers at the conference. We talked about food.

While Pat and I were raiding the refreshments, my friends wandered off to seek more intellectual conversation. No doubt it was a relief to them, not having to witness my babbling humiliation any longer. Something unexpected had occurred over the bruschetta and cheese spread, however; Pat Conroy was so laid-back and friendly that I forgot to be awestruck. We chatted easily, as if we'd known each other all our lives. Which is not to say that being with him wasn't intimidating. Pat had an imposing and vibrant presence, an undeniable aura of magnetism and charm. No doubt part of it was his size. Almost six feet tall, he had the rugged build of a linebacker and shoulders wide as a tree trunk. His coloring was wonderfully vivid, with the snow-white hair, ruddy face, and pale blue eyes. Although not conventionally good-looking, he was undeniably attractive.

Soon my and Pat's conversation would wander from food to writing. It was, after all, a literary conference. As Pat munched on the glazed pecans that I'd urged him to try, my mentor Bill came back over to us. (Later Bill would tell me why: it occurred to him that I was too shy to tell Pat about my book, and he wanted to brag on me since he'd been my thesis director when I worked on it. Bill was right; I would've never mentioned it otherwise.)

"Since my favorite student's got you cornered, Pat, I guess she's telling you about her new book," Bill said in his distinctive, West Alabama drawl. "Her first novel, and it's coming out in a few months."

Grimacing, I tried to motion for Bill to shut his mouth, but it was too late. Pat turned to me in surprise, eyebrows raised.

"Why didn't you tell me you were a writer?" he demanded. "All this time, I thought you were the caterer or something."

"I-I'm not!" I stammered, red-faced. "I mean, it's just a small press. I'm not really a writer—"

Pat waved off my protests with his napkin, as though swatting at an annoying insect. "What'd you mean, you're not *really* a writer? That's the most ridiculous thing I've ever heard. You've got a book coming out. You wrote it, right? Therefore, you're a writer."

With a self-satisfied smile, Bill bade us goodbye and resumed his socializing with the other guests, pleased that he'd done his good deed for the day by connecting one of his former students with such an eminent writer. No doubt he was thinking to himself, *Maybe he'll give her some advice. God knows she needs it.*

"Now then," Pat said, his bright eyes focused on me like laser beams. "Tell me about your book."

I started off stammering, not sure where to begin. But Pat helped me along, drawing me out with his questions, until I'd relaxed enough to tell him the whole story—not only about the book but also about how I'd worked on it in one form or another for a long time. Intrigued by the unusual title, Pat asked me to explain the significance. (Originally *Making Waves in Zion*, the title was shortened to *Making Waves* when it was reissued by my new publisher a few years later.) Making Waves, I told Pat, was the name I gave a beauty shop in the little community of Zion, the book's setting. The inspiration came from a story I heard about an automobile accident that changed the lives of two young men. One walked away unharmed; the other one was crippled but would discover a long-buried talent during his rehab. I'd written the story partly to explore the idea of redemption through art, which would be a theme that I'd return to in each of my books. It was my story as well, in that writing had been redemptive in my own journey. That night was the first time I'd talked to anyone, even Bill, about why I'd been compelled to write the book I'd written.

Pat was so easy to talk to, and seemed so genuinely interested in my writing, that I forgot whom I was confiding in, a world-renowned author whose work I fervently admired. He prodded me to put into words things about my writing—inspiration, character development, and recurring themes—that I'd never articulated. After the book came out and I found myself speaking to audiences, Pat's insightful prodding helped me to develop talking points that I returned to again and again. Nothing could've been more helpful to someone like me whose main experience in addressing a group had been standing before a classroom of yawning, hungover college students.

When I realized I was not only jabbering again but, even more embarrassing, going on and on about my book, I quickly changed the subject. I told Pat how much I loved his work, and how I thought I'd discovered him. I'd read his memoir of teaching, *The Water Is Wide,* right after it came out in the early 1970s. It inspired me to become a teacher. "Lots of people tell me that," Pat said with a shrug. *Oh well,* I thought, hiding a smile, *so much for originality.* I didn't tell him that my boys called their father the Great Santini when he had a temper tantrum, or that my oldest son's favorite book ever was Pat's second novel, *The Lords of Discipline*, which had been assigned reading in my son's Honors English class.

Our conversation turned to publishing, and first books. Pat told me the story of the first writer he asked for a blurb, and how the famous author turned him down by saying he couldn't put his name on such an insignificant work by such an insignificant writer. "I hope you've had better luck with your requests," he said with a chuckle.

I didn't know many writers, I admitted, but the few I knew had been kind enough to respond favorably to my pleas for blurbs. "But if I'd had your experience," I told him with a shudder, "I would've never gotten up the nerve to ask anyone else."

Pat studied me a minute then said casually, "Have your publisher send me your book, okay? If I like it, I'll give you a blurb. If not, I'll pretend it got lost in the mail."

Before I could respond, the hostess interrupted our conversation to take our picture together. She then motioned for Bill and Loretta to come over and took one of the four of us, a copy of which Pat and I would later frame as a reminder of our first meeting—which came to an abrupt end after the photo-taking. The hostess took Pat's arm and reminded him of the announcement he'd promised to make for her.

Before he left to fulfill his obligation, Pat and I exchanged phone numbers and addresses so I could send him an advanced reading copy of my book. He held my card at arm's length and studied it a minute before saying, "Oh God, another hyphenated three-named woman writer! But I like the sound of King-Ray, so I'll just call you that."

I tried to tell him that, actually, it wasn't hyphenated but he didn't hear me because the hostess yanked his arm again to urge him on. Before he left, Pat gave me a warm, friendly hug and said, "It was great meeting you, King-Ray, and I really enjoyed our conversation. I can't wait to read your book. If I don't see you at the conference tomorrow, I'll call you, okay?" He patted the pocket of his plaid shirt where he'd put my number.

I didn't believe it for a minute, but I smiled and waved goodbye as the hostess dragged him away. The paper on which he'd written his address as Fripp Island, South Carolina, was clutched in my hand. Watching him write it, I remember being surprised that he lived in the part of the country he'd written so beautifully about in *The Prince of Tides*. I could've sworn the article in the paper about his Birmingham appearance said that he lived in San Francisco. All I knew was, I dared not lose his address or my publisher would kill me. I could only imagine how thrilled the publisher was going to be at the prospect of my getting a blurb from a writer he'd often said topped his list of favorites.

Pat wouldn't be seeing me at the conference the next day, however. It would be years later, when we were reminiscing about our first meeting, before I told him why I wasn't there. Although I'd been invited to the party, I couldn't afford to purchase a ticket to the conference. (Rather than admit it to anyone, even Bill and Loretta, I'd pretended to have another commitment that weekend.) In the process of a divorce, I was struggling to make it on my own. Literary events, even the most reasonably priced ones, were luxuries I simply could not afford.

CHAPTER 2

LONG DISTANCE

I didn't expect to hear from Pat Conroy again, nor did I have any reason to think I would. What took place the night of the party has happened many times in the past and would happen many more in the future. We've all done it—met someone at a party and instantly became new best friends. Phone numbers are exchanged, get-togethers planned. *Next time you come this way, let me know and we'll have lunch!* I've found names and numbers on pieces of paper in my purse and had absolutely no idea who they were or where we met. Pat and I had connected at the party, and during those moments I'd felt as if I'd known him forever, but that was it. It'd make a better story—certainly a more romantic one—to say that our eyes met across a crowded room while "One Enchanted Evening" played in the background. It wasn't that way with us. Maybe those scenes only happen in romance novels.

I let my publisher know right away to hold the presses—there might be another blurb coming for my book. As I figured, he was beside himself and said that a quote from an internationally best-selling author could be a big help for publicity. In the years to come I would read with amusement how Pat and I met when I asked him to blurb my first novel, which tickled us both. It wasn't that I'd been afraid to ask him for a blurb; it just hadn't occurred to me. I had a lot to learn about the publishing business. Josephine Humphries (one of my favorite writers ever, and a dear friend) once told an audience in Charleston that if it were true and I hadn't asked Pat for a blurb, then I was the only writer in the South who hadn't.

Later that week my publisher called me and, without even saying hello, began to read Pat's blurb over the phone.

"He just called me," the publisher added, "to say how much he loved your book. We talked on and on about the book, and about you. What a great guy he is! He couldn't have been nicer, and we must've talked for an hour. He wanted to hear about my press and the other books we're bringing out. You did a great job networking, by the way. Keep it up."

I hung up thrilled about the blurb but distracted by a new worry. *Networking*! Surely writers didn't have to do things like that when a book came out, did they? If so, I was in deep dooky. I wasn't good at schmoozing. Not for the first time, I wondered if I had what it took to be a writer. Writing was all I'd ever wanted to do, but the business of being a writer was another thing altogether. What if other writers weren't as nice as Pat? If they were all as snotty as the one who refused Pat his first blurb, how would they treat a nobody like me? Originally, I'd been excited about my book coming out; now the thought filled me with apprehension.

One thing I *had* to do, however, was write Pat a thank-you note. I'd sent cheesy little thank-you cards for my other blurbs (all three of them), but hesitated with Pat. For such a big-shot writer, should

I also send a box of candy, or bottle of wine? It'd be even nicer if I baked something—my rosemary-shortbread cookies, maybe?—and mailed them in a pretty tin. I couldn't decide.

I pondered the options but hadn't done a blooming thing a few days later when I arrived at the English department to find a note in my box: "Call Pat Conroy." It included a number, but I didn't know if it was his home, his office, or an assistant's.

I took the note to my office and closed the door to make the call, chagrined. After Pat had been so gracious to me, I couldn't believe that I hadn't even thanked him! Thankfully he didn't answer, and I left a message on the machine, stating only my name and that I was returning his call. The voice on the recording was a woman's, very professional sounding, and I wondered if it was his assistant. Probably she'd been the one to call me on his behalf to make sure I got the blurb. I was preparing for my upcoming class when the phone rang again, and I answered unsuspecting.

"King-Ray!" Pat boomed out. I recognized his voice immediately because, like his presence, it was distinctive—warm, friendly, and exuberant. He would call me by my last name until we married and he came up with a more suitable nickname (according to him, anyway). Without wasting time with how's-your-day niceties, Pat jumped right in to the reason for his call. He wanted to talk about my book. And as he would do in his future calls, he picked right up from our previous conversation as if it'd only taken place a few minutes before.

"*Making Waves in Zion*! The title works perfectly now that I've read the book," Pat said jauntily. "But tell me where the hell you learned to write like that and why you haven't written more?"

Instead of answering his questions I began blathering like a fool yet again. I groveled on and on about the blurb and his generosity in sending it, then apologized ad nauseam for not having thanked him. I was so embarrassed that I lied and said I'd written him a note but hadn't gotten it in the mail yet. Pat was having none of it and wanted only to talk about the book. I'd find that one of his favorite topics of conversation would always be books.

"Those fucking voices you used!" he cried. "Of both an eighty-year-old woman and a twenty-year-old guy? Gimme a break. That's some hard shit to pull off. I've never been able to write in different voices. Tried it, but it's never worked for me."

I stifled a giggle at his language. At the time, none of my friends used the once-forbidden F-word in ordinary conversation, nor with such gusto. (In a few years it'd become as common as dirt but was still somewhat taboo in those days.) Pat, a former altar boy, would later blame his more colorful expressions on the formative years he spent attending The Citadel, the military college of South Carolina. Some of the expressions I'd never heard before, such as *shitbird, fuckhead, wad waste*. Pat still holds the distinction of being the most expressive cusser I've ever known, before or after.

His mention of voices led us into a lengthy conversation about the merits of multiple points of view as opposed to third person, and before I knew it, I had to interrupt him. "Ah, Pat?" I said reluctantly. "I've got a class coming up, so I need to run."

"Give me your home number, then," Pat said, "and I won't bother you at work. But don't write me a fucking thank-you note, okay? Those go straight to my assistant and I never see them anyway."

~~~~~

As I walked home after work that day I kept thinking about my conversation with Pat, as well as the talks I'd had with my publisher lately. The closer it came to my pub date, the more I wondered how much, if at all, my life would be affected by the book's release. Because of my long friendship with Bill Cobb, who'd published several novels, I probably knew more about publishing than a lot of first-time novelists did. I even had a hotshot New York agent (thanks to Bill's introduction), who I hoped would sell my next novel. I knew that small presses did very limited book tours, though my publisher had plans to send me to a lot of regional events. Even so, I couldn't help but wonder how touring—even on a small scale—would work out with my crazy family life, which had recently gotten crazier than ever. And that was saying a lot.

When I reached my house, a cute little cottage only a block from campus, I went around to the back to let myself in. If the neighbors wondered why I didn't use the front door, I'll never know. No one asked, and I wasn't about to tell them. At the time, my family life was too complicated to explain.

Several years earlier my husband and I had bought the house as an investment, a good rental for college students. Since we lived in a parsonage in Birmingham, furnished by the church where my husband was senior pastor, we didn't own a home. Instead of renting to students, however, we ended up renting only the separate wing in back, so we could use the main part of the house as a getaway. When I finished a graduate degree and got a job at the college, I began staying in the house during the week and returning for church activities on the weekend. When our youngest son started high school, we decided he'd stay with me and attend Montevallo High School.

I've seen studies that say living apart puts too much strain on a marriage; since mine was already troubled it's hard to pinpoint when or how it fell apart. When counseling failed, I filed for a legal separation as the first step toward divorce. The preacher man was so opposed to giving up the house that I moved into the rental in back. Living in a separate wing was my pathetic and misguided attempt at a stable family life after we split up.

It wasn't working out as I'd hoped, and why I ever thought it would is still beyond me. But at the time my guilt for breaking up my family was such that I would've done anything, no matter how misguided, to make things better. As I saw it, I'd been the one who wanted out of the marriage, so I should be the one to make it easier for the family. If living under the same roof while leading separate lives would do it, then it was worth a try.

For a short time, I thought it might work. My son, by then a high school senior, occupied the other part of the house, and during the week his father came down to spend time with him. Since I no longer went to the parsonage, the house also provided a place for family get-togethers when our two older sons visited. The oldest was away in medical school; the middle one had two little boys, making me a grandmother since age forty-four. Just when it seemed my plan would work out for everyone, things between my ex and me began to deteriorate. My experiment in familial normalcy teetered on the brink of failure. The lab rats were still alive, but barely.

Foolishly, stubbornly, I kept trying. I had another motivation as well, one that shames me: staying in the same house with my ex was also my way of keeping up appearances. If I'd learned anything in my two decades as the wife of a preacher, it was the importance of putting up a good front. Putting up a good front was so deeply ingrained in my psyche that only a few close friends knew my true situation. After Pat and I started seeing each other on a regular basis, he told me that from the first night we met, he'd been interested in getting to know me better. But when he asked the librarians hosting the party about me, they said that he might as well look elsewhere. I was not only happily married, my husband was a prominent pastor of a local church. Pat got the message: I was about as unavailable as anyone could be. He wouldn't find out otherwise for several months, and only after the two of us had become friends.

But I didn't know that on the afternoon of my first phone call from Pat, a couple of weeks after our meeting in Birmingham. I entered my living quarters in a state of anxiety and exhaustion. The tension between my ex and me, which was higher than ever, was taking its toll on all of us. At least I'd be home alone that evening, I thought gratefully; my son was rehearsing for a school play and my ex was supposed to be at the parsonage. As usual, I carried home a stack of essays to grade. I looked forward to kicking off my shoes, pouring myself a glass of wine, and getting started on them. Nothing like a hundred student essays to take your mind off your troubles. A blessedly quiet, uneventful evening was just what I needed.

It was not to be. No sooner had I changed into my sweats than I heard a car in the driveway, the slam of a door. I knew with a sinking heart that the preacher man had arrived. He wasn't supposed to be here tonight, but lately he'd been driving down more often, trying to reason with me. The sermon was always the same: I needed to stop this foolishness and return to the fold. If I could put aside my sinful ways, then forgiveness was possible. At the sharp rap on my door, I cringed and braced myself for the inevitable.

~~~~~

A week or so later, I was closed off in my quarters grading yet another stack of essays. The second semester of the required freshman English course, Composition 102, was dedicated to research.

Instructors usually assigned their classes to write about a famous writer or historical figure, but I'd developed what seemed to me more of a true research project. (If nothing else, my students couldn't plagiarize a former student's work. And thankfully the internet wasn't a factor then.) I gave my classes the Myers-Briggs personality assessment test then applied the results to their unique writing and learning style. Based on the results, I asked each of them to come up with a self-improvement project, do the research, and write the conclusions as their paper. To my surprise, the students really got into it and worked enthusiastically. The first batch of essays in the project were their personal analyses of their learning styles, which I was marking for stylistic problems.

A knock on my door startled me, but it had to be my son Jake, since no one else was there. Rare for Jake, he'd been home that evening and we'd had a nice dinner together. Sure enough, Jake stuck his head in and motioned for me to pick up the phone. "A man for you, Mom," he said with a wink. I picked up the phone with a frown. Occasionally male colleagues called about school matters, but it was pretty late. Fearing it might be my ex's lawyer, I took a deep breath before answering. One reason I'd stayed in a troubled marriage for so long: there was no question how a custody battle between an upstanding preacher and a runaway wife would turn out in the Deep South. It had been a potent threat. "Hello?" I said in a small voice.

I was taken by surprise to hear Pat's hearty "King-Ray! I tracked you down at home. So, how're things going?"

Once I regained my composure, I forced myself to match his bright, cheery tone. "Everything's great, Pat! And how're you doing? It's nice to hear from you again."

"Hope I'm not calling too late. Is it a bad time?"

"No, no. I've been grading essays and couldn't be happier to take a break."

"Oh? What's the dreaded essay topic this week?"

And so our conversation went, or at least somewhere along those lines. Although neither of us could've known it at the time, Pat's call that night was the beginning of what would become a two-year relationship between us—conducted solely by phone. It was the damnedest thing and wouldn't make sense until later when I got to know Pat and his quirks. I'd find that most of his social life took place over the phone. He hated going out, but genuinely loved people and had a whole slew of phone buddies whom he talked to regularly, mostly other writers he'd met on the circuit. Somehow, I became one of them.

At the time, however, I didn't know *what* to make of his calls. After that night, Pat began calling fairly regularly, and he was prone to end our conversations with what came across as "Hey, it's been nice knowing you, King-Ray. Hope you have a good life. See you, kiddo." I'd hang up bemused, staring at the phone and wondering what just happened. Had I said something he didn't like? But it couldn't be that—he'd sounded much too jovial and upbeat. I'd tell myself that we'd talked for an hour or so; maybe he just got tired. *Oh well*, I'd think with a shrug. *Guess he's just weird that way.* Then to my surprise, a week or so would go by then he'd call again, out of the blue. And we'd pick up right where we'd left off in our last conversation.

It was also odd how long it took for us to discuss anything of a personal nature, despite the fact that we talked for hours. Neither of us knew that we were operating on false assumptions about the other. Based on the dedication he'd written to his wife and children in his latest book, *The Prince of Tides*, I assumed Pat was a devoted family man. (His calls had started early in the spring; *Beach Music*, which was a bit more revealing, wouldn't come out until the summer.) Pat's phone calls were always strictly friendly, not flirty or suggestive in any way whatsoever. I told him next to nothing about my personal life, and he didn't ask, having been warned off by the librarians. Instead, we talked about the books we were writing and reading, the classes I taught, and the essay topics I assigned my students. He especially loved the unintentionally funny things my students wrote and would hoot with laughter when I quoted them. ("I think Hemingway must've written this story before he died.") I loved his great big laugh and would find myself still smiling after one of his calls.

From the first time he called, Pat drilled me about my writing. He never failed to ask how my book was doing, or what I was working on. I told him about whatever articles or short stories I had in the works. I'd had a couple of short stories published in literary journals and had another one rejected, probably because of the cheery subject matter. It was about a dying woman who goes to a Native American medicine woman for a suicide potion, digs a grave that she fills with flowers, then crawls in to drink the potion. The last thing she hears is the medicine woman playing a lute in the distance. The editor's comment on the rejection slip amused me, asking if I was Native American and, if not, if I was familiar with their burial rituals.

I wasn't yet ready to talk to Pat about the novel I'd started. Taken from my journals of my life with the preacher man, it was the most personal thing I'd ever written. But I wasn't at the point where I could share it with him or anyone else. Since I wasn't sure I'd ever be, I'd put it aside and started another novel, a made-up story about a female rodeo rider. (Whose grandmother, incidentally, was a Native American medicine woman. Not sure how I got stuck on that twist.) That one wasn't far enough along to talk about either, though later a chapter from it would be published as a short story then reprinted in an anthology from Milkweed Press, which made me proud.

Scholarly papers were a safer topic for Pat and me at the time, and we talked about those as well. I'd helped Loretta edit an article on linguistics, which couldn't have been more boring. But Pat wanted to hear all about it. If it had anything to do with reading or writing, he was interested. Or rather, he was if it was about someone else's writing, not his. Try as I might, I couldn't get much out of him about his work. After finishing the final edits of *Beach Music*, he hadn't had the energy to start anything new. About the edits, he said his editor, Nan Talese, was fantastic and had guided him every step of the way.

Because we talked mostly about teaching and writing, it would be several months later before Pat had his first inkling of how things were on the home front for me. As I'd feared, my relationship with my ex had only worsened. Despite our best efforts, we just couldn't seem to be civil to each other. Eventually I had no choice but to get my own place. I waited until after Jake's graduation that May before giving up all pretense of normality, then I packed up and moved out. I'd found a great place, a two-room efficiency close to the campus where I worked. That summer, Jake left for college in North Carolina, where he'd earned a full scholarship in theater. For the first time in more years than I could remember, I was completely on my own. I couldn't believe how much I cherished my hard-earned solitude, especially in my cozy little efficiency, just the right size for me. Despite my lame excuses and explanations, I couldn't understand why I'd been so reluctant to seek out being on my own sooner. All my life, I've needed solitude in much the same way I need air, or water. It's essential for my soul.

Later that fall, Jake happened to be home for the weekend and visiting his dad when Pat called me. He'd used the only number he had, at my old house, and Jake had answered the phone. *Yet another fateful moment?* Pat and I would ask each other later. The way things were between my ex and me at the time, I can't imagine him giving anyone my new number if he'd been the one to answer the phone instead of Jake. The caller would've more likely gotten a litany of my many shortcomings instead.

When I picked up the phone at my new place, Pat's voice was less exuberant than usual. "Ah . . . King-Ray?" he said tentatively. "Your son gave me this number for you?"

Yeah, I said, I'd gotten my own place, a studio apartment closer to the college. I said nothing about the divorce, nor why I'd moved out. Neither did I tell him that shortly after I settled in, someone slashed all four of my tires. The police immediately suspected my ex, despite my shocked denial. No way, I told them—he was a respected man of God! Oh, you'd be surprised at the crazy things divorce would drive even the most respectable folks to do, they responded.

The police turned out to be right. Eventually the holy man would confess that he'd complained about me a tad too bitterly to a friend of his. In a moment of male solidarity, the friend had gotten drunk and done the dirty deed late one night. (In the upcoming years the preacher man and I would become friends again, but that time was yet to come.) I accepted my ex's apology without comment, though I didn't buy it. How had his friend known where I lived or what kind of car I drove? It had hit me hard. If one of my friends hadn't helped me finance new tires, I would've been stranded. A car was a necessity for me, not a luxury. Teachers' pay is abysmal at best, and to make ends meet while trying to help out my kids with their college expenses, I'd started teaching a night class at a community college thirty miles away. Monday through Thursday I left work at the writing center and drove straight to the six-to-nine class, eating a peanut-butter sandwich on the way.

But I didn't tell Pat any of that when he called me that night. My book had come out, and he wanted to hear everything—where I'd signed, how I liked the bookstores, which writers I'd met at various literary festivals. He sounded downright disappointed to hear that everyone had been fairly nice to me. Next time, I said, maybe some snooty writer would snub me, so I'd have a good story to share. Although we laughed about it, Pat warned me that it'd happen eventually. Stay midlist and nobody bothered with you; but land on the bestseller list and earn a target on your back. Unfortunately he proved to be right. In every field, success breeds jealousy, and writing is certainly no exception.

Only later would I look back and divide others' treatment of me into two camps, pre-Conroy and post-Conroy. It became a test of character, the way I defined a writer, bookseller, or critic to Pat. "I met a friend of yours at the book festival," Pat might say to me, "and he seems like a nice guy." If my response was "He was really nice to me when my first book came out" (the subtext being, before I married Pat), then said person passed the good-character test. On the other hand, if my response was more like "He claimed to be a friend of mine? That's odd. He never spoke to me until I married you," it was another story altogether.

On a more cheerful topic, that evening I had an adventure to tell Pat about, and a good one: the English department had sent me to a two-week workshop at a college in Vermont that specialized in teaching learning-disabled students. It'd turned out to be one of the most profound experiences of my life. Because I not only taught freshman classes but also worked in the writing center, I ran across a lot of students with various learning disabilities. Most of them were mild, certainly in comparison to the severe cases I saw at the Vermont college. Some of their stories were heartbreaking, like the student who told us how his disability made reading so difficult. When he was in the third grade, his teacher, a nun, made him stand in front of the class in the position of Jesus on the cross for hours every day because he couldn't complete his reading assignment. When he got home from school he was afraid to tell his parents why his arms hurt so badly he couldn't hold them up. He failed third grade twice and was put into a class for the "mentally retarded." He was dyslexic.

Pat, whose first job had been as a teacher, asked me a dozen questions about the school and their methods. I wasn't really surprised by the intensity of his interest. Recently I'd reread *The Water Is Wide*, about his experience as a young man teaching black students in a Gullah community off the coast of South Carolina, during the early years of integration. His unconventional teaching methods and outspoken criticism of the educational system cost him his job. Rereading the book now that I knew the writer, I understood something that would be proven to me over and over: first and foremost, Pat was a teacher. Although he never returned to the classroom, his love of teaching came out through his mentoring and support of other writers. I couldn't help myself; I had to laugh when I asked him why he didn't teach after *The Water Is Wide* came out. I'd assumed since the book was a success and had been made into a movie that he didn't need to. Not so, he said. "It's kind of hard to get another teaching job," he told me with a laugh, "when you've been fired for gross neglect of duty and conduct un-becoming a professional."

After he and I said our goodbyes, my mind kept wandering back to our conversation, which had been as lively and stimulating as ever. Not to mention long—we'd talked past midnight. Ours was a unique relationship. We had met one time and knew little about each other, yet I considered him a good friend. Involved in my own chaotic and busy life, I wouldn't think about him for ages, then he'd call and once again, we'd pick up where we left off. He had a remarkable memory. Sometimes he'd ask about a book I'd mentioned the last time we'd talked, or a new essay topic I'd assigned my students. It blew me away, how he could recall such details of weeks-old conversations. It was also embarrassing. I faked my way through half our phone calls by pretending to remember stuff that I'd totally forgotten.

I'd only told a couple of my closest friends about Pat's calls, and Loretta's reaction made me think twice before sharing with anybody else. "Don't give me that friendship crap, girl," Loretta smirked. "He's coming on to you." I swore he wasn't, but she didn't believe it. If she'd been privy to even one of his calls, I argued, she'd understand. Pat wasn't like that. "He's a *man*," Loretta said. "Of course he's like that. God, you're so pathetic."

While it might've been true that I wasn't overly worldly in the ways of men, I relied a lot on intuition. I wasn't so inexperienced that I couldn't tell when someone was romantically interested. And if the signals got hazy, I wasn't beyond seeking outside help: I read the tarot cards. Loretta challenged me to take it to the tarot, but I insisted there was no need. I trusted my intuition on this one: Pat Conroy wasn't a player. His only interest in me was as a friend.

CHAPTER 3

FIRST STEPS

Doing a signing for *Beach Music* sometime in 1996, Pat came to Birmingham, but I was teaching a night class and didn't get to go. Based on my own signings, I foolishly assumed his would only last an hour or so. I still had a lot to learn about the publishing business. Although Pat had left a message several days before the signing to say when he'd be in my neck of the woods, I hadn't called him back. He was traveling and said in his message that he'd call back when he could. He'd also mentioned that he'd only be in town briefly—flying in for the signing and out the next morning. I'd devoured *Beach Music* and looked forward to talking about it with him. But his calls were so sporadic that I never knew when (or if) we'd talk again.

A couple of weeks after Pat's appearance in Birmingham, which went on so long he had to have a hand massage before it was over, he called me from New York. And said breezily (as though it didn't matter to him one way or the other), "Hey, King-Ray! I kind of hoped I'd see you at the bookstore in Birmingham."

I explained about the night class then quickly launched into my glowing review of *Beach Music* before he could get on another subject. I'd tried to talk to him about it before—it'd been out almost a year by then—but he would always brush me off by asking how things were going with *my* book. It was hard to get him to talk about his work, except in a vague or general manner. When he did say something more specific, it always caught me off guard. About *Beach Music*, his shocking comment was "My brothers are all characters in the book, except Tom. Well, he was in it, but he committed suicide before I finished the first draft."

"*What?*" I said when I found my voice. "My God! What happened, Pat?"

His response was calm and measured. "Tom was mentally ill and had tried before. Truth is, I hardly knew the kid because of our age difference. I was gone from home by the time he came along. But it was still godawful."

"Of course it was. What a terrible thing. I can't imagine how you ever finished your book after that."

Following a heavy silence, Pat said, "You know what, King-Ray? I'd planned for John Hardin, the character based on Tom, to commit suicide in the book, but I changed his story afterward. And it helped me, to be able to give the fictional Tom a better, happier life."

"John Hardin's a wonderful character, Pat. What a lovely tribute you gave your brother."

"It's the only thing I ever gave him. Poor kid. He never had a chance." As though catching himself before revealing anything else painful, Pat quickly changed the subject. "But enough of that! Tell me about your day. What're your students like this semester?"

On other occasions, my attempts to talk about his work had led one or the other of us to reveal personal information. When I told him that my oldest son could quote passages from *The Lords of Discipline*, Pat'd asked how many kids I had, and he perked up to hear I had three boys. Except for the time when he helped to raise a stepson, he said, his house had been made up of girls—four daughters. "Funny," he said with a chuckle, "I can't talk any of them into going to The Citadel. Seems like some shitbird wrote an uncomplimentary book about it."

(The "shitbird" in question was Pat himself. In *The Lords of Discipline*, Pat exposed the hazing and abuses he experienced as a student at The Citadel, the military college of South Carolina. After reading it, I would've never let one of my boys go there, but I wisely refrained from sharing that thought with him.)

Instead we laughed and moved on to another topic. I would soon discover that jokey, dismissive banter was Pat's favorite way of avoiding painful subjects. Nothing he'd said in any of our conversations revealed the terrible turmoil he was going through during that time, or that the family he'd mentioned so casually had been split apart only a short while before we met.

That particular evening, he interrupted my yammering about *Beach Music* to ask a question. "King-Ray? Have you moved again, or just changed phone numbers? I got a recording when I called your old number."

It hit me then that he didn't know. Since our last conversation, I'd taken a job at a community college in eastern Alabama and moved halfway across the state. Such was the nature of our relationship that it hadn't occurred to me to send him a note with my new address, like I'd done with other acquaintances. He and I were buddies, true; but casual, long-distance ones. In those days, the phone company gave out a new number when the old one was called, or Pat and I would've lost touch with each other completely after my move—which he didn't hesitate to point out.

"And you didn't think to let me know about your move—or the new job?" he asked, sounding more bewildered than hurt by my oversight.

"Yeah, I should have," I muttered, chagrined. It sounded lame and was. I loved our conversations and valued his friendship, yet I'd been unintentionally careless with it more than once.

Pat chuckled. "You're not very forthcoming, King-Ray. I've had to drag every bit of information out of you, kicking and screaming. Anybody ever told you that?"

"All the time," I said lightly. "Now, tell me what you're doing in New York."

Eventually Pat would claim to have found the perfect nickname for me. He started calling me Helen Keller because he said I saw nothing, heard nothing, said nothing. It was typical of Pat's blarney, of course, since Helen Keller had been very vocal in her own way and for many causes. But the nickname, a tongue-in-cheek dig at my natural reticence, stuck. Even my sisters would ask to speak to Helen Keller when they called, claiming Tanna (their own nickname for me) never told them anything either. Over time it became a family joke, with everyone joining in. Even I got into it and signed my notes to Pat Helen K. It amuses me now to think of Pat's papers, which are at the University of South Carolina's special archives collection, and the questions future scholars will have when they come across the sweet little love notes Pat wrote and addressed to Helen Keller.

I have to admit, Pat wasn't wrong to poke fun at my taciturnity. Although I'm not intentionally tight-lipped or unforthcoming, I've always been private to such a degree that my reticence can come across that way. It's something I assume all introverts deal with. In the life I led before meeting Pat, I'd worked hard to overcome what could be perceived as aloofness. A pastor's wife lives in a goldfish bowl, where personal privacy is practically unheard of. During my two decades as a preacher's wife, I coped by developing a public persona that was as different from the real me as possible. It took me a while to realize that's why I enjoyed my conversations with Pat. I was myself with him and could talk about things in a way I've never done with anyone else. It took us a while to get there, but once we did he became my closest confidant.

One time early on, our conversation turned to religion. Pat'd been surprised that I'd read a book by a female theologian he'd just discovered and said most folks had never heard of her. "On the contrary," I responded. "All good Episcopalians know her work."

"You're lucky to be Protestant," he said, sounding truly wistful. "I was born and raised Catholic. You can't imagine how it screwed me up."

"Oh, I think I can," I said with a smile.

~~~

In my new job I had less time to chat because my teaching load was heavier. The two-year college was large and sprawling with many more students than the four-year school where I taught before. I was teaching not only night classes in creative writing, thanks to my credentials of having published a book and a couple of stories, but also an early morning class for returning adults (6:30 A.M.!). In addition, I had the usual freshman and sophomore composition classes. With that many classes, I spent weekends and every free evening grading essays. I loved my new life, though, and fit in easily with my colleagues, whom I came to adore. Being in a new environment helped my recovery from the bitter divorce more than anything else. (No slashed tires, at least.) After the turmoil of the preceding few years, I relished my hard-earned freedom and swore to never give it up again. Any landing you walk away from, I told myself, is a good landing.

My new town, about halfway between Birmingham and Atlanta, was larger than Montevallo—it even had a mall—but lacking in the small-town charm I was used to. I was far from a regular at the stately Episcopal church I joined, but no one there spoke to me. Even so, I didn't mind the anonymity of a larger place at that stage of my life. Being away from everything familiar forced me to start over and take on a new persona. I rented an unassuming little town house in a development built next to a wooded, derelict graveyard. When my sons visited, we roamed it searching for the fallen-over tombstones hidden in the brambles. I wouldn't dare go in it alone.

I even started going out with men again, though I cringed at the word *dating* and refused to call it that. I'd never liked dating, hadn't enjoyed it even as a teenager. Nevertheless, I got involved with a colleague much sooner and more seriously than I intended. I was out of practice, I chided myself, or I would've seen it coming and pulled away before getting in so deep. In truth, I wanted nothing more than my freedom. I wasn't ready for a relationship and getting into one with a colleague was a mistake that caused me a lot of remorse and guilt.

Later, I would find out that Pat had done the same, which explained his off-and-on phone calls. In typical Conroy fashion, his involvements were even messier than mine.

While still married, Pat had gotten involved with another

woman, a major factor in the breakup of his marriage and hers as well. Once both Pat and the "other woman" were free, however, their relationship soured, and they went their separate ways. He started seeing someone else right away, a newly widowed woman he'd known for a long time. Soon he'd become a father figure to her kids, who were still grieving for their own father. Like me but to a much greater degree, Pat found himself caught in a situation that he couldn't get out of without causing everyone involved a lot of pain.

At that time, however, neither of us knew those things about the other. When I first moved to East Alabama, most of what I heard from Pat came from my answering machine. It took him a few tries to learn that the best time to call me was late at night, after my classes and just before bedtime. In many ways, those late-night calls started a different phase of our friendship. Because it was late and both of us were tired (having had a few glasses of wine didn't hurt, either), we talked much more freely. When he questioned my move, wondering if I'd been unhappy at the other college, I told him no, it wasn't that. I admitted that I needed to relocate after an extremely difficult divorce. "No kidding?" was his response. "I went through one of those myself not too long ago. Aren't they *fun*?"

~~~

Christmas 1996. My relationship with the colleague was still on, the one I needed to find a graceful way to exit, when Pat called me one night. How far was this new town of mine—Gadsden, right?—from Atlanta, where he might be over the holidays, he asked. Maybe a couple of hours, I replied. Why? Oh, he might come over and see me, he said in that overly casual tone I'd heard so often. That'd be nice, I'd said, but he needed to let me know because I'd be away for most of the holidays. I'd planned on seeing the grandkids then going to South Alabama to visit my widowed father, where my two sisters would be with their families.

Pat's plans were still uncertain, he told me, but he'd call if his visit to Atlanta worked out. We said our goodbyes with nothing settled, just a lot of maybes floating around. Even after that, it did not occur to me that he was interested in me in any way other than as a friend. To this day none of my friends believe that, but they weren't privy to our conversations. He still hadn't said a single thing to suggest his interest was anything other than companionable, even with his suggestion of a Christmas visit.

No calls came from Pat during the holidays, however, not even to wish me a Merry Christmas. So I was caught off guard when the new year, 1997, kicked in and he called to say that he'd be coming to Alabama in February. First, he was speaking at Auburn University in Montgomery (AUM), then going on to the Birmingham "literary thing" where we met two years ago. He wasn't presenting; he'd only agreed to come so he could introduce Anne Rivers Siddons at the awards dinner. Since he remembered me saying that I loved Anne's books, he wanted to let me know that she was getting the award Pat'd gotten when we met. Would he see me at either place? he asked.

"Ah . . . maybe," I said, hedging. No way I'd tell him that, yet again, I couldn't afford to attend the writers' conference. Even with the new job, better pay, and living frugally, I barely scraped by on my own. It was my fault: I'd stubbornly (and stupidly) refused to take anything from my ex in the divorce agreement. Because I still helped my youngest son with college expenses not covered by his scholarship, there were plenty of times when I wondered how I'd manage.

"I'm not sure about the conference," I told Pat, "but I can probably make it to the talk in Montgomery. I'll let you know, okay?" Because the event was held at a university, I figured it'd be free.

Then he said something unexpected. "Maybe we can have dinner together next time I'm in your area."

"Sure," I said. "That'd be fun."

"Really?" There was genuine surprise in his voice. "I'm no good at asking women out."

Okay, you'd think I would've known then, right? He had flat out said it, for the first time. He was asking me out. Instead, I found it touching that a man as successful as Pat would admit to being shy around women. If it was advice from a female friend he wanted, though, I was hardly the one to ask. I'd made too much of a mess of my own relationships to advise anyone else on how to handle theirs. I hung up, bemused by Pat's contradictions. On the surface he was affable and lighthearted, always in a joking and self-deprecating manner. But I'd read his books and knew a much darker side lurked beneath, no matter how he tried to cover it up. Each of his five semiautobiographical books dealt with disturbing subjects: abuse, both systematic and domestic; rape and violence; mental illness and suicide; horribly dysfunctional families.

I called him a few days later to say that even though I wouldn't be attending the conference, I'd come to his speech in Montgomery if it fell on a night I didn't have classes. But he needed to let me know when the speech was. As his phone rang it hit me that I had never called him before, except that first time in my office when I returned his call about the blurb. It felt strangely awkward doing so; women of my generation didn't call men friends except on business. Thankfully he wasn't in and I was able to leave a message.

No surprise, I heard from Pat only once before his speech, and only on my machine: "Aw crap, King-Ray—I forgot you're in class, sharing your vast knowledge of lit-uh-rah-ture with your adoring students. I wanted to talk to you about my trip to your fair state, fill you in on some of the details, but . . . you ain't there. So. I'll call you back, okay?" He didn't.

I didn't know the date of Pat's speech, and in those days, information wasn't readily available on the internet. But surprisingly, the week of the speech a colleague stuck her head in my door to ask if I wanted to ride with her and a couple others to AUM (ah, fate!). "Pat Conroy's giving a speech at AUM and I heard that you're friends with him," she said.

I'd avoided talking about Pat with my new colleagues because it felt like name-dropping. But at a talk I'd given not long after my move, someone in the audience asked about his blurb on my jacket cover, and how I'd "pulled it off." The new sassy me, freed of the preacher's wife image, resisted the urge to wink and say, *You'd be surprised*. Instead I related the story of meeting Pat at the Southern Voices conference, and the audience laughed in sympathy at my klutziness. On the ride to hear Pat's speech in Montgomery, one of the women asked if he and I were close friends. No, we were more like acquaintances, I answered. Not wanting to sound coy, I added that we talked occasionally, but I'd only met him once.

The speech was held at AUM's basketball gymnasium, which indicated that they expected a big crowd. Even so, my companions and I were shocked at the number of people there, shocked that we barely found a place to sit. The bleachers were full and chairs were set up on the gym floor as if for graduation. We were then pleasantly surprised that Pat's speech was so entertaining; being at a university, we'd expected a scholarly discourse, I suppose. I shouldn't have been surprised; his calls were light and funny, but I always felt a deep undercurrent of melancholy beneath his jovial demeanor. There was no trace of anything of that nature in his talk, which had the audience in stitches the whole time. He even made his family dysfunction humorous. Describing his childhood memories of his father's arrival home, he said his father "got out of the car with his knuckles dragging the ground" and his sister called out to her siblings: "Everybody hide—Godzilla's home!"

After Pat's talk, my companions stood for a couple of hours in a very long line to have their books signed, but I hadn't thought to bring mine. While watching the line inch slowly along, I spotted a writer friend in the front row of the bleachers and went to sit by him. I had no way of knowing that he was Pat's host for the evening. We were seated close to the action but angled in a way that we could see only the backs of Pat's fans as they gathered around the table. I caught a glimpse of Pat every so often and was surprised to see him laughing and talking even as he signed.

I poked my writer friend with an elbow. "I couldn't do that in a million years, could you? Talk to folks while signing books? No telling what I'd write."

My friend smiled in agreement then turned his head to study me. "It's funny to see you here, girl. When I picked Pat up at the airport this afternoon, first thing he asked was if I knew you and if I'd read your book. He said y'all were friends and that he was looking forward to seeing you tonight."

I couldn't help but laugh and motion to the hundreds of seats in the gym. "He's got better vision than me, then," I said. "I couldn't pick out anyone in this mob."

My friend shrugged. "He'll see you at the reception. You know where it is, or do you need to follow us?" When I told him I'd come with some other folks and we had to get back, he inclined his head toward Pat with a frown. "Aw, Pat's gonna be disappointed to hear that. Go break in line and tell him that you're here, at least."

That was the last thing I wanted to do, so I asked if he had any paper. I'd write Pat a note that he could give him at the reception, I said. He searched his pockets but didn't even have a card; I'd brought my little wallet-purse and had nothing either. It took forever but I finally got a scrap of paper from someone, wrote a "so sorry I missed you!" note, signed it King-Ray, then made my way back to the front row. My writer friend was nowhere to be seen.

I stood flummoxed for a moment, not sure what I should do. My traveling companions were almost to the signing table; I could ask them to hand him the note. I decided I was being ridiculous. Note in hand, I crept up behind Pat's table, waited to catch him as the next person in line made their way forward, then quickly passed him the note. He looked up startled and seemed genuinely pleased to see me. After two years, I wondered if he'd even recognize me.

"King-Ray! I'm so glad you made it," he said as he grabbed my hand and squeezed it in greeting. "I'll see you afterward, okay? Come to the reception."

I gave him a little wave and scurried off, not wanting to hold up things to explain that I couldn't stay. Everyone was already staring daggers at the brazen hussy who dared hold up the line even for a couple of seconds. Red-faced, I made my way past the line and went to wait for the others by the box office. On the ride home, they jabbered in excitement about how much they'd enjoyed the event, what a great speaker Pat was, and how friendly he was to everybody in the line. We were halfway home when the driver glanced my way and asked if I'd even gotten to say hello to Pat. I told her that I was able to get a note to him.

"We should've gone to the reception!" she exclaimed. "You could've introduced us to him." The others chimed in, dismayed that it hadn't occurred to them before. The woman sitting next to me in the back seat grabbed my arm. "If he ever comes to visit you in Gadsden, promise you'll invite us over, okay?"

I smiled. "Now there's a promise I can safely make." The way our wires had crossed this time, I couldn't imagine he and I ever meeting face-to-face again.

~~~~~

It was late the next night, after I'd finished grading essays and gotten ready for bed, when Pat called to invite me to the awards dinner in Birmingham the following evening. He'd obviously forgotten that I wasn't attending the conference.

"Hey! Why don't you come with me to that dinner thing they're having Saturday night?" he said without bothering to identify himself. Not that he needed to; I'd recognize that upbeat voice of his anywhere.

"Oh! Well, I-I'm . . . ah . . . not registered for the conference," I stammered. "And I'm pretty sure you have to have an invitation to attend the dinner."

He laughed. "So? I'm inviting you. Aw, c'mon, King-Ray. Don't make me go by myself. I'm a stranger here, remember?"

I agreed to attend with him, and we arranged to meet in the lobby of his Birmingham hotel, where the participants were being bused to the dinner. When I arrived, Pat stood by the door watching for me and called out, "King-Ray—you made it!" as soon as I entered. I went to him smiling and we hugged like long-lost friends. He stayed close by my side until we got in the bus, even when I stepped away to greet folks I recognized from other literary occasions. Oddly enough, instead of feeling weird to be face-to-face with him after two years had gone by, it felt like the two years had only been a couple of days. He looked the same, the cherubic round face and unruly white hair, those twinkly blue eyes. Instead of the rumpled khakis I remembered from our first meeting, he was properly attired and quite distinguished in a dark suit and white dress shirt.

As gallant as I remembered him being, Pat kindly told me that I looked a lot better than he recalled.

"Hmm. I'm not sure how to take that," I said, and we laughed together.

It was my first experience with Pat's astonishing blarney, but it certainly wouldn't be my last. *Stranger, my arse*, I thought, as he dragged me around to meet friend after friend, despite his having told me that he'd be all alone and pitiful if I didn't go with him. I met his buddies from Atlanta, Cliff and Cynthia Graubart, and felt as though I knew them since both Pat and Anne Siddons had used them as characters in their books. Then I was thrilled to meet Anne Rivers Siddons and her husband, Heyward. Never could I have imagined that we'd end up becoming close friends one day. Everyone was friendly, but I was uneasy. It was a fancy-dress affair given exclusively for the honored guests. This time I was properly attired in a black velveteen pantsuit, so it wasn't that. I just hoped and prayed Pat had let them know that he'd invited me.

He hadn't. Red-faced, the librarian in charge pulled me aside at the restaurant to confess that Pat had "forgotten" to tell them he was bringing a guest. There was no room at his table, which they'd crammed with big donors. Did I mind terribly sitting elsewhere? A leggy blonde with Kim Basinger–like hair was an associate of Pat's (his publicist, I guessed; she didn't say) and she was standing nearby. The librarian gestured frantically to her for help, and it was arranged that I'd sit with her.

The next obstacle was Pat, who scowled and said no way; he'd look like a heel if they put his guest at another table. I leaned in and whispered, "Pat, listen—I've been on library boards before and they need you to woo their donors. I'm perfectly happy sitting elsewhere." Pat scowled but agreed, ambling off to the head table with the relieved librarian steering the way.

During the predinner mingle, I purposely detached myself from Pat to chat with other guests, not wanting him to feel obligated to stick tight just because he'd brought me along. Occasionally he'd show up and ask if I was okay, which I found surprisingly thoughtful. I began to form a different picture of the famous writer who'd somehow befriended me. It amused me to see him as a chick magnet, for one thing. It was as if Fabio had shown up, the way women flocked around him. But Pat didn't appear to be a womanizer, unlike others of his breed that I'd heard about. Instead he just seemed to genuinely enjoy the company of women. He was certainly a study: a chivalrous, old-fashioned man who fairly radiated magnetism and charm. I wasn't unaware of what a dangerous combination that could be. From time to time our eyes would meet and I'd give him a little wave to let him know that all was well.

It seemed that every time Pat and I got together, a librarian ended up pulling us apart, and that evening was no exception. (Got to be a metaphor there somewhere!) After the dinner, everyone lined up to board the bus back to the hotel, and Pat sought me out. We were about to board when Linda, the head librarian who would later become a dear friend of ours, approached Pat. She was literally wringing her hands as she cried, "Oh, Pat—you've got to help me!" She looked absolutely frantic. "One of our poets has disappeared."

The rustic, mountain-themed restaurant sat in the midst of a dense hardwood forest; evidently the poet had wandered off while everyone waited for the bus. Pat shrugged and said to Linda, "One less poet in the world doesn't sound like a bad thing to me."

"This is not a joke," Linda hissed as she pulled Pat away. "Come help me find him."

The bus driver waited until Linda and Pat reappeared with the slumped-over poet, one on each side of him. As they helped the guy into the bus, I heard Linda telling the others that the poor thing was sick. Tugging on Pat's arm, I whispered, "Oh dear! Is it bad?"

Pat snorted. "Sick, my ass. Drunk as a skunk. Never known a poet who could hold his liquor."

As soon as Pat and I got on the bus, the Kim Basinger–looking publicist appeared. Pulling me into a seat next to her, she motioned Pat toward a seat across from us where a man jumped up eagerly and held out his hand. Kim Basinger introduced the man to Pat then said to me sotto voce, "Please forgive me. That man's a Conroy fanatic and begged for a few minutes with him."

"He has an amazing fan base, doesn't he?" I said.

She nodded wearily. "You wouldn't believe it."

I sure wouldn't, I thought, stifling a giggle. It'd been a thrill when my book had gone into a second printing, but I wasn't likely to ever experience anything like the hordes of swooning fans I'd seen around Pat.

Back at the hotel, Pat and I reunited in the lobby and smiled at each other ruefully. "God, what a night," he said with a groan. He appeared to be wiped out. Another thing I'd learned by watching him in action: when you're at the top, everyone wants a piece of you. It had to be utterly exhausting.

"We didn't get to spend any time together, King-Ray." Pat frowned, then peered down the hall. "The bar's closed, but I've got some booze upstairs. Let's have a drink and talk for a few minutes, at least." When I hesitated, he held up his hands. "Don't worry. I won't put the make on you. I'm too damn tired."

I laughed and told him it wasn't that. It was late, and I had a two-hour drive ahead of me. Pat looked alarmed. "Oh, hell no. You're not driving home this time of the night, King-Ray. There's no need to anyway. I've got a room for you. C'mon—I'll show you."

"I don't even have a toothbrush!" I protested as I began to back out the lobby door. "Really, I'll be fine." With an exasperated sigh, Pat marched over and took my arm to stop me. "Okay, okay," I said, holding up a hand in surrender. "I won't drive all the way to Gadsden. I'll crash with my friends in Montevallo instead."

His eyes narrowed suspiciously. "How far?"

Before I could lie and tell him only a few miles, Pat sighed again and led me rather forcefully to the elevator, where he refused to listen to my protests. "Looks like I've finally met someone as stubborn as I am," he muttered as he jabbed in the floor number.

On the top floor, he showed me the setup of his two-storied suite. The bedroom was upstairs, and the living area downstairs had a king-sized pullout sofa. "See? And the upstairs bedroom has a door with a lock," he said, pointing. "So your virtue will remain intact. I'll take the sofa—"

I stopped him. "You'll do no such thing. I'll stay, but under one condition. No—make that two."

For some reason that tickled him, and he raised his eyebrows with an impish look on his face. "Here's the deal," I said. "I won't take your bedroom, but I'll sleep on the sofa." He groaned but asked what the second condition was. "You cannot *ever* tell anyone that I stayed here," I told him.

Pat was still chuckling when he called the front desk for a toothbrush, and I ducked into the bathroom when they delivered it. After they'd gone, I came out to see Pat rubbing his face wearily. "Go to bed," I ordered. We hadn't had our nightcaps, but he needed sleep more. "We'll talk tomorrow."

He was too exhausted to argue, so he said good night with a little wave and started up the stairs. When he reached the top, I couldn't resist calling out, "Hey, Pat—don't forget to lock your door!"

When I curled up on the sofa with a blanket, not bothering to pull it out, I realized how tired I was. A two-hour midnight drive would've been stupid. Dozing off, I wondered why it mattered so much to me that no one knew I was sharing Pat's fancy suite. I was fifty-two, divorced, and hardly a prude. I'd never been one to sleep around but had friends who did, and I'd always figured it wasn't anybody's business but theirs. When would I *ever* stop caring what other people thought? And why was I so obsessed with keeping up appearances? It was an unfortunate trait that my mother had drilled into me. My father sure didn't give a jolly good damn what anyone thought of him and never had. Before I fell into an exhausted sleep, I decided that things were going to change. I was sick of myself—or I would've been if I had any idea who I was. All my life I'd tried to live up to what others expected of me: first my mother, then my husband and the good folks of the church. I couldn't do it anymore.

When I woke at eight the next morning, I splashed water on

my face, brushed my teeth, and ran my fingers through my hair. I looked like a fool in the same pantsuit I'd worn to dinner, but too bad. Nobody'd see me. When I heard the upstairs door open, I brewed coffee in the little hotel pot.

Pat came downstairs dressed in his suit, and I smiled as I handed him a cup of coffee. Without asking, I figured he'd like it with plenty of cream and sugar. "You didn't have to dress up on my behalf," I teased.

He sipped the coffee eagerly and gave me a thumbs-up. I'd guessed correctly. Then he sat on the sofa and motioned me to sit beside him. "You're not going to believe what I have to do today," he said.

"Preach a funeral?" I guessed, then froze at his expression. "Oh God, Pat—don't tell me—"

He nodded. "Yep. I'm giving the eulogy for a friend in Atlanta this afternoon. Going straight there from here." He waved me off as I stammered my regrets, wondering if I was doomed to stick my foot in my mouth every time I saw him. Maybe we were better off staying phone friends.

After asking how I'd slept on the sofa, Pat picked up the phone and called room service. Without asking, he ordered the All-American breakfast for one. I couldn't resist teasing him again and said, "For one? You're not eating anything?"

"Can't," he said. "I'd hoped to spend some time with you this morning, but I've got to get on the road."

"You drove from South Carolina?" I asked, confused. Hadn't my friend at AUM picked him up at the airport? Pat went on to explain that the funeral had changed his plans, then he reached for the phone again to call for his rental car and a bellman to take his suitcase down.

As we waited, Pat said, "If my friend had died a few days later, I would've been out of the country. I'm about to travel to Asia and will be gone for a couple of weeks."

"Asia? How fabulous! Have you been before?"

He hadn't, and we talked about his trip, where'd he be and what he hoped to see. He asked for my address and said he'd send me postcards from exotic locales. He didn't mention if the trip was business or pleasure, and I didn't ask. Although we chatted easily, there was a bit of a distance between us that morning. He was preoccupied, his mind already on the road to Atlanta and the sad occasion that awaited him.

The bellman arrived to pick up the suitcase, and Pat told him that he'd be right down. I joined him by the door to say our goodbyes. He gave me a long hug, then patted my back. "Sorry things turned out this way, kiddo. Typical of my shitty life. I didn't even get a chance to hear what's going on with you."

"Not much to hear," I told him. "I'm just sorry about your friend but hope your trip to Asia turns out to be good. Maybe you'll get some rest."

He frowned down at me. "I shouldn't have invited you to come all the way over here for this. After last night, the least I could've done is gotten my fat ass up and taken you out for a proper breakfast. I'm sorry that things didn't turn out the way I planned."

"Don't be ridiculous. I had a great time. It was a thrill for me to meet Anne Siddons and see her receive the award. Your introduction was fabulous." I gave him a gentle nudge out the door. "But you'd better get on the road so you'll make it to the funeral in time."

He'd barely gone when the breakfast arrived, and I realized how hungry I was. Sitting down to the lavish spread, I thought again about Pat and what an incredibly nice person he was. Despite having to go to a funeral for a friend, he'd thought to order me breakfast. I wished I were half as thoughtful; if so, I wouldn't have let him get off without making sure he took some food with him. I couldn't help but feel guilty enjoying the breakfast that the conference provided for him—though not guilty enough to turn it down. I should've made him take some coffee, at least. Oh well. As Lady Macbeth said, what's done is done and can't be undone. Next time, I'd do better.

If there is a next time, I thought as I closed the door of the fancy suite behind me and headed toward the elevator. Pat was off to Asia, and me back to my teaching. Who knew if our paths would ever cross again?

A couple of days later, a surprise. I came in from my night class to see the answering machine blinking. Pressing the button, I heard a familiar voice and I smiled, remembering.

"I'm about to leave for Asia but I'll be back in two weeks, and I'd like to see you again," Pat said. "I had a really good time, King-Ray. I liked having you with me. I mean that. Having you with me felt . . ." There was a pause as he searched for the word. "*Right.* It felt right."

CHAPTER 4

GOING COURTING

Our potential romance (or whatever you wanted to call it) was far from smooth sailing after such a tenuous start. In March 1997, Pat called when he returned from his two-week trip to Asia. His call wasn't as unexpected as it'd been in the previous two years; while he was away he'd sent a couple of entertaining, albeit impersonal, postcards. (One said, *I've been making waves in Hong Kong and Thailand and have been loving my first trip through Asia. I loved seeing you in Montgomery and Birmingham and delighted that you're happy in Gadsden.*) Despite the fact that we hadn't spoken for a few weeks, Pat plunged right in to the reason for his call, without preamble or as much as a how-d'you-do. When was my spring break? he wondered. He would like to pay me a visit.

It was coming up the following week, I told him, but unfortunately I wouldn't be home then. I was speaking at a writers' group in Savannah and would be traveling with my friends Bill and Loretta. Pat groaned in frustration. Ordinarily he'd be at his home on

Fripp Island, only an hour from Savannah, but that week he had to be in Atlanta on business. It was one of the reasons he'd hoped to arrange a visit, he added, since Atlanta was only a couple of hours away from where I lived.

The man whom I'd found to be as awkward and inept with pursuing women as he'd claimed was surprisingly insistent. When I expressed regrets that things wouldn't work out for him to visit, he ignored me and pushed on. Wait—wouldn't I be traveling through Atlanta on my way to Savannah? he demanded. Matter of fact, we were, I told him, and we'd be staying overnight with some friends there. Pat thought a minute then asked the question: Would it be okay with my friends if we met up somewhere so he could take me out to dinner? He'd been trying to find a time to take me to dinner for so long that it'd be a shame not to at least give it a try.

It was a date, and the arrangements made. My friends dropped me off at a prearranged place convenient to them, where Pat waited in his car. From there he and I went on to have dinner at an authentic Italian restaurant called Abruzzo's. Small, dark, and charming, Abruzzo's was exactly as I imagined a restaurant on a backstreet of Rome to be (strictly in my imagination since I'd never been to Italy). Looking back, I can't believe that I wasn't more apprehensive about the evening; the last time he and I were together had been pretty awkward, what with the table arrangements at the awards dinner, the drunken poet, the hotel room, and his rush to get off the next morning. But strange as it was, I felt like I was meeting up with a dear old friend, and he appeared to be equally relaxed with me. Pleased to hear that I loved Italian food (an understatement!), Pat described the dishes he ordered for me and entertained me with stories of his years in Italy. During the 1980s and his unfortunate second marriage (his words), he and his family had lived in Rome for three years. They'd loved it and planned to live there forever, until his mother got sick and they moved back to be with her.

To my surprise and without prompting from me, he began to open up as he talked about the joy of the Italian years, and how terribly things fell apart after their return to the States. "My ex-wife and I went through a nasty, bitter divorce a few years after moving back," he told me. "We were in San Francisco then. I'd been so crazy in love with her that it seemed impossible that things could turn so ugly and sordid. But we were both such damaged people that the chaos of our life together finally drove us apart."

I sat back in my chair, stunned. Thinking about my own marriage, I wondered if he'd hit on something profound. Maybe it didn't really matter how much two people loved each other when they pledged to be together forever. Despite the love and passion they felt, forces already in play could tear them apart. Wouldn't bringing two damaged souls together only create twice as much chaos? Could it be that some lovers are just doomed from day one because of what each brings to the other? Even though their own union might be ill-fated, they could marry someone else and live in perfect harmony. I asked Pat if that's what he was saying, and he considered it, frowning.

"Hmm. It's certainly something to think about." He swirled his wineglass around and stared off into the distance. "My former wife and I? Our lives were chaotic from the first day we met. We lived in such a toxic environment it's a miracle any of us survived. Both of us came from failed first marriages, and we were emotional messes when we met. Lenore's ex was a madman, and he did everything imaginable to tear us apart. She'd tried to run him over in her car; he and I fought and I ended up in jail for assault; he sued over and over for custody, then their daughter accused him of sexual abuse. Things went from bad to worse."

"*Worse?*" I stared at him in disbelief. "Jesus Christ!"

"Oh yeah, it got a lot worse. Their godawful custody battle was one of the reasons we moved to Rome, to get away from him. We were happy there," he added, his voice wistful. "If we had stayed, I think we'd still be together. Our daughter was born there, and I fell in love all over again."

"Your youngest daughter, Susannah—the great gift of your middle age," I said with a smile, quoting from the dedication page of *The Prince of Tides*.

Pat's face fell and his pale blue eyes darkened. "Ah! That's another story, King-Ray."

I was taken aback by the change in his mood. "Oh dear. And I'm afraid it's not a happy one. Right?"

When he didn't respond, I put a hand on his arm. "I'm sorry, Pat. I didn't mean to pry." I cast around desperately for another subject. Holding up my glass, I motioned to the waiter for a refill. "What kind of wine is this? It's really good."

Pat motioned for a refill as well, then he smiled ruefully at me. "It's okay, King-Ray. The truth is, I need to talk about all this shit. It's going to kill me otherwise."

For the next hour or so, over course after course of fabulous Italian specialties that the chef had prepared just for him, Pat told me more stories of his tempestuous life. From time to time I interrupted with "Wait a minute, you lost me," or "Remind me who this person is?" Otherwise I listened wide-eyed. It was as if he were reading from the books he'd written, and I found my head spinning as I tried to keep fiction separated from real life. The old adage "Write what you know" took on a whole new meaning that night. No writer has ever taken that advice quite so literally as Pat Conroy.

He'd written *Beach Music*, Pat told me, as a love letter to Susannah, whom he called Leah in the book. "She was the most magical kid you've ever seen." His voice was filled with so much longing that it broke my heart for him. "God, I adored her! But I knew if I left her mother, I'd never see her again. She was eleven when we split up, thirteen when the divorce went through."

I did a quick calculation. "And you haven't seen her since then?"

He shook his head. "Barely. We were living in San Francisco at the time. In California, a thirteen-year-old can choose whether or not to see either parent."

"That doesn't sound right to me. A child that young shouldn't have such a burden."

"I don't blame her for refusing to see me," Pat admitted. "I was severely depressed and drinking too much—and I mean, *way* too much. Then I got involved with someone else, which was another nail in the coffin. I was a mess, a suicidal mess. Most of my time I spent trying to come up with the best way to kill myself."

I found myself telling him something I'd never told anyone, except a therapist I saw after my depression got so bad it scared me. "I've been there, Pat. A few years ago, I had my final exit all planned out, down to the last detail. It was a good one too, foolproof. The only thing that stopped me was my boys. I was afraid their father'd be so mad at me for offing myself that he'd take it out on them."

"I'm glad you didn't," he said, and reached for my hand.

"I'm glad you didn't either."

Before we parted that evening, me to Savannah and Pat back to the business that had brought him to Atlanta, he insisted I schedule a time for him to visit Gadsden. Here was the thing, he said. He saw on a map that Gadsden was about an hour's drive from the little town his mother was born in, where he'd been planning to visit for a long time. Might as well kill two birds with one stone, right?

Much later, Mr. Romantic would tell me that was sheer malarkey; he had no desire to see either his mother's old homeplace or Gadsden. He could've fooled me (and did, obviously). But he seemed so sincere that I had no reason to doubt him. Once again we parted ways with nothing more than a friendly hug, friendly goodbyes, and friendly plans to get together again.

~~~

I had my first real indication of where we stood when Pat's long-awaited visit finally came about, a couple of weeks later. After our heart-to-heart in Atlanta, I was anxious to talk to him in depth again, and not just on the phone. His revelations about his "screwed-up life" had both haunted and intrigued me, and I wanted to hear more. A longer visit would be the perfect chance for us to talk in more depth.

Typical of our unusual relationship, I had no idea what to expect from his visit, however. When he'd called to ask where I wanted to go to dinner when he came to town, I told him I'd rather cook. Surely he was tired of eating out, right? He'd love nothing more than dinner at my place, he responded enthusiastically. That was settled, but I didn't know if he planned on staying with me, nor could I think of a polite way to ask him. He hadn't inquired about a hotel, but neither had he asked about my living arrangements and whether I had an extra room. Giving him the address,

I'd described a small circle of town houses and told him that most of the occupants were other old ladies like me.

I was equally unsure of what we'd do during his visit, how long he'd stay, or anything else. Nothing of particular interest was going on in Gadsden that weekend; no plays or concerts or water events at our one great tourist attraction, the majestic Coosa River. Should I plan on our doing something in Birmingham? I wondered. I figured my illustrious guest would end up so bored he'd run back to South Carolina the following day. I led a blissfully quiet life, bound to be dull compared to his in the fast lane. Each night when I got in from classes, I poured myself a glass of wine and turned on bluegrass music. Because I was a recovering vegetarian, my supper was usually pasta and a salad, which I ate while marking essays or making lesson plans. Things had fallen into a predictable pattern, and I reveled in my cherished solitude and new sense of serenity. I'd been standoffish enough with my other involvement that he'd gotten the hint and wasn't coming around as often.

How could I possibly know that after one lovely but platonic dinner date, Mr. Conroy was about to come storming into my placid life with the force of a category 5 hurricane, and that nothing afterward would ever be the same?

Friday evening, Pat arrived at my door starved and appreciative of the fancy dinner I'd labored over half the day. At the community college, the faculty's forty-hour workload was crammed into four ten-hour days, Monday to Thursday, but no one complained about having Fridays off. I spent most of the day cooking, cleaning, and arranging flowers from my little patio garden. Since I had mostly herbs, I used rosemary as greenery to fill in my scraggly bouquets of daisies. Centerpiece in place, I ironed napkins and pulled out the pottery dishes I used for company. Because the kitchen only had room for a small breakfast table (a yard sale special), I decided we'd eat on the patio by candlelight. At a thrift store, I'd found a couple of wicker chairs with a table and turned the patio into a lovely place for alfresco dining.

My town house had two identical bedrooms upstairs, so I fixed up the guest room with fragrant rosemary and fresh flowers, bottled water, and fluffy towels folded on the daybed. Just in case. I still had no inkling of whether or not Pat planned to stay with me. Late afternoon when he arrived with wine, a bouquet of roses, and an overnight bag, I figured it out. "Come upstairs," I told him after we'd greeted each other with a hug, "and I'll show you where the bathroom is. And you can put your stuff in your room." Paying no attention whatsoever to my gesture toward the guest room, Pat plopped his overnight case down in my bedroom across the landing. *Okaaay*, I thought, hiding a smile. Looks like I'd be taking the daybed, then.

After all my fretting and worrying, Pat's first visit to Gadsden went much better than I could've imagined. As we'd done from the start, we fell into cozy, comfortable conversation and could've spent the whole weekend sitting on the patio or sofa talking, talking, talking. But I was determined to be a good hostess, so I showed him the sights, what little there were to see. He loved the Coosa River as much as I did, and Noccalula Falls Park, with its trails and caves, aboriginal fort, and re-created pioneer homestead. The ninety-foot falls was where an Indian princess (of course) had flung herself over the rapids rather than agree to a loveless marriage (a lesson to be learned there, I told Pat). He and I tossed crumbs to the ducks at the foot of the falls, just like my little grandsons did on their visits. At our only museum in town Pat lingered over old pictures of the Coosa when it teemed with steamboats.

Then we visited Bill and Loretta in Montevallo, where Loretta prepared dinner for us. It turned out to be one of those evenings we'd joke about in the years to come. Although Loretta had entertained many visiting writers over the years, including Eudora Welty, having Pat as a dinner guest flustered her—maybe because she'd read *Beach Music*, where the character based on Pat is a food writer. Although primarily a novelist, Pat did his share of writing about food and would eventually get a James Beard award for it. Loretta put her trademark Greek stew in the oven, set the timer, and shooed us outside for cocktails on the patio overlooking their pool. After a lively hour of laughing and gossiping, we filed inside to the dining room, famished. Loretta put on her oven mitts then froze in dismay in front of the stove. She'd forgotten to turn it on.

Back in Gadsden it was late Sunday afternoon before Pat and I said our goodbyes. Would it be okay, Pat asked, if he came back the next weekend? Sadly, we hadn't made it to Piedmont, his mother's hometown. He still longed to see it, he said so sincerely that I didn't see through his innocent-looking expression to the sheer bull beneath. He was welcome to visit anytime, I told him. And I answered his other question in much the same vein: Yes, of course I'd be glad to accompany him to Piedmont. Poor thing was so anxious to see where his mother was born, how could I not?

On his next visit, Pat came in with flowers, then he handed me a small gift bag. Inside was an oblong gift box from a Beaufort jeweler. I opened it in astonishment to find a long string of perfect pearls, the most beautiful I'd ever seen. Being Pat, it hadn't occurred to him to remove the receipt, which I spotted when putting away the bag. It was as much as I made for a whole month of teaching, which confused me even more. I still couldn't read him, couldn't tell what kind of relationship we were in. Last time he'd visited, it had moved swiftly from friendship to romance, and in typical Conroy fashion. When we finally went upstairs to bed, having exhausted ourselves talking half the night, Pat stopped me on the landing outside my room. "I took your room on purpose," he confessed, "hoping you'd get the message."

I couldn't resist teasing him. "Oh? And what message is that?"

Pat grimaced. "Don't make me say it, King-Ray. You know I'm not good at this kind of thing." Determined not to laugh, I raised my eyebrows and watched him expectantly until he gave in. "Okay, okay. Shit!" he said with a heavy sigh. Pulling me in close, he murmured, "I don't want to be your friend anymore, and I'm tired of pretending to be. I want to be with you. That night in Birmingham? It took every bit of willpower to make myself stay upstairs. I've wanted to be with you ever since."

I looked up at him. "Oh, I wouldn't say you're not good at this, Conroy."

~~~

The main thing was, we just enjoyed being together. We talked for hours and we laughed a lot—about everything and anything. In the past I'd learned to suppress my dark sense of humor, but with Pat, I could just be myself, which is why I loved being with him. I've never felt as comfortable with anyone else. Going Zen, I shrugged off the uncertainty of our relationship by repeating the mantra I'd adapted for uncertain situations: it would either work out or it wouldn't.

We finally made a visit to Piedmont, where Pat's mother had been born. Her family, the Peeks, was having a big reunion that Sunday after church, he told me, and it'd be the perfect occasion for him to reconnect with relatives he rarely saw. His mother claimed Rome, Georgia, as her hometown because the family moved there shortly after her birth; so she'd never really lived in Piedmont. Nonetheless, Pat couldn't *wait* to see it. (I was astonished to find out later that he'd been there several times before. The whole thing had been an excuse for him to visit me. Why he felt the need to fabricate an excuse I will never know.) It was obvious that Pat had worshiped his mom, who'd died of leukemia in her fifties, and he told me about her on the drive over. When we pulled into the church parking lot, he warned me that his dad would be there. I guess he feared I wouldn't go if he'd told me in advance.

"Oh, how sweet," I said, "that he keeps up with your mother's family." At our dinner in Atlanta, Pat'd told me how his mother had finally left his father, a few years before her death. Since then his father had lived in an apartment complex in Atlanta, but he'd never remarried. Pat doubted that his dad would ever love anyone else like he'd loved Peggy Peek.

Pat snorted. "Shit. Dad's a lot of things, but *sweet* ain't one of them."

I was apprehensive about meeting his father, but who wouldn't be after reading *The Great Santini*? As soon as we arrived, Pat dutifully took me by the arm to make the introductions. Colonel Don Conroy turned out to be a good-looking man in his midseventies. He had a regal bearing and the piercing, ice-blue eyes that his son had inherited. Despite my fears, Colonel Conroy couldn't have been more charming or attentive to me. Although he and Pat joked around with each other quite a bit, an undercurrent of tension lurked beneath their conviviality. It was the first time I'd seen Pat, usually peppy and outgoing in a crowd, so tightly wound. Understandably, being with his dad still made him jumpy.

The family reunion was held at a church fellowship hall, and I felt right at home with the down-home folks I met there. They were my kind of people. The good old country food laid out on long tables was familiar as well: fried chicken, ham and redeye gravy, field peas, creamed corn, butterbeans, okra. I'd brought a plain old pound cake, which quickly disappeared despite the dozens of other cakes. In addition there were pans of banana pudding; pies of pecan, chocolate, egg custard, or apple; and peach or blackberry cobblers big enough to feed most of East Alabama. Pat's dad, mingling with his former wife's relatives as though they were his own kin, told me that I simply must try the baked bean dish he brought. "I'm famous for it," he told me solemnly. "It's an old family recipe."

"Old family recipe, my ass," Pat muttered as we piled our plates. "I'd steer clear of it if I were you."

"Shh!" I chided. "You'll hurt his feelings."

"Not a chance," Pat said dryly. "He doesn't have any."

To compensate, I took a double portion. The beans were in a scratched-up old Pyrex dish, which made me sad. I pictured Pat's poor dad in his lonely apartment laboring lovingly over his prized heirloom recipe. Sitting across from him, I smiled and took a big bite of the beans he was so proud of. Watching me, Colonel Conroy beamed. "It's an old family recipe," he repeated. "I take it everywhere."

I managed to swallow it down without gagging as Pat watched me with a smirk. Someone came to sit beside his dad and engaged him in a lively conversation, which gave me the chance to whisper to Pat. "It's pork and beans right out of the can! He didn't even warm them up." Thankfully his father's conversation lasted long enough that I was able to dispose of the remains on my plate without getting caught. Seeing the vacant spot on my plate, Colonel Conroy tried to refill it for me but I demurred. Oh, no—it'd be too selfish of me to deprive everyone else, I purred, ignoring Pat's snort of derision.

Later a relative would report to the family that Pat had shown up at the reunion with a "young filly," which tickled both of us. I was a year and a half older than Pat, which bothered me more than it did him. Later when we discussed marriage, I would argue that my age should be a factor in the decision. Who knows, I said—he might want to start another family. Pat had hooted at that notion. The last thing he needed, he said, the *very* last thing, was another frigging family.

~~~~~~~

Pat kept coming up with reasons to return to Gadsden, but at least I began to see through them. It amused me that he thought it necessary to invent excuses, though I couldn't imagine why. As comfortable as I felt with him, I couldn't think of a nice way to say *Cut the crap, Conroy; If you want to see me, just say so.* He called after his visit for the family reunion to ask if I'd be home the following weekend. The thing was, he'd been in touch with a young writer in New York who he was just *dying* to meet, and the kid was going to be visiting his mother who lived—surprise!—not far from Gadsden. Sure, I said; I'd be home. He'd seen firsthand how uneventful my life was. Both times he'd visited, he'd had to entertain himself while I marked essays. Every Thursday, my students wrote in-class essays, and regardless of what else I did on the weekend, those essays had to be given back for revision on Monday. If I got behind, it threw off my whole week.

One time Pat looked on as I graded essays and was appalled by what he saw. "I'd hoped things had changed more since my days of teaching," he remarked. "But some of these kids can't even put a sentence together."

I looked at him in surprise. "Pat, these are college freshmen. You should've seen the papers from my remedial English classes."

He blinked at me, then sighed. "Jesus. I'm glad I didn't."

That Saturday, Pat and I drove north to meet the writer he'd told me about, a *New York Times* reporter who'd written his first book. I wasn't sure I wanted to spend the day with some hotshot reporter but kept that to myself. When Pat told me about the young man's book, however, I changed my mind and couldn't wait to meet him. "It's about his mama, and the publisher sent it to me for a blurb," Pat said. "After I read it, I wrangled the address and sent his mama flowers. She's had a really rough life." The book, *All Over but the Shoutin'* by Rick Bragg, became the big bestseller Pat'd predicted. Instead of flowers, I brought his mama a chocolate cake I'd made from scratch that morning.

Driving a little sports car, Rick Bragg came varooming into the driveway of his mother's farmhouse just as Pat and I were getting out of Pat's car. I loved Rick on sight; he was adorable and as down-home country as every good old boy I'd ever known. His Deep South accent was as thick as mine. Holding Pat in a long embrace, Rick must've thanked him a dozen times for the blurb and flowers for his mama, whom he couldn't wait for us to meet.

Like her son, Mrs. Bragg was a sweetheart. Although she was shy and unaccustomed to entertaining her soon-to-be-famous son's friends, Pat set her at ease with his usual joking and teasing about Rick, and what a disappointment he must be to her. After she found out that I'd been born and raised in LA (Lower Alabama), she relaxed with me as well. She proudly showed off her new house, the first thing Rick had bought with the advance from his book. One thing touched me so much that I had to blink back tears. Although Rick was almost thirty and lived in New York, Mrs. Bragg had fixed up a room for him. With navy-and-green plaid curtains and the walls decorated with banners and sports memorabilia, it was the little boy's room that she hadn't been able to give him in her hardscrabble life. My eyes met Pat's, and I saw that it moved him as well.

I understood that Rick's devotion to his mother had struck a chord with Pat, and it saddened me to think I'd never meet the mother he'd so adored. Neither would he meet mine. I'd lost my sweet mama only five years before, just after she turned seventy. I decided to give each of my boys a copy of Rick's book as a reminder to cherish their mama while they could. Like Rick, they were good boys and fiercely protective of their mother, even overly so on occasion. I'd learned the hard way not to tell them if someone hurt my feelings because they'd swear vengeance. For the first time, I wondered what they'd think of Pat. I'd taken care not to introduce them to anyone I'd been involved with since the divorce, not sure how they'd react. *Oh well*, I thought, turning my attention back to Mrs. Bragg's home tour, *I'll cross that bridge when and if I get there.*

The end of spring semester freed me from classes until summer sessions started, so Pat proposed a trip. "I've got a great idea—let's go to New Orleans!" he called to say. I have no idea what made him think of New Orleans that time of year, but I guess he'd run out of excuses to come to East Alabama. The heat in New Orleans is unimaginable in early June, but fools rush in where angels (or saints, I guess) fear to tread, so we went anyway. I look back on that trip as the first time Pat got to see the real me. And it wasn't pretty.

Decked out in my new pearls and sipping sauvignon blanc as I showed off my knowledge of Renaissance poetry (based solely on the graduate courses I'd fallen in love with years before), I tried hard to pass myself off to Pat as a sophisticate. Trust me, with a southern accent that sounds like you're speaking with a mouthful of corn pone dipped in sorghum, it's not an easy thing to do. "We'll get to know each other better," Pat announced as we set out on the drive. I dared not tell him what I was thinking: that's what I was afraid of. In comparison to him, I was a rube when it came to travel. My last two trips to New Orleans had been strictly business—once to present a paper at a conference, another time to conduct a business-writing seminar with a couple of colleagues. The benefactor of the writing center had been a successful businessman with holdings all over, and he'd sent Loretta and me to do seminars for his corporate executives all over the South. In New Orleans, he'd put us up in a grand hotel in the middle of the French Quarter, but we'd stayed too busy to step out on the town.

Even though I'd visited New Orleans several times in the past, it'd always been on a limited budget. I'd never set foot inside Commander's Palace, Antoine's, Brennan's, or any of the other upscale eating joints Pat and I discussed on the drive down. I wasn't about to let Pat know that, though. I figured I could play the sophisticated lady without flat out lying if I took care with wording. "The Commander's Palace," I gushed with a carefree flap of my wrist, "might have a lot of ambiance, but nothing quite compares to Antoine's. Don't you think?"

Pat had reserved a swanky hotel for us, a suite in the Windsor Court with our own balcony overlooking the Mississippi River. I'd never stayed in such a place, although naturally I pretended otherwise. My first misstep was out of Pat's line of vision: I almost knocked the bellman down when he appeared to open the passenger door for me. Handing over his car keys to the valet, Pat missed the moment when I pushed the car door into the poor bellman's face as I crawled out unassisted. *So that's what those guys do*, I noted. The startled bellman quickly regained his composure and fetched our luggage from the trunk. Unfortunately for him, he hadn't seen the last of me.

Pat learned that the restaurant at the Windsor Court Hotel was one of the most highly ranked in the city, so we didn't have to venture out for dinner our first night. He was thrilled to find that oysters on the half shell were available, even though it wasn't an "R" month. Having been weaned on the famed Apalachicola oysters, I was equally delighted. Plus I wouldn't have to wonder which fork to use with foie gras or how to pry escargots out of their shells.

Either of which might have been a better choice for me, as it turned out. The oysters on the half shell were incredible, topped with a ginger-shallot sorbet and washed down with shocking shots of ice-cold vodka. The tiny vodka bottles were served embedded in a block of ice that centered the table in a footed silver dish. Pat raised his eyebrows when I ordered another round, but I waved him off. For the first time in my life, I was daring and urbane, a Zelda-like sophisticate, dashing down oysters and vodka with the finesse of a true bon vivant. Pat had been right, I realized, about our getting to know each other on this trip. I'd discovered that he was a knowledgeable, cultured person to travel with, and he was learning the same about me.

The sin of self-indulgence always exacts its price from the sinner. I don't remember the rest of the evening, except for a vague, humiliating flashback of Pat half walking, half toting me to our very elegant suite, where I promptly passed out, drunk on oysters. (*Oysters*, for God's sake. Could anything be more embarrassing?) I awoke the next afternoon when he returned from sightseeing with a knowing smile on his face. "Don't get out much, do you, King-Ray?" he teased.

———

What both of us recalled most about the trip to Sin City (or so I tried to convince myself) was how much fun we had. It'd be hard not to, with New Orleans being such a fun place to visit. Playing tourist, we went on a carriage ride, then to Café Du Monde for the traditional beignets and chicory-laced coffee. I finally made it to Antoine's and some of the other landmark restaurants, which were every bit as fabulous as they were heralded to be. We listened to jazz and watched the street artists at work; then after our excursions, we cooled off in the pool at our hotel. We were so hot the water sizzled when we jumped in.

In many ways that time was the highlight of the trip for me. No one was ever in the pool but Pat and me, and like a kid before bedtime, I made him tell me stories. "Just one more, pleeeze," I'd beg, despite my skin wrinkling like a prune from being in the water so long. I couldn't help myself. Pat was on a roll, Scheherazade held captive in a rooftop pool, and he answered all my questions and then some. How much of what he told me was Conroy blarney I'd have to find out on my own, but it was vastly entertaining regardless. Most of his stories about his screwed-up life (the only way he ever referred to it) were hilarious, but occasionally he got serious. I was beginning to get a better picture of how the damage of childhood abuse is carried over into adulthood. I'd been unbelievably fortunate to grow up with loving, uncomplicated parents. Pat was at the top of his game, where every writer dreams of being, but beneath the successful facade would always be a hurt little boy.

One afternoon, we were passing through Jackson Square on our way to Café Du Monde for more beignets when I grabbed Pat's arm and asked him to wait for me a few minutes. There was something I needed to do. He eyed me suspiciously, then shrugged and said he'd step in the cathedral to cool off while I did my thing. I waited until he was safely out of sight before making my way to the group of fortune-tellers set up around the fountain. I never came to New Orleans without having my fortune told, but I knew Pat would scoff at such foolishness. If only I'd selected one of the unremarkable-looking women instead of the seven-foot-tall, dark-skinned man in flowing robes, Pat probably would never have been the wiser. But this guy, with his burning black eyes and long hair in a topknot, was hard to miss. Pat reappeared just as the fortune-teller instructed me to bow toward the north, south, east, and west while chanting "Ohm" three times in each direction. My hands folded as in prayer and cheeks burning, I twirled, bowed, and chanted as Pat watched me with a mocking smirk.

Pat not only didn't tease me about the fortune-teller, though, he surprised me by buying what he said was the perfect souvenir for me. He'd spotted a crystal ball in a store window earlier and went back for it while I finished my coffee at Du Monde's. "Can you read it?" he asked when I unwrapped it. Despite his twinkly-eyed curiosity, I believed he was more intrigued by the occult than he professed. "No, but I can read the tarot cards," I retorted, then braced myself for his derision. Instead his face lit up. "No kidding! Will you read mine?" Sure would, I told him, soon as we got back to Gadsden. I didn't tell him that I'd almost brought my cards with me, just in case I needed to pick up some extra spending money on the Square.

Our last night we decided to eat at the Windsor Court Hotel restaurant again. Instead of the oysters, Pat wanted us to try the chef's signature dish, lobster on some kind of creamed spinach. It sounded like the least appealing way to do lobster. Instead, it was absolutely amazing. I spooned foie gras on a cracker without knowing what it was until I'd taken a bite and Pat, laughing, told me. After years as a vegetarian, I'd started eating a little meat again, but goose innards was a bridge too far. Suppressing my gag reflex, I boldly took another bite in a pathetic attempt to reclaim my thin veneer of culinary sophistication.

I convinced myself that I'd fully recovered my cool after the humiliation of getting passed-out drunk on oysters, never suspecting that our last morning would be my downfall.

Ordering room service breakfast one morning earlier in our visit, Pat was genuinely surprised to find that I'd never had bagels and lox. I enjoyed them so much that he requested a double portion for breakfast for our final meal at the Windsor Court. It turned out to be way more food than either of us could finish. After breakfast, Pat suggested that I do my primping while he went down to check out and get the car. He'd send a bellhop up for our luggage.

The nice young porter from our first day pretended not to recognize me when he came to get the luggage. I was following him to the door when my eyes wandered wistfully back to our breakfast leftovers. It was too much to leave behind. With a smile I said casually, "Ah, I need to get a few more things. You go on and I'll be right down, okay?"

I'm notoriously tightfisted, something that Pat didn't know about me but was soon to find out. I'd already stuffed my suitcase with shampoo, soap, lotion, and several bottles of condiments from previous orders. No way could I leave the remains of such a fabulous breakfast behind! *We can have it for lunch and won't need to stop*, I told myself. How pleased Pat would be that I'd planned ahead.

I realized with a groan that I had nothing to put the leftovers in since the bellhop had taken the suitcases and tote bags with him. The dry-cleaning bags were already loaded with dirty clothes and packed. I wasted precious minutes—they'd be wondering what on earth happened to me—looking for something to use. Finally I found a Styrofoam box from the day before, which I'd brought back my leftover lunch in. It'd been tossed in the trash, but fortunately had landed on top. Though not very big and pretty flimsy, it'd have to do. I dumped the stale po'boy and fries in the trash can, washed out the box, then dried it with a washcloth. Carefully I arranged several toasted bagel halves on its now-clean bottom. On top of them I piled slivers of smoked salmon, squares of cream cheese, finely diced tomatoes, purple onions, and capers. When I got the top closed and started toward the door, I did my best not to think about the half dozen or so miniature jars of strawberry jam left on the table. I could eat those for a month.

With a sigh, I went back to the table to retrieve the jam. This time I had to force down the top of the Styrofoam box. Or rather, it refused to cooperate with my efforts to close it, so I held the top down with one hand while balancing the bottom with the other.

I was almost to the door when the box collapsed in my hands and spilled its contents all over the floor. Staring at the mess in horror, I played with the idea of tossing the box and making a run for it.

With jars of jam rolling around my feet, I was down on my hands and knees scraping up bagels, cream cheese, tomatoes, onions, and capers when I heard a key in the door and my heart sank. I knew without a doubt who it was. Sure enough, I looked up from my unladylike squat to see the bellhop and Pat standing there staring at me in wide-eyed astonishment.

He'd waited for me in the car, Pat explained, avoiding the bellhop's eye, then decided that I must've been waiting for him to escort me down like a proper gentleman. Since he'd already checked out, he had to enlist the services of the bellhop to open the door. Eighteen stories up, and he finds me on my hands and knees stealing food. I quickly finished cleaning up then followed the two of them down, silent and shamefaced. In the car, I saw that Pat was struggling to keep a straight face, and when he burst into laughter, I did too. As I'd feared, he had finally seen the true me.

CHAPTER 5

WHERE DO WE GO FROM HERE?

After our trip to New Orleans—a special place for us that we'd return to many times in the years to come—I packed up for a writers retreat in Black Mountain, North Carolina, and Pat headed out to a cousin's wedding in Florida. On his drive down, he did something that both surprised and touched me. I'd answered the phone to hear his voice even heartier than usual. "King-Ray! You'll never guess where I am."

"Uh . . . your cousin's wedding in Orlando, where you're supposed to be?"

"Nope. I'm in your hometown of Pinckard, Alabama."

"You are not."

"I'm across the street from First Baptist church, calling you from a pay phone by the Shell station."

"Now I know you're lying. Pinckard doesn't have any pay phones."

"They've obviously come up in the world since you left."

"Tell me what you see."

There was a pause and I pictured him stepping away from the phone booth and looking around. "Nothing. There's nothing to see," he said.

I conceded defeat. "How on earth did you find Pinckard . . ." I began, then stopped myself. "Or more importantly, why?"

"I wanted to see where you were raised. Where's your daddy's farm? I might pay him a visit."

I smiled at the thought. "I wouldn't recommend it. He's half deaf and might mistake you for a revenuer." I'm sure Pat thought I was kidding, but a sign at the entrance to the King farm says THIS PROPERTY PROTECTED BY SMITH AND WESSON. In case trespassers don't get the message and enter anyway, there's another one closer to the house: NEVER MIND THE DOGS—BEWARE THE OWNER.

"Tell me about Pinckard." Intrigued as always with the prospect of a story, Pat thankfully forgot about the surprise visit to the farm. Of course, neither of us could've imagined then that had he done so, he would've met his future father-in-law—even if at the other end of a shotgun.

~~~~

Years later, I found an undated letter I'd sent to Pat and was able to place it as written shortly after that conversation. The mention of Black Mountain helped me date it, as did the reference to his diabetes. He'd been diagnosed with type 2 diabetes before our trip to New Orleans, but he wisely waited to tell me until we were heading home so he could eat all the rich food he wanted. He'd told me that a friend of his had suggested it might turn out to be the best thing that could happen since he'd always been so careless with his health. (As for the letter's salutation, I sometimes referred to him as Conrack, which was what his students called him in *The Water Is Wide*.)

Dear Conrack,

Something told me you might need one of my warm, supportive, witty, fun letters on your return. I'm anxious to hear how it went but not sure when I get back from Black Mountain. By the way, I love your honey-toned voice calling me from exotic places like Pinckard. I still can't believe you found a pay phone there. What's the world coming to? Next thing you know they'll have an ATM machine.

The purpose of my writing is to discuss a subject dear to both our hearts—food. I've told you that my friends used to hate me because of my metabolism. Then I hit middle age and they had to find other reasons. But I was determined to stay slim. So I got on a vegetarian / health-food kick for a while and eliminated fats, sugars, etc. If you're into cooking like the two of us are, it seems like all the fun's gone, but the challenge can be kind of fun too. (I can see you rolling your eyes, but bear with me.) Tackling the new diet like everything else I do—by reading everything I can get my hands on—I got interested enough in nutrition to consider going back to school for a degree. So I wasn't just running my mouth when I said I could help you with your new diabetes regimen. Well, maybe I was. But I still think it won't be as bad as you fear.

I agree with your friend who says that this will turn out to be a good thing for you, though it may not seem so now. Wait and see—you'll get healthy, live to be an old codger, and turn out many more fabulous books. I'll stick some of the notes from my reading on nutrition in here, along with a picture of the man I ran off to New Orleans with. He's precious, just precious, a broad-shouldered, blue-eyed Irishman. I'm so grateful to him for such a fun and fabulous escape.

And I'm grateful to you, dear friend, for encouraging me to stay home and work on my book this summer instead of teaching the second term. Taking your advice has made me realize how my depression is linked to my frustration over not having time to write. Time to write is a luxury, which I'll try not to get too used to before classes start back in September.

I'm looking forward to your upcoming visit, but don't forget your swimsuit this time. The little old ladies at the pool have yet to recover from you floating around in your drawers.

Take care of your fool self,
King-Ray

Looking back over old letters and notes and remembering how crazy things were at the beginning of our relationship amuses me, and I find myself either groaning or chuckling. Although my breezy note clearly reveals a deep fondness for its recipient, it can hardly be called a love letter. That would come later in the summer. The only letter that I got from Pat during this time contained a poem; he preferred to call in response to my notes. I know when our friendship changed but doubt I'll ever know why. If love is truly a mystery, as I believe it to be, then that's as it should be, I suppose.

The light tone of my letter verifies what I recall most from the early days of our courtship, how playful our relationship was. Evidently we were both desperate at that time in our lives for a bit of plain old fun. I found Pat hysterical, and we spent most of the time together cutting up and acting the fool. Pat joked so much, and his wit was so deadpan, that it was hard to know when he was serious. Some folks never got it. I did, and in the early days we concocted some really silly games. He joked about being diabetic (nothing was ever sacred to him) and how all his appendages would eventually fall off. Initially I was horrified, then proceeded to beat him at his own game. I'd make up scenarios where I had to help him into the pool because he'd lost his limbs. He'd bob around like a cork, I said, and occasionally I'd have to nudge him into an upright position so he wouldn't drown. Then I'd pull the poor limbless thing through the streets in a wagon so he could enjoy the sights. I cringe now remembering such carrying-on, but that was the kind of dark humor we both had. Until I met Pat, I'd had sense enough to keep that part of myself well hidden.

Looking back, it's obvious that such foolishness was a much-needed emotional release for us. Each of us had come from situations that had left us wrung out, depleted, despondent, and hollow-eyed with despair. Pat's depression was so extreme that he'd later describe it as a mental breakdown. He wrote and spoke freely about his suicidal urges, and how "surviving" a divorce took on a whole new meaning for him. He was in such a bad way after his last marriage that suicide felt like the only relief from the mess he'd made of his life. It's no wonder that gallows humor became one of the ways he coped during his recovery.

It'd take me much longer to write about my own suicidal thoughts. (The first reference I can find is in an essay I published fifteen years later.) As hard as it is for me to open up, I'd been proud of myself for telling Pat about the depression I'd battled for years. I knew that he'd understand, more than anyone. At times it'd gotten so bad I no longer connected with anything that had once given me joy, even my writing. I functioned mostly on autopilot; placid on the surface while beneath I was a seething cauldron of anguish and self-loathing. I had yet to learn that keeping everything bottled up, as I'd always done, was the worst possible way of coping. I would only discover that later, when I began to work my way out of the misery my life had become by embarking on a feverish journey of self-discovery and recovery. I didn't purposefully set out on such a journey; it came about when I began to write again, and only when I began to write about my inner turmoil and struggles instead of denying their existence.

That journey began a few years before I met Pat, when I'd turned to my journals to record the difficulties I was dealing with in my marriage. But putting my feelings in writing was such a difficult and painful process that I could only endure it a little at the time. Disclosure didn't come easily to me, so I would put my journals aside to write an article, or a light little short story. (It was during this time that I published "My Life Is a Country Song," a vapid story about a good old girl whose cheating boyfriend wins her back with classical music.)

The summer of '97, my and Pat's first summer together, was one of those times when I had turned from my journals and toward easier endeavors. Ever since *Making Waves* came out I'd been half-heartedly working on a novel about a preacher's wife. But revisiting that part of my life had depressed me so much that I'd put it aside. So I went back to the novel I'd started about a female rodeo rider. As a girl, I had loved riding and adored my horse whom I'd unimaginatively named Black Beauty. A rider himself, my father encouraged my hobby and took me and my little sisters to rodeos in Florida. My sisters weren't particularly into it but I was enthralled. I idolized the rodeo riders, especially the sequined cowgirls who led the parades. So the idea of writing such a novel wasn't totally out of nowhere for me, and the research was a helluva lot more fun than reliving a pain-filled past. That fall when the rodeo came to Birmingham, I was the first in line.

───~~~───

During our courtship, Pat was honest with me, in his fashion. Although the relationship I'd gotten myself into had come to its inevitable end, Pat was still in the process of breaking free of his. He told me about it one night over supper at my place, after I'd had to take the phone off the hook when my former "friend" kept harassing me. Avoiding Pat's eye, I gave him the short version, saying only that I'd unintentionally gotten myself into a bit of a mess. At first Pat teased me, which was his knee-jerk response to everything. "Aw, poor bastard," he said with that wicked grin of his. "He must be an idiot not to have seen it coming. I pegged you as a heartbreaker the first time I laid eyes on you."

When I shot him a look of exasperation, he got serious, confessing that he'd done a similar thing. The problem he had in terminating his relationship with the "other woman" was guilt. "Because you've strung her along?" I asked suspiciously.

Pat shook his head. Although I wasn't about to let him off the hook, it was obvious that he truly felt bad. "It's not that," he said. "She's a wonderful person who's had a sad life and deserves more happiness than I can give her. According to my shrink, I have a knight-in-shining-armor complex and go into full rescue mode when I perceive a damsel in distress. Goes back to me trying to rescue my mother from my father's wrath as a kid. Show me a woman with a sad story and I fall in love. It's my siren song and my curse." He grew pensive then said, "It's one of the things I like about you, King-Ray. You've worked out your shit and are more together than anyone I know."

I let out a shout of laughter. "If that's the case, your other friends must be serious nutcases."

Pat admitted that he'd always been attracted to chaos, which had almost ruined his life. "I'm a jaded old man who's made a mess of my life and everybody's I've ever been involved with."

"Remind me why I should be with you, then?"

He threw back his head and laughed, his mood suddenly lighter. "That's another thing I like about you, the way you always cut through my bullshit." He reached across the table for my hand, serious again. "King-Ray? What I'm saying is, I need someone to rescue me for a change."

It would only hit me later that was the most profound insight I'd heard from Pat, not to mention the heart of our relationship, but at the time I treated it lightly. Giving him a sugary smile, I squeezed his hand. "Aw, that's *so* touching. But it's also the worst line I've ever heard. Surely a hotshot writer like you can come up with something better."

Pat sighed in exasperation before agreeing to give it another try. Then he drew back in the chair, his eyes narrowed. "Wait a minute! I'm getting the short end of the stick here. From now on you'll think anything nice I say to you is nothing but a line."

"Naw," I assured him. "I can tell when you're sincere."

"How?" he demanded.

"Where would the mystery be if I told you all my secrets?"

Pat studied me for a long moment then said, "Let's put it to a test. I'll say something and you tell me if I'm sincere, okay?"

When I agreed, he took both my hands and stared deeply into my eyes. "King-Ray, I say this with complete sincerity and from the bottom of my heart. You're as bat-shit crazy as I am."

~~~~~~

As time went on I didn't ask Pat about his other relationship because it not only made me feel bad, I didn't really want to know. I cringed the next time he brought it up, but he said he was trying to be honest, not exactly what he did best. He started off poorly by telling me that he'd canceled so many get-togethers with her that he'd run out of excuses. "And you want me to help you come up with some new ones?" I said, trying not to sound too sarcastic.

Pat flinched. "I just feel like such a jerk."

Because I'd been in his shoes I felt for him, but I also knew better than to say anything one way or the other. If he truly wanted to break things off, then he wasn't doing her any favors by staying in. It seemed like the least he could do was come clean and admit he wasn't ready for a serious relationship. I didn't suggest it, though, determined to stay out of the whole thing. It was a situation only he could work out, no matter what.

But I had wondered how he explained his absences in the last few months to someone he'd been seeing before I came into the picture. Several of Pat's friends would tell me later that he was incapable of a clean break with anyone. His pattern was to simply disappear and leave the poor woman to wonder what on earth happened. Pat inadvertently verified that by telling me he'd had so much trouble ending his relationships that he'd sworn to never start another one. The whole thing made me uncomfortable but bemused. Why was he telling me that? Anytime he wanted to end ours, all he had to do was bugger off. I certainly had no intention of tracking the dummy down if he disappeared on me.

Pat's old buddy Cliff Graubart told me that after Pat's breakup with the woman in California (the one he'd planned to marry once his divorce went through), the woman called Cliff numerous times looking for Pat, who'd abruptly cut off all contact with her. He wouldn't return her frantic calls or answer her letters. (According to Pat's version of the story, their parting of ways had been mutual.) "Sounds like she failed to get the memo," I said dryly to Cliff, who threw his hands up in exasperation. "That's Pat for you" was his astute assessment.

The memo I got on hearing this was loud and clear, however. I'd finally gotten myself out of a toxic relationship and had no business getting into another one. Pat might be lovable and a lot of fun to be with, but it was obvious that he could also be a real pain in the ass. I heard the stories of his failed relationships as cautionary tales, to be ignored at my own risk.

The funny thing was, I *still* didn't know where he and I stood. Despite his frequent visits, our trips together, the gifts he brought me, and his almost-nightly calls, I couldn't figure out what was going on with us, much less with his other entanglement. At that point, I wasn't even sure how I felt about him. No question that his mixed signals kept me from getting too emotionally involved; it's certainly easier to remain detached when you can't read the other person. I adored Pat, enjoyed our time together immensely, and felt a strange kind of peace when we were together. But how did I feel about him? I suppose I was like the teenaged Emily, the character in Thornton Wilder's play *Our Town*, when asked by her new boyfriend how she feels about him. Emily gives it careful consideration before responding. "I think about you, George," she says earnestly, "as one of those people who . . . I *think* about."

No question, however, that things had changed between us since New Orleans. Some of our conversations and notes to each other could even be called mushy. Pat called me one time when he knew I was in class just to leave a message: "I have absolutely no reason for calling you, King-Ray. I just wanted to hear your voice on the answering machine." When he came to Gadsden, he started arriving on Wednesday evening, stayed at my place to write while I was teaching the next day, and left late Sunday afternoon. One time he stayed until Monday and left shortly after I did early that morning. I got home late that night to find shrimp salad for my supper, a bottle of wine, and a short note: "King-Ray the stingray . . . being with you was a life-changing experience."

Now what did *that* mean? I wondered. Life-changing in what way, pray tell? Another time on the phone he told me that he was often accused of giving mixed signals and putting up all sorts of barriers to intimacy. I laughed and said, "You *think*?" His response was "So I can't tell you how I feel about you. If I do, I'll be too embarrassed to ever face you again."

No wonder I was confused. Shrugging it off, I coped by doing what I did best. I went into full Helen Keller mode, kept my mouth shut, and just enjoyed the ride. *It would either work out or it wouldn't*, I reminded myself. Either way, it was certainly a fascinating journey.

Despite my laissez-faire attitude, Pat's inability to make a clean break with his other relationship caused a couple of miscues with our plans for me to visit him in South Carolina that summer. I couldn't imagine how difficult the daylong drive was on him, but my teaching schedule had made it almost impossible for me to make the trip instead. Even so, I was willing to give it a try, I was so curious to see where he lived, the places he'd described to me and talked so much about. I'd never been to Beaufort, the picturesque little town closest to Pat's Fripp Island home. A few days after our New Orleans trip, he called to cancel my tentative visit because the other woman had surprised him by showing up. She had some relatives visiting her who loved his books and wanted to meet him. "Guess it'd be better if you came another weekend," Pat said sheepishly. I refrained from reminding him that *he'd* been the one to invite me, not the other way around. "No biggie," I said instead. "We'll try another time."

Ironically, another male writer I knew only casually had asked me to go to a bluegrass festival with him in Tennessee that same weekend. I hadn't returned his call because of my tentative trip to South Carolina, but I called back to say I'd love to go. Sauce for the goose, sauce for the gander. I continued to go out with other guys occasionally, though I still hated everything about dating. Looking back, I'm not sure why I did it. Except when I was with Pat, I was fidgety and couldn't wait to get home. It's where I preferred to be, home and at work on my new book, vicariously leading a rodeo parade on a golden palomino.

━━━━✕━━━━

Despite my big talk and even bigger resolve, Pat and I kept getting closer. The problem was, we just plain *liked* each other and liked being together. Even while I was telling myself not to get involved, something began to shift in our relationship without my being able to articulate what it was, or why it was happening. Although it made no sense, everything kind of fell into place when we were together. Apart, we stayed busy and went on with our lives; together, neither of us felt the need to be anywhere else.

Finding the time to be together, though, was another matter. Pat was determined that I visit him on Fripp Island, but the summer was halfway over before we could make it happen. As if my class schedule and Pat's other entanglement hadn't complicated our plans enough, family matters threw other obstacles our way. Late in the previous spring, Pat's dad had been diagnosed with colon cancer, about the same time that my ex-husband had. I'd stayed with my ex in the hospital during his surgery and visited him after his release whenever I could. By that time, the animosity between us had dissipated, as those things tend to do, and we were getting along. Meanwhile, Pat had brought his dad to Beaufort for treatment. Pat's youngest sister, who lived in Beaufort, was a nurse and could help care for their father. That whole summer, Conroy relatives from far and near flooded Pat's house on Fripp Island for visits with the ailing patriarch. I didn't want to come during that time. Although it wasn't stated, I knew Pat wasn't quite ready to introduce me to his family. We weren't there yet. Where we were, neither of us could've said, nor did we try to. Pat slipped away to Gadsden when he could, and we were content with whatever stolen moments we found.

My first visit to Fripp Island came about in early August. I'd barely begun my eight-hour drive to South Carolina when I wondered if the gods were trying to tell me something. After driving through thunderstorms and torrential rains the entire trip, I got disoriented and ended up halfway to Hilton Head. A friend had given me my first-ever "car phone," but I couldn't make the blamed thing work. When I drove onto Fripp Island much later than expected, the pouring rain made it so dark that I saw nothing of the famed scenery. I arrived bedraggled, hungry, and exhausted. When I climbed the steps to the front porch, drenched, I saw that Pat had left a vase of white roses by the door with a welcome note taped to it. Or so I assumed. The rain had left the note a soggy, unreadable glob, the roses drooping.

Having no way to call me, Pat had decided by midnight that I wasn't coming and gone to bed. I entered the house carrying the vase of wet roses and my suitcase, only to be greeted by a sight that would become familiar in the years to come—not just to me but to other visitors to the Fripp house. In his own home, Pat saw no reason to stand on ceremony. His only concession to the presence of houseguests was to put on his drawers when he made an appearance after bedtime. Hearing a guest arriving late, Pat had no qualms about venturing out of the bedroom to say hello. I can still see him coming down the dark hallway in his boxer shorts; barefoot, bare chested, and calling out a hearty welcome.

It was our first time together with Pat as host, a role he was born to play. He couldn't wait to show me his favorite place on earth. I'd been to the general area many years before; once to Charleston with my parents, then later with my former husband and the boys on vacations in Savannah. But I'd never seen the Lowcountry with the Prince of Tides. "The only way to see Fripp Island," Pat told me on my first morning there, "is by golf cart. And wear your swimsuit because when it gets hot we'll take a dip in the Atlantic to cool off."

On the grand tour, Pat pointed out all the things he'd been telling me about during our conversations over the past two years. I finally saw where he swam every day, where he walked on the beach, and where he went for the best sightings of osprey nests. Enchanted, I drank in the wild beauty of Fripp Island as though it were nectar offered from the cup of God. Accessible only by bridge or boat, Fripp is a private residential island that doesn't have the feel of a resort. Low-key instead of posh and ritzy as I'd expected (and feared), it's a tropical paradise: lush, verdant, and dense with saw palmettos, towering palms, and spreading oaks. On Fripp you'll see weather-beaten cottages rather than columned mansions. Like most of the other dwellings there, Pat's house was so well hidden by moss-hung oaks and oleander that I'd driven past it twice the night before.

Later, folks would tell me that they were surprised by how modest Pat's Fripp house was. Modest it might have been, but it was also cozy and welcoming, a comfortable, low-slung bungalow the color of driftwood. I soon discovered that alligators lurked in the dank waters of the lagoon in the backyard when they weren't sunning themselves on the banks, just a few feet from the house. Fripp's a virtual game preserve. Herds of deer roam around the island as tame as house pets. In the low-hanging branches of trees growing by the lagoon, dozens of snowy egrets perched, which made the trees appear to be laden with giant white blossoms. At some invisible signal the egrets raise their wings gracefully and soar away together, a wondrous sight that took my breath away the first time I saw it.

The following night on Fripp couldn't have been more different than my first one. The rain had gone, and a full moon hung high in an ink-dark sky. On a lark, Pat proposed that we swim in the Atlantic in the moonlight. Although we'd already been swimming at sunset—the water we swam in a fierce pink—we pulled on our soggy suits and headed out again. The island was bathed in moonlight, bright enough to light our sandy path down to the beach. We had it to ourselves, but I just wanted to sit on the shore and stare in awe.

The full moon left such a startling expanse of silver on the gently rolling waves of the dark ocean that I sat watching it spellbound, not wanting to move. The only sound was the splash of the waves on the shore. Pat plopped down beside me and placed an arm around me to shield me from the strong, chill wind. "How could anyone see this and not believe in God?" he said in a low voice.

I shook my head and leaned into him. "Thank you for bringing me here."

"Thank you for coming," he said simply. "I love having you with me."

We must've stayed that way for an hour, neither of us daring to break the spell by talking. Finally Pat nudged me. "Ah, King-Ray? Could you move your lovely ass over a bit? My arm's numb."

With a laugh, I jumped up, ran headlong into the surf, and dived in. Surfacing, I called out, "Is this far enough for you?"

He lumbered to his feet groaning. "I didn't mean for us to actually get *in* the damn water. It's cold out here."

"Suit yourself," I said. "But when's the last time you went swimming in moonbeams?"

On our golf cart ride back home, Pat told me another of his stories, reminding me of our time in the pool in New Orleans when he kept me entertained with tale after tale of his life. His story that night came about after I tried to get him to turn around so I could retrieve a beach towel I'd left on the sands. He shrugged it off, saying it'd be there the next day. "But what if someone gets it?" I cried. "That's a really nice towel, Pat." It was his, not mine, but I couldn't believe he'd blow off something so obviously expensive. The beach towel I'd brought with me was a Kmart special I'd had for years.

He let out a weary sigh. "Oh God. Not you too. I might've known."

"Known what?" I asked, wary.

It was a Conroy thing, he explained. Not too long ago, his brother Jim had come up with the Conroy version of one of Aesop's fables. Everyone, Jim observed, was by nature either extravagant or thrifty—in other words, each of us was either a grasshopper or an ant. In the fable the industrious ant was busy storing up for winter while the grasshopper fiddled and frolicked and frittered away his resources. According to Jim, most Conroys were ants. Jim and his brother Mike, both ants, had married outside their species by hooking up with grasshoppers. Their sister Kathy was an ant married to an ant; while brother Tim and sister Carol were ants with their provisions and grasshoppers with other people's.

"You, my dear," Pat said with a glance my way, "are obviously an ant. I've never met an ant who wasn't proud and pious about it. You'll fit right in with my family."

"And what are you?" I teased.

"Now what do you think? Unlike you stingy, miserly ants hoarding your last dime in your tight little fists, we grasshoppers are life-affirming, Zorba-like creatures. My family calls me the Jurassic Grasshopper."

~~~~~

It was early fall before Pat and I arrived at the point where fate seemed to have been taking us all along. During the summer Pat's other relationship had ended as amiably as he'd hoped, and now ours was out in the open. The next time I came to Fripp I met Pat's closest friends there, Gregg and Mary Smith. On my first visit

Pat had intercepted Gregg at the door but not invited him in, which hadn't fooled Gregg one bit. "I guarantee you that son of a bitch has got a new woman with him," Gregg had reported to Mary, who told me later. Why would Pat hide a new love interest from them? Mary had asked her husband, since they hardly knew the other one. Gregg's response was "Why does that crazy fuck do anything he does?" Gregg had been at The Citadel with Pat and knew him well.

One bright day we took off for a picnic on Pat's boat, aptly named the *Grasshopper*, with the Smiths and another couple, friends of theirs visiting from Georgia. Although our picnic was mostly liquid—a choice of either vodka tonics or Bloody Marys with pickled onions instead of celery sticks—no one got soused, which might have saved our lives. With Gregg at the helm, we boated for hours, basking in the warmth of the sun and strong salt breezes. We were in the middle of the St. Helena Sound, a few miles from Fripp, when a dark cloud formed overhead. In the hands of an experienced skipper (Gregg ran the marina in town), we nonchalantly headed back toward Fripp.

The marina at Fripp was in sight when the bottom fell out. Lightning flashed around us as a sudden squall blew in and turned the water we'd just peacefully floated on as wild as a tempest. The *Grasshopper* was a good-sized boat, but the squall tossed it around like it was a toy. Huge angry waves splashed over the sides and soaked us. Squealing, Mary and her friend Becky grabbed for the picnic items, which were rolling all over the place. From his perch near Gregg, Pat yelled at me to hang tight, which I was doing with both hands. Maybe it was hysteria, but each time a wave—the water was now freezing cold—sloshed over me, I screamed with laughter. The wilder it got, the more I howled. Evidently it was contagious. By the time we'd reached the dock,

Mary Smith and I were bent double with laughter. None of the guys were able to join in, as they were working frantically to get us safely docked. By the time that was accomplished, the rain had stopped. It hardly mattered then since we couldn't have been any more soaked.

Safely ashore, we all laughed and hugged one another in relief. When we posed for pictures, Mary and I bent over to turn our wet rear ends to the camera. In the midst of a storm, I'd found a soul sister, my first Lowcountry girlfriend.

The storm seemed like nothing compared to what happened when we got back to the house. Few things have ever caught me so completely off guard. Even though Pat and I had wrapped in towels on the golf cart ride home, we were still dripping wet when we entered the house. My teeth were chattering as both of us rushed toward the shower. He headed to the master bedroom while I opted for the one closest to the guest bedroom. When I passed by Pat in the hall, he paused to smile down at me. He was looking at me so intently that I said, "*What?*"

"I just want you to know, King-Ray," he said in a tone I'd never heard before, "that I love you. I think I've loved you from the first time we met."

"I love you too," I mumbled as I ran into the bathroom. Leaning against the door, I closed my eyes and took a deep, trembling breath. *Did we just say what I think we said? Oh God. What on earth will we do now?*

~~~~~

Pat's answer to that question was simple: we were in love, we didn't want to be apart, and we were too damn old to be traveling back and forth to see each other. Once my classes started back, the traveling would have to be all on his part again. He wasn't in the best of health and the frequent drives to see me had about killed him. Plus there was the situation with his father, who'd be staying in Beaufort for treatment. Colonel Conroy's stay would be divided between Pat and Kathy, but Kathy worked full-time so Pat would be the one taking his father most of the time. Our long-distance relationship was about to get a lot more complicated.

It would make more sense for me to move in with him than for him to move to Gadsden, Pat said. Only his earnest expression kept me from laughing out loud in sheer astonishment. Him in Podunk, Alabama, when he could be on a tropical island? Surely he wasn't serious! Although the invitation to move to Fripp Island was certainly tempting, I couldn't see giving up a great teaching job at a time when they were so hard to come by. I'd somehow lucked up and landed a teaching position over hundreds of other applicants, probably because I was a published author and could teach creative writing as well. The joke in my profession was, What does the PhD in English say on his/her first day on the job? Answer: Would you like fries with that? Or worse, what do you call a male PhD without a girlfriend? Answer: Homeless.

It wasn't a good idea for me to give up such a hard-to-come-by job, I told Pat reluctantly. He scoffed, saying I could teach in South Carolina. He knew plenty of folks at the local colleges and could get me a position, if that's what I wanted. My reluctance bewildered him. Where was my sense of adventure? Women always claimed to be more romantic than men, but obviously that was nothing but bull, he said in frustration. Couldn't I give it all up for love?

Apparently not. I told myself I had better sense but the truth was, I was scared. Pat had been involved in two other relationships since he'd separated from his ex-wife, and neither of them had worked out. Suppose I threw caution to the wind and the pattern repeated itself? He had a way of disappearing on people, and if he did, where would I be? Answer: I'd be out of a job and in a strange place where I knew hardly anyone.

Nope. Wasn't going to happen.

Even so, I began the 1997 fall semester back at my teaching job haunted by an image of Pat that I wasn't able to get out of my mind. He'd invited Bill and Loretta to come to Fripp with me on Labor Day weekend, our last stretch of time together before my school year began. We'd had a thoroughly enjoyable time, but as we packed the car, Pat pulled me aside. "So you're really going to leave me here all by my lonesome?" he said. I repeated what I'd told him before, that I felt it was best for both of us. If he still felt the same way at the end of the school year in May, then we'd talk about my moving there again.

"Go ahead then, break my heart. I knew you would," he said, throwing his hands up in the air. It was so typical of him that I laughed and got in the car. As usual, it was impossible to tell if he was serious. Was he? Was I crazy to turn down a chance to be with the man I knew now that I truly loved?

As we pulled out of the driveway, waving, Pat stood on the porch and watched us, hands in his pockets. He looked so forlorn I could barely stand it, and I blinked to keep from boo-hooing. Eyeing me in the rearview mirror, Loretta gave me a sly smile. "Oh, girl, you got it bad, don't you? And I think he does too."

"I don't know, Loretta." I sighed. "Maybe. But how can I be sure?"

This time it was Bill, my former teacher, who caught my eye.

My Alabama friends had another nickname for me, K.B. (Don't ask.) "Aw, c'mon, K.B." Bill snorted. "You know better than that. How can any of us be sure of any damn thing in this life? You love the guy, he loves you, and neither of you are getting any younger. If you throw that away, you're nuttier than I thought you were."

~~~~~~

Pat and I were miserable apart, and we talked for long hours every night like a couple of lovesick teenagers. As much as I enjoyed teaching, my mind was elsewhere and I knew I wasn't giving it my best. I felt bad for my students, which made me try even harder not to let my mind-set interfere with my job. But I was distracted, preoccupied, and troubled. Even worse, I had absolutely no idea what to do about it. All I knew was, sometime during our crazy, unpredictable journey together over the past couple of years, I'd fallen in love with a crazy, unpredictable man. It must have been the storm.

I was only able to make one trip to Fripp that fall, in October, a visit that Pat would tease me about for years to come and that would be added to his repertoire of stories about me. Pat collected stories in much the same way he collected books; he'd pull one of them out from time to time to share if he deemed it either funny or wise. During my visit in early October, Gregg and Mary invited us to go with them to a Citadel football game. Pat had been a fine athlete during his college career there. Lousy cadet, but good athlete, Gregg hastened to tell me. Unlike the affable, easygoing Gregg, Pat had a complicated relationship with his alma mater. After his novel *The Lords of Discipline* revealed some unsavory truths about the school's hazing practices, Pat was no longer welcome on campus. Then he'd made matters worse by defending the first female cadet to attend, which caused an even bigger stink and made him more unpopular than ever. He even got a few death threats on that one.

My initial hesitation about Gregg and Mary's invitation to the game was based on Pat's response. "You love football, so let's do it," he said to me. Then he added, "It's probably safe for me to go back now."

Probably? Probably wasn't good enough for me. During my previous visit, Pat had driven me around The Citadel campus, which was surreal, like entering the set of a movie. (The campus in the movie made from *The Lords of Discipline* was actually in England because the school wouldn't allow it to be filmed there.) It was a formidable place. Scary even, if you'd read Pat's book. Pat stopped the car, rolled down the window, and called out to two young knobs (freshmen) marching past us. "Hey, dumbasses! Great choice of schools you made. Love the haircuts." I saw the moment of startled recognition on their faces, and they saluted him sharply. "Yes, sir, Mr. Conroy, sir. Great choice, sir! Thank you, sir!"

Pat pulled the car away laughing.

But our safety wasn't my only concern about going to the game. "I couldn't go anyway," I wailed. "I didn't bring anything nice to wear."

It took Pat a minute to get it, then he groaned. "This ain't Alabama football, sweetheart. Dressing up for a Citadel game means wearing a shirt."

He was right about both. We were not only safe but welcomed, and everyone was in shorts, T-shirts, or uniforms, without a dolled-up sorority girl or preppy fraternity boy in sight. We had a great time tailgating with the Smiths and other former classmates of Pat's, a rowdy bunch that made me feel like one of them. They descended on the food Mary and I brought like a swarm of locusts.

We filed into the stadium, where the atmosphere was even more electric with excitement and camaraderie. When the team ran out on the field, I gasped. "Those boys don't look big enough to play football," I whispered to Pat, who reminded me again it wasn't the SEC.

Telling our story later, Pat claimed he could pinpoint the exact moment he knew for sure that he had to marry me. When The Citadel's opponent lined up defensively, I grabbed Pat's arm. "Uh-oh. They'd better watch out for a safety blitz."

Pat turned to stare at me in astonishment. "Would you kindly repeat what you just said?"

But there was no need. I pointed to the field and winced when the quarterback was hit by the defensive safety so hard he fumbled the ball. "Yep," I said with a sigh. "Safety blitz. I can spot 'em every time."

A woman who could talk football, Pat said to Gregg. Where had I been all his life?

───◦◦◦───

I came for Thanksgiving with the entire Conroy clan and met the folks who had already become mythical figures in my mind, having become acquainted with them by their portrayals in *Beach Music*. Pat had five younger siblings—his brothers, Jim, Mike, and Tim; and two sisters, Kathy and Carol. Their names, Pat often said, told you all you needed to know about the Irish Catholic imagination when it came to naming their kids. (He wasn't even the only Patrick in the family: Jim was James Patrick, and the brother who died, Thomas Patrick.) It was an effort for me not to call Pat's brother Jim by the name of Dallas, or the others by his/her character's name in the book. Although I knew Pat had an on-and-off relationship with his sister Carol, the poet from New York, she was perfectly lovely to me, and told me that my southern drawl was a lot like her mother's. I especially liked Pat's sister Kathy, and the sisters-in-law, Janice, Terrye, and Jean.

It was a delight to meet Pat's oldest daughter, Jessica, who looked like the actress Drew Barrymore to me; and little Elise Michelle, Pat's only grandchild at the time. Another daughter, Melissa, was in graduate school at Georgia; Pat would take me to meet her later for one of her art shows. His two youngest daughters, Megan and Susannah, lived in the Bay Area of California where Megan had her first teaching job and Susannah was a junior in high school.

I'd find that all of Pat's girls were artsy and free-spirited. Jessica and Melissa had graduated with art degrees; Megan had a degree in art history, and Susannah had published poetry. On one of our golf cart rides, Pat had told me about the time he took his father to Melissa's graduation at RISD, the Rhode Island School of Design. Typical art students, the graduates paraded across the stage to get their diplomas mostly barefoot, and in various other degrees of undress. It amused Pat, their graduation speaker, but the colonel was so horrified he almost walked out. When Don Conroy, strict military man that he was, lamented the loss of values in American culture, he'd blame it on the way the younger generation was raised. Spare the rod, spoil the child, was his creed, making him a popular guest on conservative talk shows. Hearing his father dispersing child-rearing wisdom, Pat dubbed him the Nazi Doctor Spock.

But the time I found myself with the large and rambunctious Conroy clan, everyone was so welcoming that I forgot to worry about whether or not they'd like me. Before the weekend was over, Mike's wife, Jean, a petite and perky kindergarten teacher, had pried my secret out. "I hope you'll be coming back," Jean said in her sincerely sweet way.

"I will," I told her. "Soon."

Something in my tone must've alerted her because Jean cocked her head and looked at me with a twinkle in her eyes. "Oh, really? How soon?"

I glanced around then shrugged, giving in. Kathy stood next to Jean and eyed me expectantly. They'd be finding out soon enough, though I hadn't told my own family yet. "I'll be here by Christmas, as soon as the semester is over at my school," I told her. "Ah . . . actually, I'm moving in."

Mr. Romantic hadn't exactly issued an ultimatum, which would've certainly been more romantic. He'd simply said he'd be damned if he'd keep driving over to see me. Like it or not, I'd have to marry him. "But I don't want to get married again," I'd protested. Neither did he, Pat assured me. "You claim you were a lousy wife, and I definitely was a lousy husband" was his argument. "Both of us have made a fine mess of our lives. But I think I can get it right with you, King-Ray." Then he had shaken his head hopelessly. "Besides, what else can we do? It seems that I can't live without you. God*dammit*."

Trying not to laugh, I'd said, "You haven't even asked me if I felt the same."

He avoided my gaze. "Yeah. I was hoping you wouldn't notice that part until it was too late."

It was already too late. I think I'd known all along, we'd both known, that I would give up my teaching job and come to live with him when the first semester was over. Like so much else that had happened since we'd met, it felt inevitable, as though we were being swept along by a fate we had no control over. And it was happening fast. By that time, whether or not either one of us was ready seemed entirely beside the point.

CHAPTER 6

WEDDING BELLS AND OTHER MISHAPS

Pat and I were married sometime in late May 1998. Neither one of us could remember exactly which day. A few years later I asked Judge Alex Sanders, who'd performed the ceremony in the beautiful gardens of their house at the College of Charleston, where he served as president. His wife, Zoe, was my matron of honor and the only other person present. No one in either my family or Pat's knew we were there, or that we were getting married that day. When I asked about the date, Judge Sanders shrugged and suggested I look on our marriage license. I had and found only the date we applied for the license. Alex shrugged again. "Seems like it was on a Sunday?"

We had reason for confusion. Everything leading up to that day, whenever it was, had been the usual Conroy drama. After a sudden decline that came on much sooner than expected, Pat's father had died the second weekend in May. When I'd first moved in, I would've bet good money that tough old bird would beat the thing. When the family gathered for Thanksgiving, he'd appeared robust and hearty, despite his doctor's grim prognosis of only a few months left. Cancer was no match for the Great Santini, I thought. Even in a weakened state he'd still been quite formidable, and despite myself, I came to love him. I believe he was rather fond of me too, though he could never express it. When he was still able to travel, he divided his time between Pat and me on Fripp, Kathy's house in Beaufort, and his old apartment in Atlanta.

Sometimes the colonel would show up for a stay with Pat and me with a "hostess" gift he'd bought me. Inevitably Pat would tease him about how cheap it was. His father was unfazed. One time he brought me a tube of luscious-smelling hand lotion. "You steal that from one of your girlfriends?" Pat asked him.

"Nope," his dad retorted. "I bought it at that place that sells women's stuff. You know, brassieres and things like that. Victoria's."

"Victoria's Secret?" I gasped. "No wonder it smells so good. Thank you, Don."

Pat eyed his father suspiciously. "And what were you doing in a place like that, Dad—cross-dressing?"

For my birthday in February, the colonel presented me with a hideously ugly running suit of green-and-purple polyester that he'd purchased at the PX. My polite *ooh*s and *ahh*s were drowned out by Pat's shout of laughter when I opened the package. "I won't even ask where you got that godawful thing, Dad," he said, chuckling, "but it sure as hell wasn't Victoria's Secret."

A good thing about the running suit, Pat was so afraid I'd wear it that he went immediately to Charleston's finest ladies wear shop and returned with three new outfits for me. His note read *Cassandra, light of my shadowy life, Pat.*

The Great Santini watched ESPN with me, but Pat, he mostly

ordered around. "Hey, fix me something to eat, pal," he'd call out from his perch in our den. Pat would appear at the door, hands on hips, to glare at his dad. I learned not to meet his eye or he'd glare at me too. But he always complied. Neither he nor his father could ever put their hard-earned affection for each other into words. Pat showed his in the time-honored way: he prepared food, wonderfully heathy and tasty food, for his dying father. As much as his dad put up a brave front, his decline was unavoidable and difficult to witness. He walked by leaning heavily on a cane, and he tired quickly. But his appetite stayed good until the final weeks before his death, and I believe Pat's cooking was part of the reason.

A lot of folks asked me what Pat's father was really like, having seen the movie or read the book where Pat depicted their difficult relationship and his father's abuse. Beneath the gruff exterior and rigid military bearing, Colonel Conroy could be quite a charmer. He had several girlfriends, lovely women in their seventies like he was, and was extremely sociable. Everyone said he was a great dancer in his day. He and Pat mostly joked around with each other, and he was easygoing with his other kids as well. He seemed to dote on the grandkids: Pat's daughters, Jim's two little kids, and Kathy's teenaged son, Willie. But I never doubted for a minute Pat's version of the father of his childhood. For one thing, Pat's siblings verified it, but even if they hadn't, my intuition told me all I needed to know. Despite the outward charm and affable demeanor, Don Conroy was one fierce old warrior.

⌁

Earlier that spring, Pat, his dad, and I had a really fun trip together, despite the dire circumstances that brought it about. Pat was driving his dad to the famed Duke University medical center for an evaluation to see if anything could be done about the cancer. Duke, MD Anderson, Sloan Kettering, the Mayo Clinic—these places hold the one thing that cancer victims so desperately need: hope. Often the hope isn't even for a cure, but simply for a little more time. Unfortunately, neither Duke nor any other place was able to offer either one to Don Conroy.

Pat thought the road trip would be a good way for us not only to spend time with his dad but also to visit his buddy Doug Marlette, who lived near Durham. I'd met Doug but not his family, although his wife and I had spoken on the phone. I'd been a longtime fan of Doug's work without ever imagining knowing him one day as a friend. A political cartoonist, Doug was best known for his syndicated cartoon *Kudzu*. He'd paid Pat and me a visit on Fripp the first of the year on his way to an event in Florida and admitted that he'd stopped by for one reason—to size up Pat's new fiancée. I must've passed muster because he and I became fast friends. Eventually Pat'd tell the story of Doug's first visit to us over and over because it had tickled him so much. A few years before, Doug had visited Pat on Fripp because Pat was so severely depressed after his divorce. No wonder, Doug observed; the house was a wreck. (No one ever accused Pat of being a neat freak.) After I'd moved in and Doug came by, he walked in the door and fell dramatically to his knees laughing at the difference. "Now this," he said to Pat, "is what a home is supposed to look like."

It was from Doug that I first heard the term "beauty disease." "I see that you have the beauty disease too," he'd said to me as he eyed the way I'd fixed up Pat's Fripp house. After he'd explained it, it hit me that I'd suffered from the beauty disease all my life without knowing what to call it. According to Doug, you fell victim if you had an incurable longing for, and appreciation of, a beautiful set-ting. Some people could live happily in less-than-attractive or even squalid surroundings, while others literally sank into depression when forced to do so. "No wonder I never liked the part of South Alabama I was raised in," I told Pat in a moment of clarity. "It's *ugly*." And it was true; I had always sought out beauty wherever I was and in whatever situation. With me, it was a deep longing, like the thirst for water. Finding myself in a spot of exceptional beauty, I literally drank it in. Thanks to Doug, I finally had a name for my affliction.

On the drive to Durham, Colonel Conroy and I had fun to-gether, mostly by teasing Pat. We begged him to stop at a cheesy tourist attraction at the North Carolina state line called South of the Border. The place has corny road signs for miles to entice the weary traveler to make it a pit stop. For pure aggravation, Pat's dad and I took turns reading the signs and laughing uproariously as though they were the cleverest *New Yorker* cartoons. "Chili to-day but hot tamale!" one of us would read, and Pat would groan. He agreed to stop there for lunch if we'd promise to shut the hell up. Although Pat and his dad thought their chili dogs were almost as good as the Varsity's in Atlanta, I suspected my grilled cheese was Velveeta but dared not tell Pat. He would've said it served me right.

Doug and Melinda Marlette threw a big brunch for us at their stately historic home and invited three hundred of their closest friends. Among them were famous writers, journalists, musicians, and other big shots, too numerous to name. I hadn't brought clothes for a party and felt self-conscious around the well-heeled guests. (A theme in my life!) In a treasured photo of me, Doug, and Pat, taken with UNC basketball coach Dean Smith, I'm wearing a plain white sweater with brown slacks, looking like Jane Eyre at Mr. Rochester's fancy-dress ball. Whenever I was introduced as Pat's fiancée to the party guests, I imagined they were wondering what on earth Pat could possibly see in such a mousy little schoolmarm.

No matter how I'd dressed I would've felt plain next to Melinda Marlette. Melinda's one of the most gorgeous women I've ever known, and she has an equally beautiful spirit. When I needed a great beauty as an inspiration for a character in my second novel, *The Sunday Wife*, I knew immediately who my model would be. I don't know if Melinda recognized herself, but Pat sure did. I was pleased when he asked me if my character Augusta was based on Melinda. Although Pat was a master at doing so, I'd never based a character on a real person before, and it's much more difficult than it seems. It was strictly Melinda's looks and vivacious personality I tried to capture, I told Pat; I knew that Melinda had better sense than my poor character, who came to a tragic end.

It surprised me to find that I wasn't the only one at the party who felt out of their element. Although I'd seen Colonel Conroy hold court at several gatherings we'd hosted where he was witty and charming and always had a crowd around him, at the Marlettes' brunch he kept slipping away to sit alone on a sunporch in the back. I nudged Pat, afraid his dad was unwell, but Pat shrugged it off. "Don't let him fool you," he said dismissively. "He'll never admit it, but a literary crowd intimidates him. That's why he's hiding out."

I fixed a couple of brunch plates, one for me and one for the colonel, then carried them to the sunporch. "So many folks came that Melinda's brought out name tags," I told him as I pulled a chair next to him and put my plate on it. "I'll go get us some, but don't let anyone take my plate while I'm gone, okay?"

To this day I don't know what made me do it, but I suppose it was Pat's claim that his father felt intimidated by the literati. I went to the table where the name tags lay in a basket and took two. On one I wrote THE GREAT SANTINI. On mine I wrote HARPER LEE, stuck it on, then returned to my chair. The colonel eyed me suspiciously as he placed his name tag on his red sports jacket, but he made no comment about my new identity.

As the crowd swelled, the sunporch filled up. Now that he was tagged and recognizable, the Great Santini attracted a crowd. Pleased, I turned my attention to the scrumptious brunch and was digging in when Colonel Conroy stopped me cold, my fork halfway to my mouth. I heard him say to the crowd, "Have you met my friend, Miss Harper Lee?" I looked up from my plate with my cheeks aflame. The colonel's blue eyes sparkled with mischief, just like his son's did when he was up to no good.

Before I could explain that it was just a silly joke, a woman knelt in front of me and clasped her hands together reverently. "Oh, Miss Lee!" she cried. "This is the greatest honor of my life. I have *always* dreamed of meeting you."

Her friends gasped and joined in, cooing and exclaiming and carrying on about *To Kill a Mockingbird* while I sat there frozen in dismay. When one of them began digging through her purse for a pen, the colonel said sternly, "No, no. No pictures, no autographs. Thank you for stopping by, but Miss Lee needs her privacy. You understand."

Practically genuflecting, the women hurried off in a flurry of thank-yous and excited titters. I heard one of them say she expected Miss Lee to be much older, but her friend whispered that with all Harper Lee's money, she could surely afford a facelift or two. I ripped off the name tag and breathed a sigh of relief as soon as they were out of sight. Pat's dad held out his plate. "If it's not beneath the dignity of such a famous writer, how about getting me a refill? But no grits. I don't eat that southern crap."

I looked around nervously. "You think it's safe? Those women are bound to tell folks that Harper Lee's here. Oh God, why did I do such a stupid thing? Pat's going to kick me out."

"If he does, you let me know and I'll brain him."

I couldn't help but smile. "Yeah, I hear you're good at that."

The colonel scoffed. "He's always been a liar. Makes his living at it."

I stood up and took his plate. "All writers do."

"So I see," he said with a snort. "All of you, nothing but a bunch of damn lunatics."

There was only one time that I saw a flash of the old Santini, and it wasn't a pretty sight. One of the colonel's girlfriends came for a visit when he was staying with us on Fripp, and I prepared a nice dinner for the four of us. Pat had gladly relinquished the task to me. He'd opted out by saying cooking a nice dinner for his dad was a waste of time that he could spend writing. He'd learned that his dad had no culinary tastes whatsoever and actually preferred canned or frozen to Pat's offerings of fresh and local. Since the colonel was a meat-and-potatoes guy (no surprise there), I fixed pork chops and gravy, mashed potatoes, green beans, and, of course, good old American apple pie.

Carrying food to the table, I missed the moment it happened, so I don't know what tripped the Great Santini's fuse or what exactly was said. Everything had been congenial when I called us to dinner and pointed out the seating arrangement. Just as I set the platter of pork chops down, the colonel turned to snarl at the girlfriend. Although I didn't catch what he said to her, his tone was sharp and vicious sounding. A deadly silence fell over the table like a pall. Horrified, I sank into my chair by Pat, who froze in place. It was like a stab to my heart to notice Pat's hands tremble as he picked up his fork. For a terrible moment, the tension was high and tight. I dared glance at Santini's girlfriend, whose face flamed red in embarrassment. But slowly and with great dignity, she nodded at me and said, "Pass the pork chops, would you, dear?"

Conversation resumed and the tension dissipated, but I was visibly shaken. Later I snuggled up to Pat in bed but said nothing of the evening. He held me close and kissed my forehead. "Welcome to my life, kiddo," he said with a weary sigh.

A big birthday feast was planned for the Great Santini's seventy-seventh birthday on April 4, 1998, and relatives from far and near came for the occasion. Most of them knew it'd be the last time they'd see him alive. He was released from the hospital just for the party, and jaundice had made him weak and yellowish. But he held court stretched out grandly in Pat's recliner, clad in a hospital gown and draped with a plaid blanket. Because there were so many folks to serve, we'd gotten barbecue from town, supplemented by dishes I'd made and others that the guests brought.

I'd not only decorated the house with birthday banners and streamers but also made three birthday cakes. Colonel Conroy looked ghastly, but not surprisingly, he kept up a good front and was as entertaining as ever. The truth was painfully obvious to his kids, however, when he called Kathy to his side while the party was still going full swing. "Hey, Sissy?" he said to his youngest daughter. "You and the boys get me out of here without anyone noticing. Think I need to go back to the hospital."

The Great Santini died almost a month to the day after the birthday celebration. Pat's daughters, as well as his nephews and niece, were heartbroken by the loss of their beloved grandfather. It had both amused and peeved Pat and his siblings to see how their father had doted on his grandchildren, like every normal grandfather in the world. Where was the brutal man they'd known? I couldn't answer that, of course, but I imagine that Don Conroy is not the only man who knew he'd messed up with his own children and looked at the next generation as a chance to make amends.

~~~~

It was several days after his father's funeral when Pat and I ran away to get married. One thing we knew for sure—we didn't want any hoopla or publicity surrounding our wedding, so we didn't tell anybody about it. Even *I* didn't know about it at first (yet Pat called me Helen Keller?). He was always one for surprises, and it would take me years to learn to read him. Not that I ever did, but it got a little easier as time went by. After I'd come to live with him, I'd written Pat's daughters and my sons a letter in an attempt to explain our insanity in joining forces at our age and stage in life. I hoped they understood it, I said in the letter, because neither Pat nor I did. Truer words have never been spoken.

Our marriage had come about as inexplicably as everything else in our relationship had. Sometime earlier that spring, we'd driven to Atlanta for Pat to give a speech. Instead of bypassing the downtown area as we always did when we drove through Augusta, Pat drove downtown and parked the car without a single word to me. I looked at him puzzled, then eyed the neighborhood. Was there a coffeehouse I'd missed? Had Pat decided we needed an early lunch?

"I've always wanted to look in this store," Pat said after he opened the car door for me. Even more puzzled, I followed him into a jewelry store called The Raven's Horde. Like most men I know, Pat detested shopping. It was hard to believe that he'd "always" wanted to look in any place except a bookstore, where he could spend hours. What he told the clerk at the counter left me speechless. "Hello, sir!" Pat said in greeting. "We're looking for a couple of wedding rings. What've you got in stock?"

A couple of *wedding* rings? Oh, really? Then pray tell, when was the wedding? My invitation must've been lost in the mail. That Christmas when Pat'd asked me what kind of engagement ring I wanted, I'd told him I didn't want one. My ex had given me one that I made him take back, and he'd been as baffled as Pat. I didn't explain, but it went back to the only engagement ring I'd ever worn. My college boyfriend had proposed and proudly given me his grandmother's treasured and beautifully set diamond. I wore it racked with guilt because the truth was, I didn't want to marry him or anyone else. When I gave it back to him a few weeks later, the experience was so traumatic I swore to never put on another one. I never have.

As we stood at the jewelry counter, I poked Pat with my elbow, hard, but he ignored me as the clerk pulled out a black velvet tray. And in the midst of all those ordinary rings were two gold bands, one large and the other small, with exquisite engraving that appeared to be Celtic. "Let's see those," Pat told the guy.

Even to this day, I don't know if the whole thing was Pat's version of the ring-hidden-in-the-chocolate-mousse trick or not, but both rings fit us perfectly. "We'll take them," Pat said without even glancing my way. Which was just as well, since I was so astonished that my mouth hung open like a fool. Had he arranged it previously, or was it sheer coincidence? I'll never know. Pat would only smile mysteriously whenever I asked, but never told me the truth.

More surprises were to come. As we drove off with the two ring boxes in my lap, I dared to ask him. "Ah, Pat? Is there something you want to tell me?"

When he glanced my way, his bright Irish eyes twinkled. "Nothing I can think of. Why?"

I motioned toward the boxes. "Oh, no reason. Just sort of wondering what I'm supposed to do with these."

"Well, the smaller one, I put on your finger, and the bigger one, you put on mine. You know—'with this ring I thee wed' and all that shit."

"Oh. And . . . ah . . . when might all this take place? Best I remember, we haven't set a date." The seriousness of his dad's illness had made wedding plans seem frivolous, and we'd agreed to wait for happier times before planning anything definite.

He shrugged. "I called Alex yesterday to see when he could marry us. I'll let you know when he calls me back."

"Yeah. Might be a good idea if you did."

After our wedding in Charleston we drove home to Fripp Island. Having done the with-this-ring-I-thee-wed stuff, both of us had our rings on. I kept glancing at mine to make sure it was real. On the drive to Charleston to do the dirty deed, I'd had a moment of anxiety. I looked over at poor Pat and thought, *Oh my God! What are we* doing? *I don't know this man. I have no idea who he is. And furthermore, I don't even want to. I just want out.* When I rolled down the window to get some fresh air, Pat asked if I was okay. Unable to speak, I stared at him in sheer panic. Surely he must be feeling the same way! Before I could let him off the hook, tell him that we were making a huge mistake and to turn the car around, he reached over and took my hand. Without taking his eyes off the road, he raised my hand to his lips, kissed it lightly, then said, "It's going to be okay, sweetheart. Trust me." And that was all it took to calm me down.

"We've got company," Pat said with a grin when we pulled into our yard at Fripp after driving home from our wedding in Charleston. I spotted Kathy's car immediately, but it took me a minute to register that the other car in our driveway—a beat-up rattletrap covered in bumper stickers—was my son Jake's. I remembered then, something about this being the weekend he was driving his girlfriend from Charlotte, where they were both in college, to her home in Jacksonville. On his way back, he might stop by Fripp, he'd told me. Unbeknownst to either of them, by showing up unexpected that afternoon both Kathy and Jake had crashed our honeymoon.

Jake was on the beach and would've no doubt been oblivious even if he hadn't been, but Kathy was another matter. To explain Pat's wearing his best suit and me a lacy blouse and skirt—unusual attire for both of us—I told Kathy as nonchalantly as I could manage that we'd been in Charleston for an event. Then both of us scampered off to change clothes. When I returned to the kitchen in my shorts and T-shirt, Kathy had curiously opened the white box I'd left on the countertop, which contained the remains of the small wedding cake Zoe Sanders had baked and decorated for us.

Instead of just asking outright what the devil we were doing with a half-eaten wedding cake, Kathy pointed to me. "Oh my God! Let me see your left hand," she demanded. When I obliged, she squealed and hugged me. Coming in from the beach at that exact moment, Jake wanted to know what all the squealing was about. "Welcome to the Conroy clan, Jake," Kathy told him. The secret was out.

CHAPTER 7

A ROOM OF MY OWN

Now that the deed was finally done and we'd committed ourselves to each other for better or for worse, Pat and I settled into our new life together with each of us praying it'd be the former rather than the latter.

"Did we really do what I think we did this afternoon?" I asked Pat when I came into our room on our wedding night. We were alone; I'd told Jake he didn't have to run off, but he'd left to stay with a buddy at the College of Charleston. Pat was propped up in bed reading as he did every night, and I pulled back the covers to join him, picking up the book I'd left on the bedside table. Not even one day yet and we'd already turned into an old married couple.

"Having second thoughts?" Pat asked without taking his eyes off his book.

"Nope." I propped up beside him and turned to the page I'd bookmarked the night before. "You?"

"Nope."

We read in silence for a few minutes, then Pat turned a page and said, "I love you, wife."

With a smile I responded, "I love you, too. Want a bowl of ice cream? I got sugarless."

Pat gave me a thumbs-up and turned another page. When I got to the door he stopped me, meeting my eyes for the first time that star-lit night of our honeymoon. "Wife? Put some hot fudge sauce on mine, okay?"

With a laugh, I opened the bedroom door. "Nice try, husband."

It would soon become clear to me that Pat was not your run-of-the-mill husband, and I mean that in the best possible way. He didn't question my whereabouts if I ran late or accuse me of running around on him. But even more important to me, he didn't demand my undivided attention and devotion—which was just as well, since he wasn't likely to get it. He had my devotion, but attention was another matter. Most of the time a writer lives in his/her own little world, creating plots and timelines and characters, which can cause problems in a relationship. It's difficult to be intimate with someone whose mind is elsewhere. Pat had more than one relationship fall apart, he told me, because he spent too much time in his "other world" and not enough with his companion. Made sense to me since I was peculiar that way as well. Because of our peculiarities, sometimes I wonder if writers should only marry other writers.

The more obvious Pat's quirks became, the happier it made me that our idiosyncrasies were compatible with each other. When they weren't, that was okay too. We'd already discovered that our circadian rhythms were out of sync; he was a night owl who read until well after midnight while I preferred to retire and rise early. He was surprised but pleased to find that his late-night habit didn't drive me crazy as it had his other wives and lovers. At first he was fidgety when I dozed off beside him and he kept asking me over and over if having his lamp on was bothering me. "It's not the light," I grumbled; "it's you waking me up every five minutes to ask." In new-wife mode, I instantly regretted my less-than-loving tone and added, "But you're sweet to worry."

Pat had other characteristics that endeared him to me. He didn't point out my annoying habits in front of others or ask at a dinner party if I really needed that second piece of cake. If I balked at going somewhere with him, he didn't sulk, pout, or refuse to go alone. He simply shrugged it off and went by himself, and I did the same with him. We pretty much left each other to our own devices. As time went on, our travels took us our separate ways more often than not. I figured that as long as we enjoyed our time together more than our time apart, we'd be fine.

Doing our own thing might've worked for us, but it tended to bother others. ("You're leaving Pat alone for a whole month?" one of my friends screeched when my first big book tour came up. "Have you lost your mind?") I understood what she was saying; there were certainly times when our schedules bothered Pat and me as well. One time Pat surprised me when I told him, laughing, that my ex went on a hunger strike anytime I had to be away from home. "Can't blame him," Pat muttered. "I hate it when you're not here. I want you with me all the time."

I was aghast; he'd not only encouraged me to do book promotions, he'd said I had no choice. Occupational hazard. When I said I'd much rather be home, his response was "Too bad." He'd said he also would rather be home, but as writers we were obliged to promote our books. I wondered if he'd been teasing about being unhappy when I was away. With Pat it was impossible to tell. He always left notes for me to find on my return, some sweet and others joking. He wrote, *Welcome home, darling. You were sorely missed. I fixed dinner and will come back and cook it. I missed you.* But the next time his note read, *Welcome back from the West Coast tour. There is boiled shrimp and a ketchup-horseradish-lemon-juice sauce in the refrigerator. I am in the bedroom becoming gay.*

In truth, it thrilled me to find that Pat was the most undemanding of spouses. If my quirks bothered him, he kept it to himself. In the early days, we were too starry-eyed and drunk on love to let petty annoyances spoil things. But I also think our laissez-faire attitude set the tone of our marriage from day one. We rarely squabbled or got into those embarrassing public tiffs some couples do, where the tension makes everyone miserable. (Though we certainly would have our moments.) Coming from relationships that felt more like combat zones, our battle-weary souls craved peace. We were ready to be done with the dysfunction of our previous lives and create our own dysfunction.

My theory is, our attitude toward togetherness worked for us at that time in our lives, though it might not have if we'd been younger, with loftier expectations. Marrying after you turn fifty, especially if you've been around the block a few times, is quite different from marrying when you're young and don't know any better. On our first anniversary I told Pat that lowering my expectations about marriage had exceeded my wildest dreams. I was only halfway joking. The truth was, I'd had enough controlling, smothering, anger-fueled relationships to last me a lifetime. To me an inattentive mate was far preferable to a demanding one, and I believe that Pat felt the same way.

~~~~~

Undemanding though he might be, Pat was insistent about one thing at the beginning of our life together, and he made sure I heard him loud and clear. I was to take any room in the house and turn it into my own. It would be sacred space—my very own writing room.

When we first began seeing each other, Pat had been appalled to hear that I'd never claimed a space for myself in any of the houses I'd occupied in my previous marriage. But where did I write? he asked. In between student conferences, advising, marking essays, and making lesson plans, my office at the English department had served that purpose. Except for the constant interruptions, and the departmental rule that one's office door remain open at all times so students would be encouraged to confer, my office had been a welcome haven that I'd been grateful to have. (Rather pathetically so, I realized later.)

In my previous married life, I'd never been bold enough to demand space of my own. (Or much of anything else either, which disgusts me to think back on. What was *wrong* with me that I ended up such a Stepford wife?) The bishop moved his preachers around to various churches, and the churches provided a nice parsonage, spacious enough for whatever size family came their way. So it wasn't a lack of room that kept me from claiming a space of my own; it was my reticence to demand anything for myself. Why, the very idea of the pastor's wife hogging a whole room for herself! Everyone knew that extra room had been fixed up by the parsonage committee as a study for their dear pastor, not his lowly spouse.

The irony was, like most instructors of freshman comp, I'd taught Virginia Woolf's landmark essay on the necessity of having one's own space, then followed up by assigning an essay on the importance of nurturing one's creativity and valuing it enough to demand time and a place for it. I'd read hundreds of student papers and scribbled words of encouragement in the margin: "Good for you, Susie! I hope you'll continue to nourish your artistic side." (Hypocrisy has always been one of my most unpleasant vices.) Despite my blathering in class, it shames me to admit that I'd never had the self-respect to make demands in order to nurture my own career. Although my love of writing was an essential part of me, as essential to my well-being as air, it took me years before I'd treat my writing seriously and respectfully, let alone nourish it.

After I moved into the house on Fripp Island, I found myself yet again hesitant to claim my own space. Although it was plenty spacious for the two of us, the house was far from palatial. Made up of a living room / dining room combo, kitchen, a small den and even smaller screened porch in back, with two extra bedrooms besides the master bedroom, the house lacked an obvious space to put down my stakes. The smallest of the bedrooms had no windows so we dubbed it the "tomb room." Since I'm claustrophobic, that one was out for me. I never liked putting guests in there either, afraid they'd be too polite to tell us they suffered the same malady. The other guest room was upstairs, the only room there, and would've been the ideal escape for writing. It was not only private but lovely, with a bank of windows overlooking the lagoon in back. But Pat had four daughters, and I didn't want to be the wicked stepmother who took over everything, including the room with a view at the top of the stairs. Then they'd have no choice but to stay in the dreaded tomb room during their visits.

But Pat wouldn't listen to my protests. I was, by God, going to have my own writing room. There was a perfectly good and private room upstairs, and he couldn't understand why I was reluctant to take it. Finally he said that if I refused the upstairs room, he'd rent me an office elsewhere. The island had several such places, built for management but unoccupied; he was sure he could work out a deal for one of them. The man knew my heart of darkness. By then I'd been busted as an ant (I preferred to think of myself as wise and thrifty). Threatening to spend unnecessarily was sheer blackmail on Pat's part, but it worked.

I took the room upstairs. After years without a space of my own, I felt guilty about claiming such a grand one—a feeling that lasted a whole minute at most. Other, less noble feelings took over. I had to admit that Pat had been right, absolutely unequivocally right on. Naturally he gloated when I told him so. I *adored* having my own space. I reveled in it. I enjoyed every minute I spent there, every butt-numbing hour that I perched on the daybed with my laptop on a wicker tea tray I'd found at the Salvation Army store. After I got everything set up to suit me, I wrote feverishly and for hours on end, as though I could make up for the lost years I'd spent denying myself.

Pat was pleased with himself for the gift he'd prodded me into taking, and it remains the best thing anyone has ever given me. Like a proud papa adorning a nursery, he brought presents for my room. "Thought this would look good in your office," he'd say nonchalantly as he handed me a first edition of one of my favorite books, *Cross Creek* by Marjorie Kinnan Rawlings. Knowing that I had a thing for birds, he bought bird prints to hang on the walls.

His first gift to me was a painting by a local artist I admired. Beautiful in its simplicity, it shows a woman alone, propped up in a chaise with a book on her lap.

Old habits die hard, however. When guests came who balked at the tomb room, I gave over my space to them, which helped to appease any lingering guilt on my part. In addition, I couldn't help but fret over the difference in my private space and Pat's. His writing room was actually part of the master bedroom suite, separated by a four-paneled screen as room divider. Although he'd demanded I have a room, technically he didn't have one himself. When I pointed that out to him, he insisted it suited him fine and had served him well for years. A hard point to argue, considering the works he'd produced there.

As long as no one bothered him, Pat was happy as a clam in his makeshift office. He was surrounded by shelf after shelf of his books, which made him happier than anything else. Since his desk faced the bay window in the back, he was turned away from anyone entering. Plus he played music full blast (mostly country music), so I could've driven a tank in without disturbing him. I rarely interrupted him at work unless I had to. He might be irritated by the interruption (an interview that he'd forgotten about), but to his credit he didn't take it out on the messenger. He'd sigh, cuss a blue streak, then drag himself up. I wasn't the only hypocrite in the family: he'd then greet the dreaded visitor with a hearty welcome and big smile, as if the interruption was the best thing that'd happened to him all day.

Although Pat didn't take it out on me for calling his attention to a forgotten appointment or visitor, it occurred to him how he could make himself look good when it happened. His method would become a bone of contention between us, but he never gave it up, no matter how much I bitched about it. Once he figured out that he could always blame it on me, he beat that dead horse over and over. The first time he did it, I couldn't believe my ears. I'd brought him out of his room for a reporter from Charleston who'd had to wait several long minutes for Pat to shower and dress. Although he'd totally forgotten about the interview, Pat greeted the reporter with a hearty handshake and a newly minted excuse. "So sorry to keep you waiting," I heard him say on my way back upstairs. "My wife forgot to tell me that I had an interview today."

Full of himself for his brilliant way of casting the blame elsewhere, he grew expansive with his fabrication. "That's why I've given my wife the nickname Helen Keller," he went on to explain with a laugh. "She never tells me *anything*." Eventually the family heard it so much that they'd beat Pat to the punch when they arrived for a visit: "Let me guess, Pat. Helen Keller didn't tell you we were coming, right?"

Since neither of us liked to interrupt the other at work, we came up with a plan. Pat told me to yell at him if I needed anything, and he'd do the same for me. Occasionally he'd bring lunch upstairs, knocking politely before entering. *You don't have to knock*, I'd tell him. Anyone bringing me food was more than welcome to barge in. If he was feeling especially romantic, he'd adorn the tray with a flower. Thanks to Fripp's deer population, which devoured anything green and growing, the only flower we had in the yard was the poisonous oleander. But it's the thought that counts.

If I was still working by late afternoon, Pat would scramble around and find us something for dinner. Unless we were having company and wanted some of Pat's fabulous Italian dishes, I'd pretty much taken over our daily dinners. Although I preferred Pat's cooking to mine, and it was a luxury to have someone cook for me, I didn't have much choice. I don't know how the man fed himself until I came on the scene. He must've made almost daily trips to the grocery store. I can truthfully say that Pat Conroy was the most scatterbrained person I've ever known. Going twenty miles into town to fetch the ingredients for an osso bucco dinner he'd been craving for days, he'd return without the veal. I learned quickly that it was a waste of time to make him a list because he always lost it. After we'd been married a couple of years, I instigated Sunday afternoon powwow sessions, me with pen and paper in hand. "Tell me what you want to cook this week," I'd say, "and I'll go into town tomorrow and get everything. Then we won't have to shop every day." That simple plan made him think of me as an organizational genius. I'm not, but I managed to look modest when he bragged about me to others.

Pat had been right about another thing as well. He said that if I had my own space to write without an endless pile of essays to grade, my creativity would be unstoppable. Having time to devote to my writing turned out to be an unbelievable luxury, and the years we lived on Fripp were the most productive of our lives for Pat and me both. Working late into the night, I wrote essays and short stories for anthologies, articles for magazines, and the books that had been percolating in my head for a long time. The first of those was my second novel, *The Sunday Wife*, which Pat took full credit for making me write. Yet again, as much as it pains me to admit it, he'd been right in insisting that was the story I needed to tell.

It came about soon after we settled down into our married life. One night after dinner, Pat asked, "Remind me—what's the book you're working on now?"

I told him for the umpteenth time that it was about a female rodeo rider, and I was about halfway done with it. (Later I'd finish the book but it remains in the back of a drawer.)

With a sly grin Pat said, "Glad to hear you're taking the age-old advice, write what you know."

"Ha ha," I said dryly, but his remark put me on the defensive. "I told you that I've always dreamed of leading the rodeo parade on a golden palomino."

"One of the great things about writing fiction, we get to be whatever we want to be," he agreed. Then he studied me for a few minutes before bringing up something that had been bothering him. "I can't believe you're not writing about the time you spent as a preacher's wife, though. What you went through to find your own identity is quite a story. *That's* the one you need to tell."

I shook my head. "I can't do it, Pat. The truth is, I started working on that book while I was living it, but it turned out to be too hard. Reliving that time took its toll on me emotionally, so I put it aside and made up another story instead. Telling the truth about your life is more difficult than I thought. You know what I mean? I don't want anyone to know what a failure I was. And I'm afraid they'll turn against me for saying things they don't want to hear."

I realized what I'd said, and who I'd said it to, as soon as it came out of my mouth. I was talking to the man who'd spent his whole career revealing the unpleasant and hidden truths that none of us likes to talk about, everything from child abuse to mental illness. And he'd paid the price with splintered relationships and emotional breakdowns (which he also wrote about). Not only that, he'd been repeatedly accused of making it all up and told me he'd been called a liar as much as any writer in history. Although tell-all books, either in the form of memoir or fictionalized stories, would later become common, early in Pat's career it wasn't done much. He had blazed his own path.

Unintentionally, I'd hit on the core of my problem as a writer. I was afraid. I'd lived much of my life afraid of everything: I feared offending others, taking a stand, going against the grain, questioning the status quo, even claiming a life of my own. After a long silence, I dared glance Pat's way. "Ah . . . you might be right. Guess it's time to pull out my preacher's wife book and have another go at it."

―᠁᠁᠁―

Looking back, it still surprises me that I spent over two decades of my life, from my midtwenties to late forties, as the wife of a preacher. It's something I could never have imagined doing. Although I'd been raised in a pious, churchgoing family, I've never been particularly pious myself. My interest had always been more with the mystical and otherworldly aspects of spirituality than with conventional religion. Not only that, I'd observed the comings and goings of the preachers in small-town churches, and everything about their lives appalled me. The pastors' families existed in a goldfish bowl, with their every movement scrutinized and commented on by the good people of the church. Who would want that?

Even so, I came from a generation of southern women born to be pleasers, to be devout and well-behaved young ladies who didn't make waves. I would never have voiced my unconventional views of religion any more than I would've voiced my views about much of anything else. As a child I'd baffled my mother by being different from my beribboned, girlie-girl peers: I was overly imaginative and dreamy-eyed, with my head in the clouds and nose in a book. I even had the fanciful notion that I could be a writer. Oh, I rebelled as a teen but always overtly, by sneaking away from my mother's watchful eye to party, drink, and raise hell. I grew up torn between being the good, compliant girl I was expected to be, and leading the artistic, bohemian life I yearned for. The first chance I got, I promised myself, I'd leave the farm and move to Europe, where I could become a writer. Only then would I have something to write about.

But, as Pat and I had both discovered, fate has a way of intervening in our carefully laid-out plans. In college I fell in with the theater crowd and became consumed with the desire to become a playwright. My obsession with theater set my sights on a different path: Broadway! Just get me there and I could make it to the big time, I knew. I'd work backstage, doing whatever menial job was needed, until one of my plays became the toast of the town. I wanted it so badly that nothing could stop me (or so I thought), and I set out to make it happen.

My head was too far in the clouds to see the curveball headed my way. To finance a move to the Big Apple, my senior year I took a lucrative summer job as a cocktail waitress at a national park all the way across the country from Lower Alabama. (My parents didn't know about the cocktail part of the job, nor did they know that I'd landed it by my willingness to dress as a miniskirted cowgirl and serve as the only female on a male-dominated bar staff.)

Away from everything familiar, I became a cliché of the worst kind, the wide-eyed country girl adrift in the big bad world, and I obligingly fell into every trap possible. To my astonishment, suddenly I became the most sought-after belle of the ball, Scarlett O'Hara at the Wilkes family barbecue. I'd landed in a place where my southern accent was considered enchanting and every word I uttered charming and delightful. For the first time in my sheltered, bookish little life, I had more attention than I could handle, and it went to my head. Prissing around in boots and short skirts, I tossed my long blond hair and flirted shamelessly with besotted customers to get big tips. Why hadn't I realized before how much fun femme fatales have? I went out with a different guy every night: park rangers, jazz musicians, frat boys, international students from exotic lands. One night a couple of cowboys got into a fistfight because I couldn't remember which one I'd promised to dance with.

Despite all the exhilarating attention, I went for the unattainable and had a forbidden love affair with a college boy who had a fiancée waiting in the wings. When that heady summer came to an end, I'd tucked away a nice savings account and was eager to start my exciting new life. Which I did; just not the one I'd envisioned. My sins had found me out, just as my mama always said they would. I came home pregnant. Morning sickness and a reluctant call to a faraway college boy changed everything, and my life turned completely upside down. My dreams of Broadway gave way to the harsh reality of bottles and bassinets.

Fresh out of college, I became a single mom with a baby boy to support. In one wild summer, life had thrown me for a loop, and

I struggled to get my equilibrium back. The Great White Way wasn't going anywhere, I reminded myself; all I had to do was put my dreams on hold. Once before I'd done what it took to start a new life, and I could do it again. This time, I'd be smarter, see the curveball coming. And I'd lower my sights. I didn't have to go to Broadway to write plays; I could start out with community theater and work my way to the top. It was a new era where women could have a home and career. I'd fallen in love with my beautiful baby, which had made me see that I wanted a close-knit family too, like the one I'd come from. Why settle for anything less when I could have it all?

The opportunity for a new life presented itself in a most unexpected way. An old college friend whom I'd corresponded with while he was in the Peace Corps had returned from Africa and called me as soon as he got home. Could he come for a visit? He couldn't wait to see me and the adorable little one. Now a theology student in Atlanta, my friend was ready to settle down. It was only later, looking back, that I realized he'd been in the market for a ready-made family by the time he crossed my threshold. A cute young preacher was nothing but trouble for a congregation, which churches avoid by insisting on a family man. Yet again, fate was throwing another curveball my way, and I was as unprepared as before. To my great surprise, my old buddy and I soon fell in love and began planning to spend the rest of our lives together.

If my mother was pleased when the preacher man and I got engaged, she was over the moon when we married, settled into parsonage life, and had our first child a year later. Praise be to God for hearing a mother's prayers! Her wayward daughter had finally given up her silly notions of becoming a writer and all that other foolishness. It had been a rough road to redemption, but surely now the prodigal daughter could see that a woman's place was in the home, just as the Lord intended, and my mother had known all along.

For a while, God was in his kingdom and all was right with the world. Once I settled into being a preacher's wife, I discovered it was a role I was made to play. In the same way some girls are educated and trained to be corporate wives for husbands-to-be, I had been groomed by the formidable church ladies of my life—my mother, grandmother, and aunts—to be the helpmate of a preacher. Plus, forsaking my old ways and becoming a new person came with an unexpected payoff: everyone—especially my husband—*liked* the new me more than the old one. It was a heady feeling. The wayward, restless daughter with her head in the clouds was now a changed person, the one God had made her to be. She had become the ideal little wife, mother, and helpmate.

And on the surface, it was a good life. I flung myself into it and tried hard to make amends. My sinful days were over, and my halo fit me better than the hoop skirt had. The preacher man and I had our last child—another boy—and I became an officer in the Preachers' Wives Club. (Yes, there really was such an organization in the late '70s. Although I knew a couple of female pastors, I guess their spouses didn't count.) As long as I stayed too busy to question how I'd ended up leading a life so different from what I'd planned, all was well.

Beneath the surface was a different story. During those seemingly joy-filled years, I was haunted by a recurring and terrifying nightmare in which a black cloth was placed over my face, and I couldn't breathe until I fought it off. Talk about a metaphor! Years later I saw my first burka and felt a cold chill of recognition. I knew I was losing my identity, lost in the role I was playing, but

I didn't know what to do about it. Somewhere along the way I became a cauldron of doubt and depression. Although I hid my true feelings, inside I was filled with guilt and self-loathing. If life was so good, then why the hell was I so miserable? During what should've been the best years of my life, I was functioning on autopilot, so severely depressed I often entertained myself with elaborate plans of suicide. For the first time ever, I was plagued by health problems and hospitalized a couple of times for heart arrhythmias that left me shaken and scared. Though I don't know what I was scared of; if the heart problem had taken me out, I wouldn't have had to spend so much time trying to figure out the best way to do it myself.

The biggest strain for me during this time was not the health issues and the suicidal depression, though; it was what had plagued me ever since I took on my new role. What would people *think* if they knew how crazy I was? Fighting depression was nothing compared to the effort I put into keeping up a good front. I'd been doing it for so many years that I wasn't about to give it up. If I ever succeeded in offing myself, it'd take the undertaker all day to get the smile off my face, it'd become so much a part of my fake persona. The poor preacher's wife had died tragically and much too young, but hadn't she been a cheerful little thing?

I didn't know at what point I'd lost myself. What had become of the girl I used to be, the dreamy one who wanted to be a writer, who filled her life with books and stories? She'd lived in her own little world, a place where she created her own characters, wrote her dramas and books. I'd taken the little girl I used to be off to college with me because she'd been so eager to learn, to sit at the feet of writers who'd achieved what she wanted more than anything in the world. She even talked me into believing I could be a playwright, for God's sake! Because of her, I'd been determined not to settle for dull and boring but to lead a fulfilling life of creativity and adventure. Where had she gone?

Who can say what happens to the dreams of our younger selves? I know I'm not the first woman of my generation to put hers aside for another life, even the kind of life I'd sworn to never lead. I came of age during the awakening of the women's movement, when we believed we could have it all. And maybe we could have, and maybe some of us did. I thought I could too, at first. I thought I could work side by side with my husband, who had his own radical and exciting dreams, to make a difference in the world. We would raise our children differently from the way we were raised. They'd come up in a free and creative environment, with a diversity of people and ideas that we never had in our stifling southern upbringings. While the preacher was bringing the liberating word of God to his congregations, I'd work my miracles with words. He'd preach sermons, and I'd create pageants and programs and books that would transform the lives of others. Together, we could do it.

Only, it didn't happen that way. As it turned out, it was our lives that were changed, his and mine, and not for the best. Now in a position where we were dependent on the goodwill of those who'd placed us there, we caved. If the sermons became too fiery or hit too close to home, an ambitious young preacher would find himself put out to pasture, serving a church in the boondocks no one else wanted. God forbid the preacher's wife offends someone by speaking her mind or not going along with the status quo! It was up to the preacher to keep an errant spouse in line. I learned many things during my tenure as a preacher's wife. One of which was what my mama had been trying to tell me all my stubborn, rebellious life. To make it in this world, to get what you want from it, you have to toe the line. Swimming against the current, blazing your own trail, leads to nothing but misery and discontent. I had everything in life a woman needed. Why wasn't it enough?

It eroded over time, of course, as those kinds of soul-searing things always will. Sometime during this period, I not only lost myself, I lost God as well. At different points in my life, I'd toyed with Buddhism and Hinduism but eventually found more meaning in the comfortable fit of the familiar, the timeless rituals of a community of believers. But even that lost meaning as the image became more important than the imagery. It no longer mattered to me what I believed. The only thing that mattered was making sure no one suspected how lost I was, how empty inside. The persona I'd created to cover up my true self had become the only me I knew anymore. A spiritual connection wasn't possible because there was nothing inside me to connect with.

Looking back, I'm not sure I can identify the turning point, the exact moment I knew I could no longer be the *me* I'd become, the depressed, suicidal person who clung so stubbornly to a self-image that was becoming less valid every day. I do know that for any new life to burst into bloom, something has to die out. I had to rid myself of the phony nonperson I'd created to please others. And I did it the only way I knew, with the only resource that has ever given my inner life any real meaning. I closed the door and started to write. This time, I wasn't writing devotionals or mission studies or Christmas pageants; I was writing my way out of a life that had stifled and imprisoned me. I wrote about my despair, my desperation, my lost identity. Word by word, I sought to reconnect with myself. No longer did I write to please or impress others—on the contrary, I had no intention of sharing what I wrote with anyone. I hid away and wrote fever-ishly, disconnected from everyone and everything. Alarmed, the preacher man demanded I get back to my church work, back to him, back to my family. The congregation had noticed and were talking about me. At one time, I would've meekly put away my silly little writings and put my false face back on.

But this time I couldn't do it anymore. Instead I stayed put and wrote about a woman's struggles to fit into the mold she'd created to please others. The playwright had written a make-believe role, then stepped in to fill it herself. God hadn't cursed her and caused her to lose her voice; she had cursed herself by denying her voice. Freely and willingly, she had given it away. *I* had given it away. My marriage began to fall apart, but my novel was taking shape.

Little did I know at the time, but during that feverish, stumbling journey of self-discovery, I was creating the underlying themes of all the books I'd write from that point onward. The loss of self, the search for identity, and the ultimate redemption through art would become the foundation for the stories I'd tell, over and over. Through writing, I finally was freed of that prison of my own cre-ation, the deadly urge to please others, to let what others think of me become more important than what I think of myself.

In the end, however, the strain proved to be too much for me, and when my marriage ended, I put the book aside. Once I'd started writing again I couldn't stop, but I could move on to easier subjects. As I'd told Pat, I couldn't bear to revisit my former life and that's where the rodeo rider came in. But Pat had sensed what I knew with all my heart but had been running from for years: I had a story to tell, and it wasn't about riding the rodeo. It was about a woman like myself, who struggled to find her identity apart from the demands of others. Whether or not I could find the courage to tell it was a question only I could answer.

――――――

Back in my writing room with a view of the lagoon where white egrets nested, I returned to the unfinished manuscript that had both haunted and eluded me for years. For the months that followed, I worked on it like a person possessed, which I suppose I was. When it was finished, I called it *The Sunday Wife* and hurriedly mailed it to my brand-new agent before I could change my mind.

Somehow it seems fitting that I'd met my new agent in the most unlikely of places, the funeral of the Great Santini. It was the first time I met a lot of Pat's friends in publishing, but most of the day remains a blur, as usually happens with funerals. A longtime colleague of Pat's at Doubleday, Marly Rusoff, took me aside to say that she'd heard about *Making Waves* and would love to read it. I gave her a copy but didn't think anything about it until she called me a few days later. She'd liked the book and was calling to see if I was represented by an agent. After years in the publishing business—at one point she'd been Pat's publicist—she was starting her own agency and wondered if I was interested. Since I hadn't gotten around to renewing the contract with my current agent, I signed on with Marly instead. It turned out to be a great decision. Not only did she sell my second novel at auction, she also sold the rights to reissue *Making Waves*, which has gone through several printings since its modest beginning.

In an unforgettable juxtaposition of horror and the fulfillment of a lifelong dream, Pat and I flew to New York exactly one month after 9/11, where I signed the contract Marly had negotiated with Hyperion for *The Sunday Wife*, scheduled to come out the following year. Our trip was bittersweet. The horrific smell of destruction lingered in the air, and the faces on the street were dark and glum. Pat visited Ground Zero, but I couldn't bear to and went for a walk uptown instead. It was a beautifully bright and crisp October day, and I searched for signs of the recovery that brave city was in the midst of.

On the way back to the hotel, my stroll was halted near St. Jean Baptiste, where a crowd filled the sidewalk. So many flashing firetrucks blocked the street that I feared there was a fire in the historic church and began backing away. It was then that I spotted the honor guard of firefighters clearing the way for a flag-draped casket to be carried into the church. When I heard someone in the crowd say that the body of one of the firefighters buried in the wreckage of the twin towers had been recovered a few days before, I fell apart. With tears pouring down my cheeks, I turned and ran back to the hotel, making my way blindly through the crowded streets.

Pat returned from his trip to Ground Zero, grim-faced and somber, to find me huddled on the bed and staring out the window. He sat beside me and placed a hand on my shoulder. "Baby? You okay?" he asked, and I shook my head.

"No. I want to go home," I told him.

"So do I, but you've got a meeting with your new publisher."

"I don't care. I don't want to go."

"Why not?"

I leaned into him. "Being here now. It breaks my heart."

Pat pulled me close and said something I would hear him say many times in the years to come. "I never expected life to be so tragic, did you? I mean, I knew it'd be hard, but *sad*? I don't know how any of us do it."

On the flight home, Pat had the window seat, and I leaned over him to say goodbye to the wounded city. At the sight of a skyline where two towers had once stood tall and proud, Pat grimaced and turned his head away. I grasped his hand but made myself look until the plane dipped and only blue sky remained. *It will rise from the ashes*, I whispered to myself as a sort of benediction, *like we all must do.*

As I settled back into my seat, it occurred to me that I too had risen from the burnt-out remains of my former life. At one point I'd lost my sense of self, my faith, and my dreams of becoming a writer, and I hadn't been sure if I could ever find my way back. But slowly, surely, I had begun to spread my wings.

CHAPTER 8

IN THE FAMILY WAY

One of the first things I did as Pat's new wife was write a letter to his daughters Jessica, Melissa, and Megan to tell them that Pat and I were no longer living in sin, and that I promised to take good care of their "maddening, crazy, irascible but lovable" father. Because of the situation between Pat and his youngest daughter, Susannah, I wrote her a separate letter. I introduced myself as the wicked stepmother, said I looked forward to meeting her, and invited her to come to Fripp for a visit. Since no specific visitations had been set up by the court, California's laws about teens being different from those in most states, I wanted to let her know she'd be welcome to stay as long as she liked.

I didn't tell Pat I'd written Susannah until I got a reply, not wanting to get his hopes up. Susannah accepted the invitation graciously and made her plans to come. In her reply she acknowledged that her relationship with her father had been troubled since the divorce, but she wanted to see him. She was turning seventeen that year, not the easiest of ages (are any of them?), but I don't recall any qualms about having a possibly moody teenaged girl in the house. I'd raised only boys, who popped each other with wet towels, told fart jokes, and got into food fights. Moody, I could handle.

Any worries I might've had were unfounded; Susannah was lovely: pleasant, mature, and overly polite. She seemed relaxed with her dad and me and was particularly sweet to my five-year-old grandson when he came for a visit, fell madly in love with her, and followed her around like a little puppy. Because I'd already decided to take the summer off from work, I turned my writing room into a guest room for her and other visitors that summer. Pat and I were creating a new life together, and I felt that concentrating on our families was the most important thing at that time. Although Pat continued to research material for his basketball memoir as well as work on recipes for a future cookbook, he too devoted extra time to family. Understandably, our kids, siblings, and friends wanted to see for themselves how my and Pat's union was working. Because our courtship had been so discreet, many of them thought we'd only known each other a few months.

At first I was oblivious to the family's conjectures and speculations, but it soon became too obvious to ignore. One evening I was sous-chef while Pat prepared an Italian meal for a houseful, and he snapped at me when I handed him the wrong pasta. "Kiss my ass," I snapped back, slamming the correct bag of pasta into his belly. As usual, everyone had crowded into the kitchen while we cooked, and two of Pat's brothers, Mike and Tim, raised their hands to high-five each other gleefully. With a laugh Tim said to Mike, "Told you, bro! She's not gonna take any shit off him."

On another occasion I walked on the beach with the sisters-in-law and listened eagerly as they gossiped about Pat's previous wives and lady friends. The first wife was beloved by all, the second less so, and most of the former girlfriends dismissed as flakes. We laughed about the stories of women pursuing Pat, including a stalker who sneaked on the island and crawled through a window looking for him.

"We shouldn't be talking about Pat's former women around you," one of the sisters-in-law said to me. When I assured her that, on the contrary, I loved gossip, they exchanged curious glances.

"Were you really married to a *preacher*?" one of the others blurted out.

"From a holy man to Pat Conroy," I said. "Talk about a leap of faith."

"What was it like, being married to a preacher?" she asked, and I smiled.

"I'm writing a book about it."

"Think you'll ever write about what it's like being married to Pat?"

"I might do that, one of these days," I told her. "Or I might just threaten to. Think that'll keep him in line?"

They exchanged glances again, then all of us giggled. "You go, girl," Terrye Conroy said, and like her husband had done a few days before, raised her hand for a high five.

───〰───

In between the comings and goings of summer visitors, I tried to make sure Pat and Susannah spent some time together, just the two of them. Although I didn't witness any particular tension between them (that was to come the following year), both seemed a bit skittish as they treaded through hazardous emotional waters. The tension was understandable. Pat'd told me about the last time Susannah was on Fripp, when she was twelve. It wasn't a pretty story. Her mother found evidence of Pat's affair, letters from his lover, and Susannah witnessed the ugly argument that followed. A terrible thing for a child to see, I told Pat. I'd never do that in front of a child or anyone else. Instead, I'd just kill him and dump his body in the ocean.

Pat surprised me by studying me seriously before saying, "No, you wouldn't. I know exactly what you'd do if you caught me running around on you."

"This I can't *wait* to hear."

"You'd leave me," he said simply. "Without saying a word. I'd never see you again." On another occasion he surprised me even further by repeating his speculation to my boys. "I'll never cheat on your mother," he told them. The boys exchanged surprised glances before one of them dared ask, "Because she'd feed you to the fish?"

"Nope," Pat said in a tone as serious as an undertaker's. "Because she'd leave my fat ass and never look back."

My oldest son laughed. "You'd better hope so. Granddaddy taught Mom to shoot at an early age and claims she's a better shot than he is."

Pat waved his hand dismissively. "Naw, she wouldn't bother to waste a bullet on me. She'd just leave."

I never understood how he came to that conclusion, or what in my behavior made him think that, and I didn't ask. I wasn't sure I wanted to know.

~~~~

As the long summer days went on, Pat and his youngest daughter became more relaxed with each other. I enjoyed their stories about friends they'd had in Rome and San Francisco, and their animated discussions of books and writing. Susannah taught her dad how to email and gave him a user name he always cherished, Atticus. She traipsed around with us without complaint when we went house hunting in Charleston. For some reason Pat had decided for us to move there. I went along with him, but in truth I couldn't bear the thought of leaving Fripp. Life on a secluded barrier island suited me to a tee. Revealing how little he truly knew me, Pat kept asking if I was *sure* I'd be happy on Fripp. His previous wife had found it boring and isolated, he told me with a worried frown. My response was *"Oh please* don't throw me into that briar patch!" Every so often he'd get a notion to relocate and we'd look again, him with high hopes and me faking it. Pondering this, I wondered if any of us could ever know the secret thoughts of another person, no matter how close we are.

The first real sign of the trouble to come occurred when Susannah's visit came to an end after a few weeks, and Pat insisted she set a time for a return visit. Her hesitancy caused him to push even harder. I felt for him because I knew why he was doing it—the thought of another long separation from her terrified him. Susannah'd already talked of returning to her birthplace, Rome, Italy, to spend her senior year, which made a long separation even more inevitable. Unfortunately Pat's fear came out the same way my father's did, with anger. Let a child run into a road chasing a ball and my father would go ballistic, stomping and yelling in such a fury he'd scare the child more than the traffic did. Pat's weapon of choice was always words, which he was a master at. He badgered Susannah for her reluctance to commit and kept pushing her. "I can't believe you're a Conroy," he'd tell her. "Don't you have a mind of your own?" I tried to catch his eye to send him a silent plea: *Don't do this. Take what she's willing to give and quit pressing for more.* To me, Susannah's being there now was a big step in the right direction. Past the age of required visitations, she'd come willingly but needed time to rebuild the relationship with her father. Couldn't Pat see what shaky ground he was on?

When we were alone, I said it aloud. Rubbing his face wearily, Pat agreed with me.

But he couldn't help himself, he admitted. He was so scared of losing her that he kept overreacting and pushing her even further away. One step forward, two steps back.

I understood his frustration. On the day he was taking her to the airport, I walked with them to the car to tell Susannah goodbye. "Don't worry, she'll be back," Pat said breezily as he tossed her suitcase into the trunk. "Hey—why don't you come for Christmas, Susannah? Remember the Christmas we spent on Fripp? You loved it."

She rolled her eyes. "Oh, Dad, you know I can't come at Christmas. We always go to Hawaii for the holidays. It's a family tradition."

Pat snorted and flung open the car door. "Oh, really? A family tradition, huh? Let me tell you what kind of a family tradition it is, Susannah. I've never set foot in Hawaii." And with that he jerked his head toward the car. "Get in. God forbid you miss your flight."

I paced the floor until Pat got back. Had they endured the hour-and-a-half drive in sullen silence, or had they cleared the air? It was a volatile situation that one wrong word could shatter. I couldn't imagine what it was like for either of them. Because my boys had always been so loyal to their mama, after the divorce I'd urged them to work on a personal relationship with their father that had nothing to do with me. I could only hope that Susannah would come to that realization as well. Although Pat blamed his ex-wife for turning his daughter against him, in truth only Susannah could work out her relationship with her father. No one could do it for her. Being torn between her mother and her father was a heavy burden for a sheltered and rather fragile girl, and one Susannah had carried since she was twelve.

Pat returned glum and slump-shouldered. There was nothing I could do but hold him and try to assure him that it'd be okay. I'd witnessed so much love between him and his daughter, I said, that even if they had trouble expressing it, things were bound to work out. Keep loving her and letting her know how much, I urged him. But Pat was inconsolable. I feared that his gut was telling him the same as mine: no matter how desperately he wanted to believe otherwise, this wasn't likely to end well.

~~~~~~

Pat and I saw Susannah again that fall when we made a trip to San Francisco. It was my first time to the Bay Area and I found it as enchanting as I'd always heard. The purpose of our trip was threefold: Pat wanted me to meet his longtime friend Tim Belk (whom he would base a character on in his next book of fiction, *South of Broad*); we were picking up some of Pat's stuff that he'd left at Lenore's house when he moved out five years ago; and best of all—we'd get a chance to see Pat's brand-new granddaughter, Molly Jean, Megan's first child.

Megan was the daughter most like Pat, so much so that I accused him of cloning her. His response was "My poor Meggie. She got all my bad traits except my temper." Except for Pat's clear blue eyes and sharply arched brows—even more striking in a female face— Megan doesn't look that much like her father (thank God for that,

Pat always said). Instead she inherited his droll wit, self-deprecating sense of humor, and absentminded approach to navigating the pitfalls of daily life. Stories of Megan's misadventures still make the rounds in the family. After each visit to Fripp, where she inevitably loses her purse, we wait anxiously to hear how she boarded the plane without an ID. Somehow she always does. Because she's not only hilarious but also drop-dead gorgeous, I figure she must either sweet-talk or joke her way through security. Either that, or they'd become so used to her tales of woe they just waved her through.

Pat's favorite Megan story was the one she told about meeting her new in-laws for the first time. Awaiting their arrival for dinner, Megan went into a cleaning frenzy getting her apartment ready. Grabbing a green can off the counter, she scoured the entire place with Parmesan cheese thinking it was Comet. "No wonder everything smelled so godawful" was her laughing response. Her good-humored attitude to the chaos of her life makes her irresistibly lovable (also like her father), no matter what kind of mess she gets herself into.

My most cherished Megan story comes from the night she called her father to tell him she was getting married. Her announcement came as a surprise because we didn't even know she was seeing anyone seriously. Pat and I were propped up in bed reading and I put my book down when Pat held the phone aside to announce in great excitement, "Megan's getting married!" Holding the receiver so I could listen in, he said to his daughter, "That's great, Megs. I'm really happy for you. Who are you marrying?"

"Hang on a minute," Megan said. Pat and I looked at each other wide-eyed when we heard Megan say to her fiancé, "Hey, Terry? What's your last name?"

In San Francisco, Megan brought six-week-old Molly Jean to meet Pat and me at Tim Belk's spacious apartment near Union Square. The apartment had a lush garden in back where wild, jewel-toned parakeets flitted around a gigantic trumpet vine drooping with yellow blooms. Dark-eyed, rosy-cheeked Molly Jean won her grandfather's heart the moment Megan placed her in his arms. With a look of wry amusement on his face, Tim watched Pat coo at his granddaughter and tried not to gag—or so he told me later. Although I'd talked with Tim several times on the phone (he was curious to find out who Pat married "this time around"), it was the first time he and I had met. I found him to be exactly as Pat'd said: a witty, flamboyantly gay man who played the piano like an angel. Although Tim was originally from South Carolina, I suspected his exaggerated southern drawl might be a bit of an affectation.

"Look at you, Pat," Tim said with a roll of his eyes, "turned to mush by a little-bitty baby. God help us all!"

"I won't ask what turns you to mush, Tim," Pat shot back. "You're liable to embarrass my Alabama bride."

Tim winked at me. "Oh, honey, I don't think so. I've read her book." One of the subplots of *Making Waves* was the homophobia of small southern towns, a theme I would explore even further in *The Sunday Wife*. After he read my first book, Tim had called me to share some of his personal experiences and it helped me in writing the second, which had a similar subplot. Initially Tim had denied his sexuality and married his high school sweetheart, he told me. "But she and I got divorced shortly afterward," he explained, "because of irreconcilable similarities."

When Tim suggested we adjourn to a bar "for a drink or ten," Megan wisely decided to take the baby home. We made our plans to meet the next day at Pat's former home on Presidio Avenue, where Susannah lived with her mother. Lenore was out of the country but hadn't objected to Pat and me coming to the house in her absence to collect the personal items he'd left behind. Somehow plans had been worked out between her lawyer and Pat's; I'd stayed out of it. The main thing Pat wanted was his handwritten manuscript of *Beach Music*. Working on the screenplay at Fripp, he'd realized it must still be at his former residence. His typist, Betty Roberts, had picked up the handwritten pages at the house and told Pat she'd returned them there. Lenore hadn't been able to find them anywhere, though. It was only later that the typist remembered she'd sent the handwritten pages to Nan Talese instead. To Pat's great relief, Nan would find the manuscript beneath everything Betty'd mailed her on finishing the job.

At the time, however, the whereabouts of the *Beach Music* manuscript was unknown, and Pat was fretting to have it in his possession, so off to his old house we went. I was curious to see the remnants of his life before me. Pat pointed out a crossing at a street a few blocks before we got to the house. "Remember I told you about my accident? That's where the car hit me. I was coming back from the store, wasn't paying any attention, and walked right into it. Brushed myself off and walked on home. I didn't realize how badly I was hurt until later."

He ended up having back surgery that laid him up for several weeks. Although the impact of the car hadn't seemed that bad at the time, the surgeon found the damage to his lower back that explained the unrelenting pain he'd experienced after thinking he was fine. "It was the perfect metaphor for my life then," Pat observed bitterly. "No one believed the pain I was in. Lenore didn't even believe a car hit me. She thought I'd made it up."

"Why would anyone make up something like that?" I asked, bewildered.

"She thought I was drunk and fell down in the street."

"Well?" I teased. "Did you tell me you were walking back from the liquor store when you got hit?"

As usual, my teasing lightened his mood. "I wasn't drinking," he said with a grin. "But as soon as the car struck me, I cradled the liquor bottles in my arms so they wouldn't break. Turns out, it was me who broke instead."

Seeing Pat overcome with emotion when Susannah let us into the house might not have surprised me, but the way it happened did. When Susannah's dogs, two sweet-faced King Charles spaniels, heard Pat's voice, they came hurtling into the entranceway and jumped him. He knelt to embrace them, laughing as the dogs yipped and danced and licked his face so ecstatically Pat almost fell over. Although he made no attempt to hide his tears at seeing the dogs again, I choked up and asked Susannah to point me to the nearest bathroom. *The heartbreak of a failed marriage*, I thought as I dabbed at my smudged mascara. *Does it ever end?*

"At least somebody's glad to see me," Pat said with a forced laugh as Susannah led the dogs away. His attempt at humor fell flat. The tension was as thick as the fog drifting in from the nearby bay, and I couldn't think of anything to do except blabber about the house and how lovely it was. While there was much to admire about the stately, three-storied Victorian, I knew how inane my compliments sounded. Unlike our home on Fripp, the San Francisco house, as beautiful as it was, felt formal and uninviting. Thankfully Megan arrived, and Pat went off with Susannah to look for his manuscript in the attic room that was once his office.

On the ride back to Tim's, I took Pat's hand, kissed it, then made a face. "I hope you washed off the dog slobber." I instantly regretted my flippancy, but Pat was too gloomy to notice. Before we left, he'd had another go at persuading Susannah to come for Christmas, either before or after her trip to Hawaii, but to no avail.

Without looking my way, Pat squeezed my hand. "I cannot wait to get home. What a beautiful word."

I put my head on his shoulder, dog slobber and all. It'd been almost a year since I'd moved into our cozy house on Fripp, and we'd made a home for ourselves. I prayed that the day would never come when one or the other of us would be forced to return to our beloved house to pick up what was left of a once-happy marriage.

In no time at all, the Christmas season was heading our way with the speed of a runaway train. Funny—when I was young, Christmas took forever to get here; after I turned fifty, I saw time in a different way. It felt like I'd been floating peacefully down a river on a small raft for a long, sweet time, then I suddenly notice that the current has picked up. When it hits me how treacherous the water has become and how fast it's pulling me downstream, I grab hold of the raft and pray it'll slow down. Somewhere in the distance is the unmistakable sound of the rapids, but there's no way for me to turn back or slow the raft down. I can't do anything but hang on helplessly and watch the scenery flash by me in a blur.

It would be my and Pat's first *real* Christmas together. I'd been on Fripp during the holidays the year before but had been in the process of moving in and barely remembered it. The few belongings I brought to my new life fit easily into the back of a small truck, which my son drove for several hours to my new address.

No sooner had he unloaded than he had to get back to his family in time for Santa Claus. Pat and I put up a tree, exchanged gifts (a nice pen for him, heart-shaped locket for me), then fixed ourselves a simple dinner of roast chicken. And that was the extent of it.

Our newly married Christmas would be memorable, I decided, then set out to make it so. Christmas has always been my favorite holiday. Pat claimed not to care one way or the other, but I was convinced I could change his mind.

I'd fallen in love with my new locale and wanted to embrace everything about life in the Lowcountry, so I went into a frenzy of preparation. Instead of the holly, cedar, and magnolia I normally decorated with, I brought in seashells, seagrass, and palmetto leaves. At an art show, I discovered the clever artisans who made creches from oyster shells as well as reindeer from palm fronds, which added local color to my decor. I made Pat help me loop ribbon around starfish to hang on our tree. It was the most fun I'd ever had decorating.

Getting in the spirit, I declared that our family dinner this year would be a Lowcountry Boil. It was a dish that I didn't especially like, but I kept that to myself. And although Christmas on the beach felt all wrong (it wasn't even cold!), I planned a Christmas Eve walk at sunset hand in hand with my sweet new husband. After a lovely candlelit supper, we'd go into town for midnight mass. It would be a special ending to a special day, I told myself cheerily. If you have to break eggs to make an omelet, to make a new life you had to break old traditions and make some new ones.

Then something unexpected happened that left me bewildered and despondent. When Christmas Eve came, my excitement flickered and died out like the proverbial candle in a gust of wind. My spirits sank, and I felt the unmistakable return of the depression

I'd battled so much of my life. It wasn't a full-blown return, just enough to make me mopey. If I didn't know better—if it weren't so ridiculous as to be laughable—I'd swear I was homesick. It *was* laughable, actually. I hadn't had a joy-filled Christmas since childhood; how could I possibly be homesick for something so long gone? My ex-husband had scorned the secular part of Christmas and found my joy in the season both childlike and irksome. Not only that, he declared it was downright sinful to spend money on gifts and I should be ashamed of myself. Every Christmas morning I'd expected to find coal and ashes in my stocking, the gift Santa brought naughty children.

The sunset walk would make everything right again, I decided, and forced myself to go about my merry way wrapping gifts and preparing for the holiday feast Pat and I were hosting for family and friends the following day. When the time came, I bounced into the den where Pat sat engrossed in a bowl game on TV. I loved football, but it was *Christmas*. I clapped my hands like a camp counselor and told him it was time for our walk. Pat wasn't having it. His eyes never leaving the screen, he waved me off. "But you'll miss the sunset," I wailed. He answered with a shrug, not even turning his head my way. "There'll be another sunset. Enjoy your walk."

So much for a romantic stroll our first Christmas Eve as a married couple, I thought in a huff as I slammed the door behind me. On the beach, the salt air was sharp and crisp, but I barely noticed. There wasn't a soul in sight, and the deserted beach appeared forlorn and sad, like I felt. Even worse, the sun had disappeared into the ocean and left behind nothing but a rosy glow on the horizon. My bad timing was all Pat's fault, I thought as my mood soured even more. If he'd come along as I'd planned, all would be well.

The sun would be hanging low on the horizon where it belonged, and we'd watch it sink into the Atlantic as we huddled together, our faces bright with happiness and love.

Muttering to myself, I trudged over wet, gray sand until I'd had enough. To add insult to injury, it was low tide, my least favorite time at the ocean. Everything had become a letdown on a day I'd planned with such hope and anticipation. Might as well go back and watch the game since my special Christmas Eve was ruined anyway. Hell, we'd just eat our dinner on TV trays instead of at the beautiful table I'd set! That was the thing about expectations. They always fall short.

Just as I was turning around, something in the water caught my eye. I stopped and blinked. Ever since I'd moved to Fripp I'd heard about the sandbar but hadn't seen it before. It was only visible during certain conditions of tide and current. And there it was, a narrow strip of white sand stretched like a long pointing finger into the deep dark ocean. Islanders were always warning strollers away from it, since sudden shifts in tides created a real danger. Walking on the sandbar wasn't worth the risk, folks were told; there was nothing to see except a bare strip of sand.

By the time I reached it, the sandbar stood out even more starkly against the gray waters sloshing around it. Then everything changed: the shocking-pink glow of the western sky suddenly deepened in color and spread out like a huge fan across the horizon. Without a thought of danger I hurried down the sandbar for a closer look, and my mood lifted. It was the blessing I'd come for, and I admonished myself for being so down in the mouth that I'd almost missed out. I stood at the tip of the sandbar for several minutes and stared in wonder and gratitude. The horizon, where vast water met vast sky, was the deep glorious pink of a Christmas rose.

After the glow faded and the sky began to darken, I turned to go and found my feet bogged down in wet sand. The tide was coming in, and I was a good distance from the shore. Already the sandbar had become an island enclosed in surging waters. It was then that I spotted what I'd failed to see in my rush to view the lingering sunset—the soggy finger where I stood was literally covered in sand dollars as far as the eye could see. With a gasp, I knelt down for a closer look. On previous walks, I'd seen the imprint of sand dollars left in wet sand by receding waves, or found brittle brown fragments on the shore. But I'd never seen them alive. Before I walked on it, the sandbar had been the bottom of the ocean; now at low tide, its sea-dwelling creatures had revealed themselves to me. Rather than the dazzling white disks that beachcombers collected, these sand dollars were dark little sea urchins, aflutter with life.

I made my way back to shore on tiptoe by maneuvering carefully to avoid stepping on the small creatures, a virtually impossible task since the sandbar was literally covered with them. My shoes filled with seawater when I crossed the tidal pool to safety, and they made a sloshing sound as I ran home. Ordinarily, running in soggy shoes would've slowed me down, but this time I ignored the discomfort. Seeing the sand dollars had made me forget my displeasure with Pat, and I burst in on the last quarter of his game.

"Patrick—you've *got* to see what I found on the sandbar," I said, gasping for breath. His alarm that I'd gone where angels fear to tread gave way to avid curiosity, which was one of the things I loved most about him. This time he came with me without a word of protest.

In the short time I'd been gone, the tide had changed. I discarded my wet shoes and waded ankle-deep into the icy, incoming waves in bewilderment. "It was right here, I swear it was!" I cried. I kept searching as darkness descended, so sure was I that the sandbar would be visible even under water. Pat waited with surprising patience but he finally reached for my arm to pull me back to shore.

"Come on, sweetheart. Whatever you saw is gone. The tide got it."

I hugged myself against the salt-laden breeze and leaned into him. "Sand dollars," I told him. "So many sand dollars. I've never seen anything like it. I wanted you to see them."

"I wish I had," he said, and I knew he meant it. He would've loved it as much as I had. "I should've come with you."

It was the perfect opportunity for wifely rectitude, a self-righteous reminder of my virtues and his failings. But instead I encircled him in a hug, loving him again, and said, "Let's go home. It's turning cold."

After our lovely candlelit dinner (at the table, not on TV trays), Pat surprised me by insisting I open the gift he'd gotten me, even though we'd planned to wait until the following day when family came for the exchange of presents. "You'll see why," he told me, and opening the box, I did. Pearl earrings to match the lovely pearls he'd given me before. "Another gift from the sea," he said. His note read, *I find the loving of you the easiest part, the nicest part, the best thing, the very best I've ever done for myself. Merry Christmas, darling.*

I showed off my pearls the next day, and I would wear them many times in the years that followed. But I never did so without remembering our first real Christmas together, and the unexpected blessings of a Christmas Eve on a sandbar, where I knelt to marvel at the wonder of sea creatures. It's a blessing I'll carry with me always.

CHAPTER 9

FROM ONE STORYTELLER TO ANOTHER

In the years that Pat and I were together following our wedding day (whenever that was), I never knew Pat to let facts stand in the way of a good story. His stories were always basically true, just embellished by the master raconteur. He'd doctor them up a bit each time depending on the reaction he got from the listener. If a different twist made the story better, or got more laughs, he wasn't beyond using it. No one relished a good story as much as Pat did.

It was something he had in common with my father. Daddy could tell a story, and he and Pat hit it off right away. I had a feeling they would. In his own way, my father was as much a character as Pat was. For one thing, Daddy was a hoot without meaning to be. As country folks put it, Elton King was a cutup, a sport, and a real card. His humor was broad; Pat's was more subtle. Daddy made exaggerated faces and gestures when telling a story, slapping his knees and holding his sides with laughter.

While it pleased and egged Pat on when others showed appreciation of his witty banter, Daddy was more apt to squawk "What's so damn funny?" when you laughed at something he said. Sometimes we couldn't help ourselves, even when it was caused by his deafness. One time my sisters and I found an old western playing on TV and urged Daddy to come watch with us. He ignored us and we called out, "Aw, c'mon, Daddy—you'll like it. Lee Marvin in *The Man Who Shot Liberty Valance*." Daddy appeared at the door scowling. "The man who shot the Liberty Bell? Who the hell wants to see that?"

Daddy also had the best sayings I've ever heard, many original with him. He'd never fly on a plane, he told us, because he didn't want to be higher than a tractor seat or lower than digging potatoes. He claimed one of our local politicians was so crooked they'd had to screw him into the ground to bury him. Some of his sayings I've used for local color in my fiction, even though they're based on unfortunate physical defects. In my first novel I described one of the characters as being so cross-eyed he could stand in the middle of the week and see both Sundays.

The grandkids would persuade Granddaddy King to tell them tales of the good old days, when he grew up during the Depression and survived hard times. The best stories came from him and his brother, my uncle Rex. Both of them told ghost stories that scared the holy hell out of my sisters and me when we were little. We shivered in delicious terror to hear about the Wampus Kitty that lived in the swampland near our house. Her terrible cry was like the scream of a woman. Both Daddy and Uncle Rex swore that they'd been chased by Old Bloody Bones one dark night when they were walking home from Aunt Fenny-Rump's. Aunt Fenny-Rump was an African American medicine woman who lived in a cabin in the woods, and they'd been sent to fetch one of her remedies. She warned the boys about Old Bloody Bones, a haunt who was wrapped in bloody rags and had a voracious appetite for children, but they didn't believe her until he came after them.

After I took Pat to meet Daddy and my sisters, Pat never let me hear the end of it. "I can't believe you, Helen Keller," he'd say a million times. (Pat was bad about repeating himself.) "You're sitting on a gold mine with that family of yours. Talk about local color! Your father's a character and your sisters right out of *Steel Magnolias*. If you don't write about them, I will." When he said that to my sisters, Beckie and Nancy Jane, they both swore he'd better think twice about it. "You married Tanna, Pat Conroy," Nancy Jane told him, "so you oughta know better than to mess with Alabama girls."

By then, Pat was learning a lot more about a certain kind of southern women than he'd bargained for. He claimed to be both intrigued and astonished by my sisters and me and what he called our kiss-my-ass sassiness, especially when one of us tangled with our stubborn old daddy, which usually ended in a shouting match. Daddy could embarrass you to death. Taking him to the doctor's office was an ordeal; if the doctor was running late, Daddy would bang his cane on the receptionist's window and demand to be seen. Poor Beckie, who lived on the farm next door, usually ended up being the one who had to deal with him. They'd return from an outing with Beckie telling Daddy that next time he needed to go to the doctor, he could, by God, drive himself.

"Those King sisters are spitfires," Pat told Beckie's husband, Reggie. "They make you walk the line, don't they?"

Reggie was quick to agree, then lowered his voice to say, "You damn straight, Pat. The truth is, you got the pick of the litter with Tanna."

Beckie came storming in from the kitchen waving a broom. "Reggie Schuler! You want me to knock you cross-eyed?" Reggie dodged the broom she tried to clobber him with while Pat eyed me nervously. Since both of his previous marriages had been to Yankee women, he had no way of knowing what he'd gotten himself into. But he was a fast learner.

A couple of times I heard Pat telling folks that he didn't meet my family until *after* we married, which is pure bull hockey. He also said that I'd told him I'd never met a Roman Catholic until I met him, but I ordered him to get his story straight. I was born and raised in the country, not on the moon. What I'd actually told him was, I'd never really known any Catholics growing up. In the sticks when I came along, everybody was either Methodist, Baptist, or Pentecostal. And in those days it was more of a class thing than a religious preference, with Methodists believing themselves higher in the social order than Baptists, and Baptists considering themselves above the Holy Rollers.

Because it always got a laugh, Pat was also fond of saying that the first time he met my family, he felt like he was on the set of *Deliverance.* While it made a better story, it was hardly true. The Kings of Pinckard, Alabama, were not only solidly middle class, we were also highfalutin Methodists. I can tell you one thing, those were *not* Methodist boys in that movie.

That's the Kings, however. My mother's family from Florida were as cracker as they come and ranged from Bible-thumpers to bootleggers. (Let it be known, I refrain from using the term *cracker* around my relations even though a historian corrected me for calling it a slur. According to him, it's a perfectly acceptable way of referring to Florida's rough-and-tumble early settlers. Maybe so, but I'm not taking any chances by riling one up.)

One time before Pat and I married we were taking a trip south, seems like to Mobile, when we stopped by to visit Daddy. To my chagrin, we landed right in the middle of a family reunion of my mother's relatives. I'd forgotten that they gathered annually for a fish fry after spending the day catching fish in Daddy's ponds. When we pulled into the yard full of pickups with bumper stickers that read "Go Seminoles" and "Get 'Em Gators," I knew we were in for it.

Nothing to be done but plunge in. I'd already caused a family scandal by divorcing a holy man; surely it couldn't get much worse. Taking Pat's hand, I took him around and introduced him as my fiancé. One of my elderly aunts reared back and looked down her nose to say, "Oh, I know who he is." Grabbing my arm, she pulled me aside to hiss, "I'm glad your poor mother is dead and gone, or she'd be turning over in her grave."

Before I could figure that one out, my sister Beckie grabbed my other arm and whispered, "I haven't had a chance to warn you. Daddy told them you've moved to South Carolina with a man."

"Oh Lord," I whispered back. "So that's why they're upset. I'm living in sin."

"Even worse," Beckie told me. "One of them looked Pat up and found out he's Catholic."

Definitely worse. Before I could decide the fastest way to exit, an uncle approached me waving my book. "Where'd you learn all them dirty words, girl? It sure wasn't from your sainted mama."

Pray God they never read one of Pat's books, I thought, hurrying toward the house and pulling Pat along with me. I was hoping Uncle Charles was there, the real character of the family, because I knew Pat'd get a kick out of him. My daddy loved to tell about the time Uncle Charles left the family reunion to run down to Dothan (ten miles away) to get more oysters for the picnic. No one knew where on earth he went because he never reappeared. Uncle Charles was a favorite with the kids because he carried around a myna bird who could sing all the verses of "I Left My Heart in San Francisco."

I adored Uncle Charles too; he played a mean harmonica, yodeled as well as Hank Senior, and buck-danced like nobody's business. I'm pretty sure I've never seen him sober. As a girl, I'd idolized his wife, Annie Mae, an Ava Gardner look-alike and Miss Florida finalist. I loved to stay with them in Pensacola because Annie Mae read movie magazines to me, which my mother considered trashy and didn't allow me and my sisters to look at. During one of my visits, Uncle Charles said something that Annie Mae found a tad peculiar. After he turned away, she looked at me and pointed to her temple. "You know Charles, he ain't right," she said sotto voce. It would become a favorite buzzword of me and my sisters; whenever someone appeared a bit off, one or the other of us would whisper, "You know he ain't right."

During the fish fry, I eyed Pat nervously to see if he was picking up on any of the anti-Catholic sentiments expressed by some of the Bible-thumpers, but he assured me later that it was nothing new to him. Growing up Catholic in the Deep South, he'd been exposed to it before, especially on his mother's side of the family. "Relax, kiddo," he said, patting me on the back. "I've made my living writing about crazy families. Yours is no crazier than anyone else's."

Although I smiled in relief, I have no doubt that his assessment would've been different if Uncle Charles had been there.

I'd given Daddy two of Pat's books, *The Water Is Wide* and *The Great Santini*, as a way of introducing him to the man I'd hooked up with. It's the complexities of families that always fascinated Pat, and my father was a study. As the oldest of five and a young man during the Depression, he didn't have the same opportunities his brothers and sisters had, and he hadn't been to college. You'd never know it, however. Although a rough-hewn farmer, gruff and grizzled, my father read voraciously and could talk about science, world history, and politics with anyone. A human calculator, he added long columns of numbers in his head. He kept wooden pencils that he whittled to a point with his pocketknife, and little lined notebooks that he wrote in, daily journals about crops and livestock. As a boy he'd wanted to be a writer too, he told me once. Pat's favorite thing about Daddy was that he listened to opera music while driving his tractor. I've never even tried to figure that one out.

After reading *The Water Is Wide*, Daddy started referring to Pat as Conrack. When he first met Pat, they sat in the den and talked about the book, and the early days of school integration in the South. My sisters and I eavesdropped from the kitchen, exchanging worried glances. Although I'd never known my father to be prejudiced, he was hardly a study in political correctness. He said what he pleased and if anyone didn't like it, too damn bad. I need not have worried, though; Daddy was on his best behavior and surprisingly honest with Pat. "Look here, Conrack," we heard him say, "I was raised to think that colored folks weren't as good as us. They were treated terrible, you know? I'm downright ashamed of it, but that's the way it was. I'm proud that most folks aren't like that anymore. It ought not make any difference what color anybody is."

The conversation moved on to *The Great Santini* and military life. A WWII veteran, Daddy had been a master sergeant in the army. Beckie, Nancy Jane, and I eyed one another in astonishment when we heard Daddy tell Pat that his father was a lot like the Great Santini, something he'd never told us. His generation was not the kind to reveal personal information about their families. "My daddy used to hit me upside the head so hard I swear that's the reason I never could half hear," my father told Pat in a low voice. "He worked me like a mule and beat me when I didn't do things to suit him."

Neither Beckie nor I was as surprised to hear this as Nancy Jane was. She was devastated. The youngest grandchild, Nancy Jane had been her grandfather's pet and had adored him. Much like Santini, our grandfather had mellowed in his old age to become more lovable. But Daddy had never said one word to any of us about his father's mistreatment. After hearing that conversation, I realized Pat had a rare gift; he could draw a story out of anybody, and they'd tell him things they'd never told anyone else. I saw this happen countless times over the years. Later my sisters and I tried to get Daddy to tell us more about our grandfather, but Daddy waved us off, closemouthed.

What Pat liked best about going to the farm was watching my father cook, which he did with great zeal. After Mother died, Daddy stepped up to the plate, so to speak, and cooked mostly from his abundant garden, which he took great pride in. My sons and nephews (my sisters and I only had boys) relished their grand-daddy's cooking for the same reason that Pat did—bacon drippings, grease, and lard. When Daddy had a heart attack in his early eighties, however, his doctors laid down the law. The next time we came for a visit, the breakfast table was different. Daddy had made his iron-skillet biscuits, but gone were the platters of bacon and freshly ground sausage patties. In their place were little links of turkey sausage, unsalted grits, and eggs lightened with extra whites. Next to the black pepper, which normally would've speckled Daddy's pan gravy, was salt substitute.

Daddy gave it a try, I'll give him that. Taking his seat at the head of the table, he broke open a biscuit and motioned toward Pat. "Pass me that play-like-it's-butter, Conrack." Gamely, Daddy sopped at the strange-looking eggs and tasteless grits with his biscuit, speared a turkey link, then scowled when he took a bite. Still scowling as he chewed, he threw down his napkin as though throwing down the gauntlet. "This goddamn stuff tastes like puredee shit," he growled.

"Daddy!" my sister Nancy Jane gasped, glancing Pat's way. He was still new to the family and she didn't want our father's language shocking her brother-in-law, the esteemed wordsmith. She had yet to learn that Daddy's colorful vocabulary was tame compared to Pat's.

My father suddenly pushed back from the table, gathered up the platters, then dumped their contents into the trash can. Next went the play-like-it's-butter and salt substitute. We watched speechless and wide-eyed, but he wasn't finished. On a roll, Daddy took his newly prescribed bottles of heart meds from the cabinet, opened the back door, and tossed the contents of the bottles into the back-yard. Why there instead of the trash can, I have no idea. Guess he was making a statement.

Squealing and jumping to their feet, Beckie and Nancy Jane ran outside to retrieve them. "You could've killed the dogs, Daddy!" Beckie screeched. Nancy Jane was more concerned with her father's health than his coon dogs. Her eyes, as electric blue as Daddy's, were flashing fire when she returned with a fistful of pills. "Don't think you're not taking these, dirt and all," she told him furiously.

Daddy stood his ground. "I been feeling like hell ever since I got out of that hospital, and I know it's those damn pills and that shitty food. I'm through with all of it." And he was. Cooking happily with all the bacon fat and grease he wanted, he lived several more years. One cold morning in January, Beckie called me early. A teacher, she always checked on Daddy before going to school. As soon as I heard her teary voice, I knew. At age ninety-six, Elton King had died in his sleep.

Pat was one of the speakers at my father's funeral, and he unintentionally gave us a gift that has carried me through many a dark moment. Even to this day, when I get down in the dumps, I remind myself of Pat's slip of the tongue at Daddy's funeral and giggle in remembrance. Although I missed it at the time, my sons didn't. One or the other of them still call me about it sometimes, sputtering with laughter. "I got to thinking about Pat at Granddaddy King's funeral," my oldest son, Jim, said recently, "and laughed as hard as I did then."

The folks at the funeral spoke of Daddy fondly, some referring to him as Uncle Elton, Mister Tony, or just Elton, depending on their relationship. He was well beloved, and everyone choked up talking about him. Even though he'd lived to a ripe old age and died the way I wish everyone could, peacefully in his sleep, he would still be greatly missed. A truly unique character—no one could take his place, or delight the kids with delicious stories of ghosties and goblins and growing up in the good old days. He was a gifted fisherman, hunter, and gardener who lived off the land, and no one else would be able to teach the boys how to do the same. My sons and nephews were devastated and wept openly at the sight of their grandfather in his casket, clad not in his Sunday best but in his favored work clothes, a denim shirt and dungarees.

The eulogy speakers brightened the mood of the funeral, as

often happens, by telling funny stories about Daddy's antics, including his throwing the heart pills into the backyard. Everyone was chuckling and smiling at one another until Pat got up to speak. True to form, Pat gave a stirring eulogy of such lyrical beauty that the audience fell silent, enraptured. No one in Pinckard, Alabama, had ever heard a eulogy like that, and folks would talk of it for years to come.

The family still talks of the eulogy too, but for a different reason. Fortunately no one else caught Pat's slip of the tongue except for the boys on the front pew. That row was reserved for the eight grandsons, who were serving as pallbearers.

"Elton King was a man who raised three beautiful and smart daughters, and his girls gave him a houseful of boys whom he adored," Pat intoned solemnly, and I saw the grandsons beam proudly. "He worked hard all his life, a farmer who listened to opera music as he plowed the fields. Nothing ever came easy to Elton John, who survived both a great war and the Great Depression."

I didn't catch it, mainly because my attention had been caught by the row of pallbearers across the aisle. Their mood had suddenly changed. All grown now, the boys were clean-shaven and suited up, and it broke my heart to see them bend over in the pew and hide their faces in their hands. Pat continued his eulogy. "No; no one could say that Elton John had an easy life. He told me stories about his boyhood that brought tears to my eyes, and I didn't have an easy boyhood either."

Stifled sobs from the pallbearers' pew caught my attention yet again, and my sisters reached for another Kleenex. Our boys were so broken up that they couldn't even raise their heads, and their shoulders shook pitifully. Pat's voice boomed out over the packed room. "Today we are here to bury Elton John, a great man whose like will not be known in these parts again. Yes, he lived a long and fruitful life, for which we are grateful, but he will be greatly missed. Rest in peace, my good man."

As Pat returned to his seat by me, the pallbearers were finally able to raise their heads and wipe their eyes, arranging their expressions into more composed demeanors. Pat leaned over to whisper in my ear. "Wish I'd told some funny stories instead, but I didn't realize I'd upset the boys so much. Even Jim was boo-hooing."

Jim, who is much more dignified than his rowdy younger brothers and cousins, told me afterward that it was the "fruitful" that did him in. And that Pat never caught himself when he kept calling his father-in-law Elton John instead of Elton King. When we told Pat what he'd said, he threw back his head and roared with laughter, even more so when he realized the boys had been stifling their laughter, not weeping. No two people in the world, Pat declared, could've been as different as his father-in-law and the colorful British musician. The boys told him it was a good thing Granddaddy King had no notion who Elton John was. Otherwise he would've risen from his coffin and clobbered Pat over the head with his cane, right in the midst of the most moving eulogy anyone in Pinckard had ever heard.

CHAPTER 10

JOINING TOGETHER, COMING APART

During our years together Pat would write six books. Previously, his books had been more like a bloodletting than ink on paper. *The Water Is Wide*, *The Great Santini*, *The Lords of Discipline*, *The Prince of Tides*, and *Beach Music* all dealt with disturbing subjects such as violence and cruelty; abuse, both institutional and individual; and mental illness. By the time he and I were together, he'd switched gears to write a memoir about his love of sports. Writing *My Losing Season* was a new experience for Pat—not the writing of a memoir, but actually enjoying the process. He loved every minute he spent reuniting with his college basketball team, reliving their glory days (or lack thereof), and capturing the experience on the page. I'd never seen my husband so engrossed and happy.

The sports memoir was also the kind of project that allowed him to work on another book at the same time, *The Pat Conroy Cookbook*, which was more food memoir than cookbook. He worked with a talented cook he'd met on Hilton Head Island, Suzanne Pollak, to develop the recipes. Suzanne, her husband, Peter, and their family of four lively teenagers moved into a magnificent old house in Beaufort, which gave me the opportunity to get to know them. The house has historic significance not just for its age and beauty; it's also one of the few remaining tabby houses in the Lowcountry. Tabby is an old-world type of concrete made primarily of crushed oyster shells and sand, which is uniquely textured and looks somewhat like stucco. I've often wondered why tabby has become a lost art in a place where oyster shells are so abundant.

It was during our friendship with the Pollaks, most likely during one of our many meals together, that Suzanne generously offered to host Megan's wedding in the expansive and elegant gardens of their house. Suzanne, who'd been raised abroad during her father's diplomatic service, was taken with all things southern, and Megan's wedding plans captured her fancy. Pat told her that Megan wanted a traditional southern wedding with all the fixings. He saw it as a return to her roots, since Megan was born in Beaufort and raised in Atlanta. But after attending college in Colorado, she'd settled in San Francisco and become a California girl through and through. Even so, her doting father set out to make her southern wedding happen, though he couldn't resist joking about it.

"You should see her billion-dollar wedding dress," he told the Pollaks with a laugh. "She showed me a picture and it looks like something Scarlett O'Hara—or more likely Melanie Wilkes—might've worn, with a full skirt and white bridal veil covering her from head to toe. Tickles me good."

Suzanne was quick to admonish him for his teasing. "That sounds lovely, Pat! You shouldn't tease her like that. Most young girls dream of a traditional fairy-tale wedding."

"Yeah, but there's nothing remotely traditional about Megan,"

Pat responded. "Take this fancy wedding she's planning. What I want to know is this: Is she planning to walk down the aisle in a snow-white dress with her baby on her hip?"

———⁓———

With Megan in California and me in Beaufort, I took on the role of unofficial wedding planner, which turned out to be a lot more fun than I feared when I made the offer. Pat got used to me cornering him with notebook in hand, firing questions like an investigative reporter hot on the trail of a big case. He soon tired of it, though, and waved me off when I persisted in asking his opinion about various details of the wedding and events leading up to it. "What part of *I don't give a shit* don't you understand, Sandra?" he said in exasperation. "The whole thing's going to be a clusterfuck, regardless."

I was indignant. "It most certainly won't be. How can you say such a thing?"

"Oh, come on, sweetheart," Pat said wearily. "You know as well as I do. Get that much family together and you're asking for trouble. Nothing sets off a family's dysfunction like weddings and funerals."

I had to admit that he had a point. Not only had I seen it in the hundreds of weddings and funerals I'd attended in my previous life as the preacher's wife, I'd witnessed it in my own family as well. I was thirteen when my great-grandfather died but remember to this day the shocking scene that took place as the family lined up outside to follow the casket into the church. I never knew what it was about, nor did anyone in the family ever mention it. My grandfather and great-aunt got into a furious, whispered argument outside the church doors, and my very dignified and elegant great-aunt reared back and slapped my grandfather in the face. Eyes straight ahead, the family marched in behind the casket as though nothing had happened.

"There's one good thing about family squabbles and dysfunction, and the nastier the better," Pat told me. "You're new to the game, but you'll find out that it's all material, fodder for our work. As a writer, you should start taking notes."

"Spoken by the master," I said. "Considering the families that God blessed us with, neither one of us will ever run out of material."

Family! What can you say? My boys inadvertently supplied Pat with the answer to that age-old question when they told him about their father, the preacher man, and his tendency to repeat everything three times. Pat was perplexed until the boys explained that sermons always have three points, so it got drummed into preachers' brains. The boys would demonstrate by doing imitations of their dad saying "Close the door, close the door, close the door" or "Wash your hands, wash your hands, wash your hands." The trilogy Pat loved most was from a eulogy my ex gave for a sweet little old church lady. What everyone needed to remember about Mrs. Grundy, the preacher man intoned, is what she loved best in all the world: family, family, family. Thereafter anytime Pat got exasperated with the difficulties, heartaches, and worries that happened in the most intimate of relationships, he'd look at me, sigh, and say "*Family . . . Family . . . Family.*"

Megan's wedding would be the first occasion in which our combined families (which Pat and I referred to as the Brady Bunch on steroids) would be together at the same time. I couldn't help but wonder how that would jibe and how folks would get along. True, our families had some things in common, but were those enough to make them enjoy each other's company? I had no idea and wasn't especially eager to find out the hard way, when everyone was under one roof without an easy escape route.

I raised the question with Pat, curious to see what he thought. Not unexpectedly, he sighed mightily and said that I worried too much. Yet again I had to admit that he had a point. I'm the kind of person who worries that something must be wrong if I don't have anything to worry about. I quickly remedy that problem by running through a list of all the things I should be fretting about, from the progress of the grandkids' potty training to global warming. Perversely, it's the way I put myself to sleep at night. Instead of sheep, I count potential disasters.

Softening his stance, Pat put his exasperation aside to ask me exactly what I was in a stew about. "Our families!" I cried. "What if they don't like each other?"

He made it clear that he regretted his half-hearted attempt to be a caring husband for a change. "Aw crap, not that again," he said with a groan. "We've been through this before. Relax, baby. It'll be fine. They'll be fine. So what if they don't like each other? I for one don't give a crap."

I let the subject drop. We'd had variations of this discussion plenty of times previously. Before my sisters and father came to visit us on Fripp for the first time, I reminded Pat that they were good, salt-of-the-earth people but not the kind of sophisticates he was used to. With the exception of the country folks I'd met on his mama's side, I was convinced that his family was much more refined than mine. (Though, granted, that wasn't saying a whole lot.)

Pat hooted at the idea and that instigated a battle of "dueling families," with each of us trying to outdo the other with if-you-think-*that's*-bad tales.

"So, your dad's a peanut farmer and your mama was a Florida cracker," Pat said dismissively. "Big freaking deal. My dad's from the Southside of Chicago, so I can tell you a thing or two about less than sophisticated relatives. I made the mistake of taking my New York publicist to dinner at my grandparents' house one time when I had a talk in Chicago. We were eating dinner when my grandma threw a meatball at me and cackled like a crazy woman. That's how uptown they are."

During our dueling-families debate, we reached an agreement on one thing: our siblings had a lot in common when it came to fine dining in that none of them particularly cared. Pat and I thought of ourselves as foodies, as were our kids and most of our friends. It was something we sort of took for granted. Our siblings, on the other hand, just weren't that interested in gourmet fixings. Pat teased his brother Mike about his preference for frozen fish sticks over fresh. Bringing in a platter of local flounder when the family gathered around the table on one occasion, Pat waved it under Mike's nose. "You don't know this, Mike, but that's what you call a fish. I bought it at the fish market. It has fins and scales and was swimming in the ocean this morning. And guess what? It's not rectangular."

At another family dinner, Pat made pasta and marinara sauce. "Okay, gang, listen up," he said to his siblings when he brought his pasta bowl to the table. "You remember how Mom made spaghetti?"

"Every Thursday night," his sister Kathy reminded him. "Spaghetti on Thursday, fish sticks on Friday."

"Well, this ain't your mama's spaghetti," said Pat. "Everybody got that? That's why it might look funny to you. Mom boiled the noodles to a clump, cut them up, and put a piece on our plates.

Then she poured canned tomato sauce over it. Makes me gag to this day just thinking about it."

"I thought it was good," Mike dared to say.

"You would," Pat retorted. Then he went around the table with the Parmesan cheese grater, liberally garnishing everyone's pasta, which he'd served in individual bowls roughly the size of a watermelon half.

Mike looked at his suspiciously and Pat sighed in exasperation. "No, Parmesan cheese doesn't come in a can and look like sawdust, Mike."

Pat returned to his chair and looked around the table in satisfaction. "This pasta"—he kissed his fingers with a flourish like the best Italian chef—"this is the real shit. You won't get anything like it except in Rome, It-ta-lee! So eat up."

My siblings were pretty much the same; there were just fewer of them for Pat to tease. Plus he was too chivalrous to pick on my sweet little sisters, neither of whom had had much exposure to the outside world. Nancy Jane had traveled more than Beckie. While a student at the University of Alabama, Nancy Jane had worked so vigorously for Jimmy Carter's presidential campaign that she not only visited the Carters at home in Plains, where she took part in one of the softball games with the press, she was also invited to the inauguration. Pat roared in delight when Nancy Jane told him the story of her first night in a hotel in downtown Washington, a country girl in the big city. Her hotel was so close to a nearby one that she could easily see the folks moving around their rooms, and she watched the occupants curiously. But to her horror, she caught the eye of a man who exposed himself to her, laughing at her shocked expression. When she came back later and dared look again, the man saw her and did it once more.

Nancy Jane called the front desk. "There's a man exposing himself to me and laughing about it!" she told them, panicky.

"A man's in your room, madam?" the snooty desk clerk asked.

"NO! He's in the hotel right across the way! And he exposes himself every time I look out the window." She was practically in tears at this point.

A pause on the other end, then the desk clerk said, "Madam, I suggest you close your curtains."

———

Unlike me, Nancy Jane had never tried to impress Pat by pretending to be sophisticated when it came to food or anything else. She was totally unapologetic about not liking to cook. What she did have, however, was an avid curiosity about food, which endeared her to Pat. My sister Beckie was another matter because she had little interest in cooking or eating, either one. I'd tried to warn Pat but he had to find out for himself. Beckie, a cute little kindergarten teacher, is one of those feisty southern girls who's pure country and proud of it. She's always tickled Pat good. Whenever I got on the phone with Beckie, Pat would take the receiver to do his best imitation of Stanley's love cry in *A Streetcar Named Desire*, calling "BECK-KEEE!" instead of "STELL-LA!" And in her thick Alabama drawl, Beckie would answer him back, "PA-ATTT!"

At one of my Birmingham signings for my third novel, *The Same Sweet Girls*, Pat took some of my friends to dinner to celebrate, along with Beckie and Nancy Jane, who had driven in for the occasion. My son Jason had been a cook at Birmingham's famed Highlands Bar and Grill when Pat and I first married, but he'd left to work with some friends who'd opened a new restaurant. Ordinarily Pat wouldn't dream of going to Birmingham without dining at Highlands, but out of solidarity with Jason and his friends, he decided we'd try their place. He said afterward that it was a bad career move on Jay's part, but he was sure glad he hadn't taken such a wild crowd to Highlands. (Remember, I'd tried to warn him.)

Beckie was seated by Pat, and I saw her eyeing the menu with a frown. It might not be Highlands, but Jay's friends had opened a first-class joint with white tablecloths, candles, and an extensive wine list. Taking charge, Pat took everyone's wine orders, moving around the table and nodding approval at some of the choices, until he got to Beckie. Nancy Jane was seated by me, so I'd had a chance to prep her, knowing what was coming. "Do *not* order white zinfandel," I'd whispered just before Pat got to her. "I'll explain later. Just tell him to pick out a nice rosé for you."

Nancy Jane looked puzzled. "But I love white zinfandel."

"Keep that to yourself. Pat will just tell you there's no such thing and make you order something else. Trust me on this, okay?"

After Pat had gotten everyone else's order, he turned to Beckie with a smile. "Okay, darling, what would you like?"

"I only drink red wine," Beckie told him, and Pat beamed in approval. Then she added, "Over ice, with half Sprite."

Pat's face fell. He cut his eyes to me, but I wasn't about to go there. Gamely, he pushed on. "What kind do you usually get, Beckie?"

She shrugged. "I can't remember but I'd know it if I saw it. It comes in a big green bottle and they carry it at Walmart?"

Pat blinked. "Okaaay." Taking advantage of the chance to educate her, he patted her back in encouragement. "I don't think they have that brand here, Beckie, but don't worry. I'll order something nice for you."

Beckie eyed him suspiciously. "Can I have it over ice?"

"Ah . . . tell you what. Try it my way first. If you don't like it, you can send it back. That a deal?"

Beckie agreed. I could tell by Pat's self-satisfied smile as he ordered her an expensive pinot noir that he was sure my sister was a rube just waiting to be transformed by his patient tutelage on the finer things of life. Henry Higgins was a role he enjoyed and played well.

When our predinner wine arrived, Pat proposed a toast to the success of my book, and we clicked glasses all around the table. I had my usual prosecco and sipped it happily, knowing it would be unusually fine and dry because the grasshopper had ordered it instead of the ant. Pat watched expectantly as Beckie took a swallow of the twenty-bucks-a-glass wine he'd picked out for her.

"Oh, yuck!" Beckie cried with an exaggerated shudder. "Pat Conroy! That wine has soured or something." She handed him the glass as though it were poison. "Here. Tell them to take it back. I can't drink that godawful stuff."

When I caught Pat's eye, I raised my glass of prosecco to him with a sympathetic shrug. You can take the girl out of the country, but you can't take the country out of the girl, Henry Higgins be damned.

～～～

Before long, our relatives would become the least of my worries. I was up to my neck in preparations for Megan's wedding in June. Lacking a daughter of my own, I figured it'd be the only wedding

I'd ever get a chance to plan and I threw myself into it. Engrossed in bridal bouquets and bridesmaids' luncheon invitations, I came late to the drama Pat had gotten himself caught up in—though *drama* falls short of describing what went on during that time. It was more of a passion play, complete with pain, suffering, and sorrow. And the resurrection scene, the catharsis of passion plays the world over, was not in the script.

I'm not sure what set this particular Oberammergau performance in motion but assumed it was triggered by the wedding plans. After Susannah had set up an email account for her father the previous summer and taught him how to use it (something she probably came to regret), Pat got captivated by the fun of sending emails and getting such quick responses back. He'd never learned to type, the reason he wrote his manuscripts in longhand, but that didn't stop him from emailing. His messages, which he painstakingly typed out with one finger, were unintentionally a hoot. He never figured out how to delete, space, or punctuate, no matter how many times I showed him. Pat claimed that he typed like a chimpanzee, but I'm pretty sure a primate would've done a better job.

Because Pat's office made up half of our bedroom, separated from our bed by a folding screen, I was used to his habit of getting up through the night to go to his desk when he couldn't sleep. Once he found that his low-wattage desk lamp didn't bother me (except when he woke me up to ask if the lamp was too bright), he often got up from bed to work. He was a terrible insomniac and roamed at night, mostly to the dining-room bar for another nightcap. But one night I woke to an odd glow coming from his office instead of the usual lamplight. Puzzled, I crept out of bed to peer around the screen and was surprised to find Pat at his computer, typing furiously with his forefinger. Who on earth could he be sending such late-night messages to? I wondered, but I went back to bed before I got myself wide awake. Whether friend or foe, nothing I could do about it till morning anyway.

The next day I had two choices in solving the mystery of my husband's nocturnal rendezvous—I could either sneak into his computer or just ask him. But if he was corresponding with a lover, would he answer me truthfully? I was being silly, I knew; if he was going to set up a tryst via computer, email would've been the dumbest way of doing it. Hardly a day went by when Pat didn't screw up whatever he was typing and have to ask for my help. He was always forgetting how to send, forward, or even open a message, and it didn't appear to bother him when he got me to do it for him. A lot of my emails contained stuff I wouldn't want anyone else to see (not even Pat!), but he didn't seem to have any such qualms. So over our breakfast of yogurt and granola, I bit the bullet and asked him who he'd been emailing through the night.

To my surprise, he pushed back his chair then went into the kitchen for more coffee. On the rare occasions when we had breakfast together, we ate on the screened porch in back. When Pat returned, he plopped down and said nonchalantly, "Was I up last night emailing? Hmm. I don't remember that."

I snorted. "Then you were either drunk or sleepwalking. I saw you."

He looked out over the lagoon. The snowy egrets roosting in the low-hanging branches fluttered their wings in solidarity, as though sensing his troubled gaze. Without meeting my eye Pat said, "Oh yeah. Last night. I must've been writing Susannah."

Instantly I wished I'd kept my mouth shut. His relationship with his youngest daughter was still shaky and fraught with tension. I'd been hopeful, despite their terse parting words last year, that they'd taken the first steps toward a reconciliation. Pat had written Susannah beautiful, loving letters that he'd shared with me, as if to say *See? I'm playing nice.* He sent flowers on her birthday and a stunning diamond necklace for Christmas, though he wasn't sure she got them since he didn't hear back. In addition to her reticence in responding to his overtures, another concern plagued him. After returning home from her summer visit, Susannah had developed some health problems. Pat didn't know until Lenore faxed him the usual household bills to pay, and an unusually high medical bill alarmed him. He surprised me by immediately picking up the phone on the fax machine and calling his ex-wife to ask what was wrong. During all our years together, it was the only time I knew him to talk to her. He demanded to know what was going on with his daughter. Before hanging up he requested, in a more polite tone, to be kept in the loop.

On the porch that morning, I leaned across the table to put a hand on Pat's and asked, "What's going on? Is Susannah sick again?"

He sighed and shook his head. "No, she seems to be okay now. It's not that."

I waited to see if he'd say more. Instead he sighed heavily again, picked up his coffee cup, and went inside. Instead of returning to the porch, he refilled his cup and went to his office. I didn't see him until later that day, when he reappeared for dinner. Instead of drilling him about Susannah, I asked about the bridesmaids' luncheon. Not only were he and Suzanne Pollak preparing the bridesmaids' luncheon, Pat was making it a chapter in his cookbook. His face brightened as he launched into menu ideas, always a safe and happy subject with him.

That night I came to bed late, unusual for me. After dinner

I'd retreated upstairs to finish a story for an anthology a friend was putting together. I'd missed the deadline but had been given a reprieve. Once I finished the story, I went downstairs to our bedroom, where I found Pat propped up sound asleep, reading glasses askew and book still in hand. I slipped into the bed, eased his glasses off, and tried to free the book without waking him. Huge and heavy, the book was *The Stories of Vladimir Nabokov*, one of Pat's favorites. I admired Nabokov but would hardly choose him as a bedtime read. At least his stories weren't as dark as some of Pat's other choices. A few nights previously he'd read a heavy tome (literally and figuratively) about the Bataan Death March, which disturbed him so much he had nightmares. Served him right, was my unsympathetic response. I no longer watched the news before bedtime for that very reason.

When I tugged harder on the Nabokov book, Pat's eyes flew open, startled, and he tightened his grip on it as if a burglar were trying to lift his wallet. Seeing it was me, he smiled a sleep-dazed smile and relinquished his grip. It was early for Pat, the night owl, but he reached up to turn out the lamp, then he wrapped his arms around me.

But it wasn't romance he had in mind. Instead, he blurted out, "I'm afraid I messed things up with the emails I sent Susannah."

I'd learned that the man who opened his heart to millions on the page wasn't always as open one-on-one and would clam up about his worries if pressed. So I kept quiet until he went on, even though I was thinking, *Oh Lord. What's he done now?*

As I feared, he'd done plenty, and it came pouring out in the moonlit darkness of our bedroom. "I always said I'd kill myself if I ever became a bully like Dad," Pat said in a choked voice. "Yet I'm more like him than you know."

"You're not like your dad," I protested. "You're a dear, sweet, and loving man. I don't like it when you beat up on yourself."

"I can be an asshole." He said it so sincerely that I stifled a laugh.

"Okay, so you're a dear, sweet, and loving man who can be an asshole. I can't relate, myself. I've never said an unkind word to anyone, my whole life."

Pat scoffed. "You probably haven't."

"Oh, please. You know how my Alabama friends call me K.B.? What do you think the 'B' stands for?"

Pat cleared his throat and said, "I'm pretty sure that I blew it with Susannah."

"In what way?"

"Just . . . ah . . . I said some harsh things to her. Really mean things that I shouldn't have said. And I came down on Megan too."

"About the wedding?" I asked hesitantly. Only a few days ago I'd come into the bedroom to find him on the phone with Megan. Since I had a dozen questions for her, I sat on the bed to wait my turn. My timing was off; Pat began to berate her for inviting Lenore to attend the wedding, so I scurried out of the room, coward that I am. Nor did I respond when he reported later how the conversation had gone. He'd issued an ultimatum: if Megan didn't withdraw the invitation to his former wife, she would have to find someone else to walk her down the aisle.

Although he and I'd only been together a few years and I hadn't seen it much, I knew that Pat had a temper. He also had a tendency—like my father—to fly off the handle and say hurtful things that he'd later regret. My boys have always said that if Granddaddy King couldn't hurt your feelings, they couldn't be hurt; later they'd say the same about Pat. But oddly enough, my father, the gruff old farmer, was better at making amends than Pat, the sensitive male writer. I can still picture Daddy, after snapping at one of us for whatever had irritated him, looking repentant and hangdog as he made his clumsy apologies. Pat, on the other hand, tended to let such things alone and hope they blew over. He wouldn't mention his transgressions in the hopes that the injured party would forget before he had to apologize. Lucky for him, it worked like a charm with me because I can't remember crap. Sometimes after Pat and I had a fuss, I'd catch myself laughing and joking with him until it hit me: *Wait—aren't I mad at him about something?*

"When I emailed Susannah last night," Pat continued, "I was really harsh about the wedding and a lot of other things. Actually it was worse than harsh. I completely lost it once I found out she's not coming for a visit this summer. She'll be here for Megan's wedding but that's it. She's off to France for the summer instead." Even in the dark, I could feel his eyes on me, feel the accusation in them. "Did you know that?"

I shook my head weakly. All I could say was "I'm so sorry, Pat. And no, I didn't know. I'd hoped she'd spend more time here. It hadn't occurred to me that she wouldn't come at all." That wasn't strictly true; in fact I'd worried about it since the previous summer. Most departures are full of promises to visit again, even if no one means it. The way Susannah'd avoided committing to another visit had been ominous.

Pat's mood shifted from remorse to fury. "Well, I'm not having it, by God. Susannah isn't making an appearance at Megan's wedding then rushing off to fucking France or anywhere else. Oh hell no! *Not* going to happen."

I had absolutely no idea what to say, nor have I ever felt so helpless in offering comfort or words of wisdom. Nothing I could do would help to mend the tenuous relationship between him and his youngest daughter. Right before my eyes, things appeared to be disintegrating like a sand castle in the path of the incoming tide. Or more aptly, it brought to mind one of the tarot cards I always dreaded to uncover. The card depicts a stone tower as it's struck by lightning in a raging storm and begins to fall apart. Even without the storm or the lightning you know the tower is doomed anyway: studying the card, you can see that the ground it stands on is too perilous to hold it up.

The wedding turned out fairy-tale beautiful, just as Megan had envisioned. Pat's bridesmaids' luncheon was a big hit, without a pimento-cheese sandwich or petit four in sight. Instead he and Suzanne prepared a cold cucumber soup and swordfish salad with garlic aioli, while I did my mama's prizewinning pound cake to serve with fresh Carolina peaches. We hosted the lunch in our dining room around the leather-topped table for twelve that had originally been in the library of Oxford University. We hosted the rehearsal dinner as well, with an authentic whole-hog pit-in-the-ground barbecue near our backyard lagoon where gators lurked like uninvited party guests. Pat admitted all that entertaining was his unabashed attempt to impress Megan's new California relatives.

Looking somewhat shaky and pale but lovely as ever, Susannah had arrived with her half brother, Gregory, Pat's former stepson who was Megan's age. I'd met Gregory during a previous visit and found him to be a quiet, amiable young man who seemed especially protective of his sister. (There was another sister, Emily, whom I hadn't met.) Pat teased Gregory about being Susannah's bodyguard, but his teasing turned hostile when he found out the two of them were only there for the wedding before scurrying off to Europe. The more frustrated Pat became, the more he ranted, raved, and threatened, which caused his daughter to retreat even further. The tension was palpable. To me, things seemed to be hurling downhill like a snowball headed for hell.

After everyone arrived, I got caught up in last-minute wedding details and the swirl of entertaining and forgot to worry about Pat's problems with Susannah and Gregory. I knew he'd been upset when he first saw Susannah, thinking she appeared sickly, but with so much going on he didn't get a moment alone with her. As long as he was preoccupied with playing host to the hordes of wedding guests, though, I wasn't about to ask him the details. I figured I'd hear soon enough. One thing I've learned about trouble—it has a way of finding you whether you look for it or not.

Despite Pat's cajoling, threats, and ultimatums, Susannah left for France right after the wedding, then spent a year in Rome finishing her high school term. During that time Pat had no way of getting in touch with her. His brothers were scornful. Cut off the money, they advised, and you'll be surprised how fast you'll hear. A former friend of Pat's lived in Rome; he intervened and reported back that Susannah had agreed to see her father if he and I would come to Italy. Pat insisted she come to him instead, resulting in an impasse where neither would yield an inch. Negotiations faltered then stopped altogether.

The following year Pat heard from Megan that Susannah had returned to California and enrolled in Berkeley. Letters, emails, and gifts from her father went unacknowledged. Maybe with her health issues, Susannah couldn't deal with Pat's demands to see her; I don't know. Without any communication, we were left to draw our own conclusions. As a means of forcing the issue, Pat was advised to cut off financial support as his brothers had suggested, but he wouldn't. (It'd be years later before he'd return to court to ease the strain of supporting two households.) Tim Belk got furious with Pat and phoned me to rant, calling his old friend a softie of the worst sort for allowing himself to be manipulated. "Pat's all talk and no action," Tim grumbled. "Always running his big mouth but doing nothing to back it up." It was hard to make others understand that Pat had no legal recourse in the matter. His daughter could either choose to see her father, or not.

At the stately old house on Presidio Avenue, a line was drawn in the sand that anyone with allegiance to Pat better not cross (or so we'd hear later). The harsh emails had the negative repercussions that Pat'd feared, and none of the loving or regretful messages that he sent could make up for them. In no time Megan, Melissa, Jessica, and the rest of the family were shut off as well. Megan, who'd been closest to Susannah, told me that once she realized what was happening, she'd gone to the house several times, where she banged on the door crying and begging for admittance. Her pleas to Lenore and Susannah fell on deaf ears, and her calls went unanswered. When she finally got through to Gregory, he agreed to meet her at a local coffee shop. After the second time he failed to show up or answer her calls, Megan gave up.

I honored Megan's request not to tell her dad how she'd humiliated herself trying to find out why she'd been cut off from her sister and the family she'd been so close to, knowing how upset he'd be. Although I didn't agree with it, I could at least understand Susannah's decision to distance herself from her father. But breaking off all contact with the rest of the family, especially her sisters, struck me as extreme, to say the least. If the estrangement was intended to hurt Pat, it worked, but the girls were hurt too. They'd done nothing but continue to love both their father and their sister. It was a tragic situation I'd seen too many times before. After a bitter divorce one parent pits the children against the other parent, and it becomes a game of *Got you, you bastard!* It's a sick and destructive game that everybody loses in the end.

Pat was fifty-three at the time of Megan's wedding. He would be a couple of months shy of seventy before he saw his youngest daughter again. During the long years of their estrangement, he pleaded with friends and acquaintances from his former life for information about his daughter's well-being. He also stayed in contact with his former stepdaughter, Emily, whom he helped support because he knew what a difficult life she'd had. But Emily's relationship with her mother, brother, and half sister was also rocky, so she didn't know much more than Pat did. Occasionally he'd get a tidbit of information from her but never knew if it was reliable.

The long estrangement from his youngest daughter killed something in Pat that he never really got over. Throughout the years, he continued to send her letters, gifts, and flowers. Even though he got no response, he never stopped hoping that one day, somehow, he and his daughter would find their way back to each other.

CHAPTER 11

IT'S A MAINE THING

A few years after Megan's wedding, Pat's daughter Melissa would have a much simpler and quieter ceremony in the backyard of her mother's house in Atlanta. Although it was an incredibly sweet and lovely affair, when the family reminisces about Melissa and Jay Shermata's wedding, the comments are always the same: *It was the hottest day any of us can remember, with one of the highest temperatures ever recorded in Atlanta.* At the outdoor reception, their beautiful, three-tiered wedding cake melted into a puddle, and so did the guests.

When Pat and I returned to Fripp, he sat me down for a heart-to-heart. "Helen Keller," he said wearily, "this ain't working for me. And you're too stubborn to admit it, but it's not working for you either. The summers are killing me. We've *got* to get out of here."

He had a point. When you live on the beach, everybody's your friend. After Pat and I had been together a couple of years, we'd start in the spring bracing ourselves for the upcoming summer, which we called Camp Fripp. And once the school year ended and relatives headed our way, that was exactly what our house felt like, a summer camp. Pat and I spent most of the summer cooking, washing sheets and beach towels, and sweeping sand off the floors. Every night we collapsed in exhaustion, worn out.

Pat came up with a way to celebrate the departure of our visitors, which he first did as a lark then later as entertainment for the grandkids. After the first couple of summers of constant visitors, Pat made up a victory dance when the last one was out the door. Big as he was, he was light on his feet and he cavorted, twirled, and jumped up and down singing *"Oh Freee-dom!"* He bent over at the waist with his arms above his head and genuflected to a sympathetic god who'd led us out of visitor bondage to the promised land of peace and quiet. It was the perfect release from the stress of endless entertaining.

"Pat Conroy," I said when he suggested that we escape, "that may be the best idea you've ever had. So here's what I think. Let's tell the kids they need to come the first part of the summer—all of them, together. Get it over with! We'll visit with them during their stay, then we'll hit the road running. And we'll stay gone until after Labor Day weekend."

"Perfect," Pat agreed. "But we'd better not tell them where we're going. They might follow us."

That's how we ended up discovering Brooklin, Maine, and Highlands, North Carolina, as our summer destinations. Not only did getting away save our sanity (and probably our marriage and writing careers as well), it was the way I became better acquainted with some of Pat's closest friends, who would become lifelong friends to me as well.

I don't recall exactly when Pat first took me to Charleston to visit his friends Anne Rivers Siddons and her husband, Heyward, but it was a happy day for me. I'd met them at the Birmingham event a few years before and couldn't believe how kind Anne was to me. Despite her success, she was as warm, charming, and unpretentious as anyone I'd ever met. I had long admired her work, especially *Colony*. I think I've read that book a dozen times. Her sixth novel, *Colony* is set on the coast of Maine and based on Heyward's family compound there. At the time I'd never been to Maine but after reading *Colony*, I would've moved there in a New York minute.

When Pat proposed that we visit Anne and Heyward at their place in Maine, I couldn't pack fast enough. For me, it was not just the beginning of a friendship with the Siddonses, it was the beginning of a love affair. In all our years together, Pat Conroy had only one real competitor for my affections. George Clooney might not get a second glance, but tempt me with a steamed lobster and I turn to mush.

Pat decided we'd make our visit to Maine a road trip— thankfully, since both of us were writing new books and had to tote a bunch of stuff, including my computer. Until his health became a factor, Pat would drive anywhere rather than fly, which he hated with a passion. He also saw this trip as a way of showing me some sights on the drive up, visiting places I hadn't been. That was not a difficult task. I'd toured the East Coast on a road trip to Quebec when I was in my twenties; visited and gone sightseeing in both New York and DC; and spent a couple of weeks at a college in Vermont when I was teaching. Even though Maine had always been on my bucket list, those scattered visits were the extent of my knowledge of that part of the country. I couldn't have been more excited if we'd planned a visit to Paris, France.

I've never gone on a road trip with anyone as easygoing as Pat. He didn't mind admitting he was lost and would even ask for directions. My father had used his deafness to pretend he didn't hear me and my sisters whining for ice cream or a Co-cola. Our wails would get louder until he'd tell us if we didn't shut the hell up, he'd give us something to holler about.

Because of Pat's frequent moves in his childhood with his ill-tempered father at the wheel, he never balked at stopping for a bathroom break, a scenic overlook, or a Hershey's bar. For whatever reason, I crave Hershey's bars (the small size with whole almonds) when on the road. They're even better if it's hot in the car and they melt just enough to get squishy. The chocolate-induced high is intensified by a bottled Coke (ice cold, of course), but I gave them up a long time ago. Drinking something that does a pretty good job of cleaning a corroded car battery doesn't seem very smart to me, and certainly not with my delicate constitution.

Some of Pat's road cravings I found appalling. It made me feel guilty since he was so good-natured and indulgent of me, but still. Even if we'd just had breakfast or lunch, he couldn't stop at a service station without getting a couple of hot dogs from the rotisserie. Some of them looked like they'd sat out all day, and probably had. Neither could he resist those hot pickled sausages that come in a big bottle, usually near the cash register. They always gave him heartburn, which is hardly surprising considering how lethal they looked. Gathering up as many bags of potato chips as he could carry with a large Diet Coke in hand, Pat'd return to the car humming blissfully. Diabetes be damned, he always sneaked in a few bags of peanut M&M's too.

Forbidden goodies weren't our only road-trip indulgences. Pat and I discovered early in our relationship that we shared a passion for country music. We stocked up on CDs by Waylon, Willie, and the Boys, and we rode the highways singing. A good country song contains all anyone ever needs to know about what can go wrong with a relationship. As Dolly Parton warns in "Jolene," if you're not careful a hussy could take your man just because she can. Or worse, you could marry a hussy who takes her love to town because you're a crippled war veteran. Maybe she leaves because of four hungry children and a crop in the field. Even so, you only stop loving her the day they put a wreath upon your door and come to carry you away. Pat was a great one for making up his own lyrics, and he'd serenade me with his version of a Waylon classic, "Amanda": "Cassandra, light of my life . . . Fate should've made you a gentleman's wife."

Both of us agreed that country songs have a lot to teach writers about catchy titles, and I find some of them nothing short of genius. Who can beat "Thank God and Greyhound She's Gone," or "Drop-Kick Me Jesus Through the Goalposts of Life." Naturally Pat's favorite were the drinking songs, "She's Acting Single (I'm Drinkin' Doubles)" or, even better, "I'd Rather Have a Bottle in Front of Me (Than a Frontal Lobotomy)." Both of us made fun of sappy songs and cracked up whenever we heard "The Wind Beneath My Wings."

Our trips were also a time for Pat and me to pick up where we'd left off telling each other the stories of our lives. On the three-day drive to Maine, Pat told me how his father wouldn't let him get his driver's license when he turned sixteen, which he saw as an obvious ploy to keep him under his thumb. It was Pat's beloved English teacher, Gene Norris, who taught him to drive and took him to get his license. He was lucky, I told him. My father taught me to drive—or rather, he started out to. He made me so nervous I waited until he was plowing the fields to learn on my own, vowing that I'd never go through such an ordeal again. When the two of us got on the road with me behind the wheel, Daddy would scare the daylights out of me by suddenly yelling for me to stop. I'd slam on the brakes and he'd go flying forward. "*Goddammit!* Just pull over and let me out," he'd holler as he grabbed onto the door handle for dear life. The time he cried out "Oh help me sweet Jesus!" and ducked down into the floor mat was the final straw for me. Driving lessons over.

After our almost-four-day drive up the coast, Pat and I got comfortably settled into the Siddonses' guesthouse. I gave my driver a day's rest before dragging him off to see the sights. Rarely has anyplace lived up to its billing like Maine did. For a nature lover, Maine's a wild and rugged paradise of ancient glacial landscapes and dense primal forest. I loved everything: the rocky, panoramic coastline; the quaint lighthouses; the picturesque fishing villages and hidden coves dotted with sailboats. Not only is Maine spectacularly beautiful, it's also a food lover's paradise. I had lobster every single day because they were five bucks each at a nearby lobster pound. It's not just the abundance of lobster; all the seafood is fantastic. The Siddonses live right on the water, where the salt-laden smells of Penobscot Bay were carried by brisk breezes into our opened windows. There's nothing like a salty breeze to stimulate the appetite, and we ate like lumberjacks the whole time.

Pat was less enamored than I was. His jovial, hail-fellow-well-met overtures that endeared him to southerners went over like a lead balloon with the good people of Maine. (Or, as Heyward so colorfully put it, like a turd in a punch bowl.) Pat's friendliness that normally had people eating out of his hand was met by Mainers with a stony silence. Anne had tried to warn him. The locals were every bit as taciturn and reticent as we'd heard, she said, and didn't warm up to outsiders until they'd known you a long time. Instead of backing off as anyone with any sense would've done, Pat took it as a challenge and set out to win them over. By the time we left to go home, the count was Mainers one million, Pat zip. Although he never gained their affection, their staunchness earned his grudging respect.

Our first encounter with the stereotypical Maine taciturnity was with Anne and Heyward's housekeeper, Lanett. Although Lanett and her husband turned out to be two of the kindest, most gentle souls we've ever met, none of us knew what to make of one another that first summer. For one thing, Pat and I had trouble with their Maine accents and mostly communicated with hand gestures. At least Pat had his deafness as an excuse. Talking with Lanett or her rough-hewn, bearded husband, I felt like I was in Scotland. I'd find out later that attitude worked both ways. After we returned to South Carolina, Anne called to make sure we'd gotten back safely. "Lanett really liked you and Pat," Anne told me. It was a rare compliment, and I took it as such, pleased. "But you know what she told me?" Anne continued, laughing. "Lanett said, 'Mrs. Conroy's real nice, but with that accent of hers, I never understood a word she said.'"

~~~~

Pat knew about my fondness for lobster, but I didn't tell him about my other Maine obsession until we got there. I hadn't told him because I knew what he'd say: *We've driven for four days so you can look for a freaking* bird?

I was dying to see the North Atlantic puffins, those cute little black-and-white seabirds with orange duck-feet and red beaks. On the East Coast, puffins are only found in Maine on small offshore islands, nesting in rocks. One day, Anne and I took off on a girls-only trip to Acadia National Park, where we took a sightseeing boat out to see puffins and, hopefully, catch sight of a whale. Neither Pat nor Heyward could be persuaded to join us, so I took dozens of photos to show them what they'd missed. We'd not only seen hundreds of puffins, we'd also had the thrill of spotting an enormous humpbacked whale.

On the drive home, Anne and I relived our fun day and the unexpected thrill of the whale. When I said I couldn't wait to tell Pat, she chuckled indulgently. "I love seeing the two of you together," she said. "I've never seen him so relaxed and at peace with himself."

"This is *relaxed*?" I said wide-eyed. "Good-natured and easygoing, I get. Relaxed and at peace, never."

"Oh, sweetie, you wouldn't believe how he was before you came along. His old Atlanta gang talks about it all the time. When we knew him before, he was so volatile and unpredictable we worried constantly about him and his self-destructive tendencies. He's a remarkably different person now. Does he even drink anymore? He's been a heavy drinker as long as I've known him."

"He seems to have gotten that under control, but he'll still self-medicate when he gets stressed out."

Anne cut her eyes my way before turning back to the narrow road she navigated cautiously down the rocky coast. "He told me about Susannah. That poor child! She's a pawn in a sorry game. Surely she'll see that as she gets older."

"I don't know, Anne," I said gloomily. "She's in her twenties now, and nothing's changed."

"This is upsetting you," she noted. "Let's talk about something more pleasant. Are you excited about us having lunch with Richard Russo this week? It was so nice of Pat's friends to include us."

Pat's friends the Millers, two of the finest people I've ever met, were close friends and next-door neighbors of the Russos in Camden (a town I'd been longing to see), and they'd invited us to meet him. "I'm excited but nervous," I admitted. "Being such an admirer of his writing, I probably won't be able to say a word and will make a fool of myself, like I did the first time I met Pat."

She pooh-poohed my anxiety, saying she'd met Russo at a book signing and he'd been extremely pleasant. "Don't let Pat scare you off with his tales of the assholes he's met," Anne added. "Most writers are good people. I'm sure Richard Russo is the same."

"It's a relief to hear that he isn't one of the crazies."

"I wouldn't know about that," Anne said with a wry grin. "I said he was nice, not sane. All writers are pretty much crazy."

My smile was more of a grimace. I'd heard that sentiment so often I was beginning to believe it. "I must be worse than crazy," I blurted out. I'd been hoping for a chance to ask her something that had bothered me the whole summer. She, Pat, and I were all working on new books, but we rarely talked shop. After our outing, I felt comfortable enough to ask her advice, so I plunged in.

"The book I'm working on now, *The Same Sweet Girls*?" I said. "It's about a group of women friends, something you've written about a lot. But the thing is, these are inspired by real people—a group of real-life friends I've had for years. I'm not sure I can do it."

Anne shot me an alarmed look. "Do they know you're writing about them?"

I shook my head. "Not yet."

"Let me guess. Pat's urged you to do this, right?" When I nodded, she sighed. "Oh, honey. Tread carefully. You know what that very thing has cost Pat. Beneath his tough shell he suffers more about the stuff he's written than he'll ever let anyone see. I worry about him. One day it's going to take its toll."

"You said that very thing in one of your books! And I copied it in my journal. Something like 'You can get whatever you want from life. Take it, and pay the price.' Do you remember that?"

"I never remember anything I've written. But I'm glad I said that." She was quick to correct herself. "Or, rather, had one of my characters say it. To me, that's the beauty of fiction. Don't get me wrong, I've done it too—based characters on people I know—and fictionalized plenty from my life. But it always comes with a price."

We rode in silence for a few miles as I absorbed her words. Then Anne reached over to pat my arm. "Don't pay any attention to me, or Pat, or anyone else. As writers we have to do what speaks the truth to us."

"I'd much rather learn from other people's pain than my own," I said, only halfway joking. "Wouldn't you?"

Anne smiled her easy smile. "Well, yeah. Too bad it doesn't work that way, though."

~~~~~

Alex and Zoe Sanders, old friends of the Siddonses, came to spend a few days in nearby Blue Hill, and the six of us got together often. The Sanders were with us the night that Pat would refer to thereafter as the time Heyward practiced dying.

Anne and Heyward had long been patrons of a place called the Lobster Pot, where we often went to dinner. It's one of those hole-in-the-wall places that only the locals know about. Perched right on the rocky shore and open to the elements, the Lobster Pot is the real deal. Because it's located on Little Deer Island and at the end of a dirt road, getting there's an adventure and made going out to dinner quite the occasion. Diners who got there at the right time could watch the staff of young men hauling in buckets of clams destined for their supper plate, sea to table.

The Sanderses followed us in their car, and Pat and I picked up the Siddonses in ours. Even though Anne decided at the last minute not to go because of a headache, we stuck to the plan of taking two cars. In his seventies and not in the best of health, Heyward had difficulty with his legs and walked with a cane, so all of us squeezed into one vehicle would've been uncomfortable for him. It wasn't the kind of place that took reservations, so we were lucky to get a table. Usually we sat at one of the tables overlooking the water, where we watched the sun sink over a picture-perfect view. That night it was packed, and we found ourselves seated at a table right in the middle of a noisy and festive crowd.

The dinner lived up to its billing. Our waitress was a cute young Mainer with a swishing ponytail and a thick brogue. Zoe, Alex, and I tied on paper bibs and dug into our steamed lobsters while Pat and Heyward feasted on the clam bake. At the center of the oilcloth-covered table was a tin bucket for the clam and lobster shells. With such a big crowd, it was so noisy that we had to raise our voices to be heard, but as usual, the two raconteurs at our table took over. I'd considered Pat the best storyteller I'd ever heard until I met Alex, who gave him a run for his money. Between the two of them, we were entertained not only through the main course but also through the blueberry pie à la mode afterward. Laughing and talking with our voices raised over the clamor, Pat, Alex, Zoe, and I failed to notice that Heyward had gone quiet.

I was seated closest to Heyward and saw that his head was bent slightly forward, as though he were studying his shoes. I nudged him. "Heyward?" When he didn't respond, I leaned in closer. At first I thought he'd dozed off, as my daddy was apt to do after a full meal. But to my knowledge, Daddy had never done so sitting straight up at the table with a piece of half-eaten pie on his plate. "*Heyward?*" I repeated.

With a heavy sigh, Heyward slumped forward as though he would land facedown in his pie. "Oh God—Pat!" I cried out as I jumped up. My ladder-back chair hit the floor, but the crowd of diners was so noisy that no one noticed. Neither did my table-mates, who were laughing at the punch line of one of Alex's stories. In less than a heartbeat I was behind Heyward's chair and had grabbed him from behind, chair and all, to keep him from falling over. This time I yelled it: "*PAT!*"

Pat was on his feet quickly and ran around the table to grab Heyward, who was too heavy for me to hold upright. The chair, Heyward, and I were all about to topple when Pat came to the rescue. Zoe and Alex both jumped up as well, and Zoe's hand flew to her mouth. All the color had left Heyward's face, and I was sure he was dead. Oh Lord, poor Anne! What would we tell her? One minute her husband was bright-eyed and full of life, laughing and enjoying himself, the next minute he just keeled over. "HELP!" I yelled out, looking around desperately. Unbelievably, the diners continued their conversations, oblivious to the drama going on at our table.

Zoe ran to the front of the restaurant where we'd stood to wait for a table. "Call 911," I heard her yelling, as Alex came around to help Pat with Heyward. Pat's eyes met mine and I mouthed, *He's dead, isn't he?* In response, Pat nodded his head sadly. I knew he was thinking the same as me: What on earth would we tell Annie? Tears started rolling down my cheeks, but I was in such a state of shock I barely noticed.

The owner, a very large man clad in a very large apron, came running over with Zoe. He'd known Heyward, a longtime regular customer, for years. At last we had the attention of the crowded restaurant. After leaning over Heyward to shake his shoulder, the poor owner raised his head to call out the classic cry: "Is there a doctor in the house?"

There was a stunned silence when not a person in the building moved. Then a woman from one of the nearby tables pushed back her chair and hurried over. "I'm a registered nurse," she said. We breathed a collective sigh of relief as she instructed Pat and Alex to lay Heyward out on the floor. Because the place was so crowded, this took a bit of doing. The woman loosened Heyward's collar and placed her ear over his heart. I expected her to start mouth-to-mouth, but instead she sat up and looked at the owner. "Have you called an ambulance?" she asked, and the man nodded glumly. It was apparent to all of us, however, that an undertaker would be more appropriate.

Without thinking I sank to my knees and leaned over Heyward, stroking his colorless face and telling him he was going to be all right, even as tears rolled down my cheeks. Waiting for the ambulance to arrive, the whole restaurant froze in place. The staff had come to stand outside the kitchen, and I saw our young waitress wringing her hands. I figured that she'd never before served a customer who died in the middle of the blueberry pie. It took forever for the ambulance to get there, but everyone maintained a reverent silence throughout the wait. The only noise was the rustle of feet and hushed whispers of the horrified onlookers. Folks resumed their places but not a one of them picked up their forks to continue eating.

Pat and Zoe had joined me to kneel beside Heyward. Pat took his friend's lifeless hand and rubbed it, looking down at him tearfully. Alex was up and down like a jack-in-the-box, alternating between going outside to check for the ambulance and returning to stand around helplessly with his hands in his pockets. Like me, Zoe was sobbing and had gone from trying to comfort Heyward to comforting Pat and me. The nurse did what she could, but a pall had fallen over the whole scene.

Suddenly the ambulance was there and the room bustled with activity again. Six muscular paramedics came in and took over. When they got Heyward strapped on a gurney, a pathway cleared for them to carry him out. Most of the diners got to their feet again. We worked it out quickly that Zoe and Alex would follow the ambulance so that Pat and I could stop and pick up Anne. Since Heyward was still alive, though barely, he'd be taken to the Blue Hill hospital, several winding and two-laned miles away.

Although the owner tried to shoo him off, Pat stopped long enough to pay our bill and to shake the hands of the staff. As we started out the door, both of us paused for a wave of gratitude for our wide-eyed fellow diners. Standing tall, Pat took it a step further. Holding his hand high like a traffic cop, he said in a booming voice, "Men and women of Maine, you were truly magnificent tonight, and I thank you from the bottom of my heart. You proved to me what I had heard for a long time, that the state of Maine produces some of the finest sons and daughters in the nation. It is a privilege to be in your state, and we couldn't be more grateful for your care and concern during this sad and unfortunate time."

The room burst into applause, and those who weren't already on their feet stood as they applauded, calling out well wishes after us as we drove away into the darkness.

The doctors would never know for sure what happened to Heyward that night. Whether a small stroke or a prolonged TIA, it would remain a mystery. Whatever, he was awake and alert by the time we brought Anne to the hospital, fearing and assuming the worst. Anne burst into tears of relief as soon as she saw him sitting up in a hospital bed, looking dazed but very much alive. Pat and I hugged each other, then turned to embrace Zoe and Alex, all of us giddy with relief.

"Thank God you were only practicing dying, Heyward," Pat said. "Now we'll know what to do when the real thing comes."

A couple of days later Pat and I were in the grocery store. As we gathered the ingredients to make soup for Heyward's homecoming from the hospital, a well-dressed young woman approached our shopping cart. Eyeing Pat, she worked up the nerve to ask, "You're Pat Conroy, aren't you?"

When Pat acknowledged that he was indeed the great man, the woman shook his hand. She introduced herself as a fellow southerner vacationing in Blue Hill from Atlanta.

Then she surprised us by asking, "How's your friend doing?" When Pat looked puzzled, she went on to explain that she was at the Lobster Pot with family and friends the other night when Heyward fell ill. She clasped her hands in relief when Pat told her that Heyward was fine, and that we were preparing dinner for his homecoming from the hospital.

"I told my family that I was sure you were Pat Conroy," the

woman went on to say. "We were surprised when so many people sitting around us agreed. Everyone recognized you from your picture on the cover of *Beach Music*, which a lot of us had brought along to read on our vacation."

Pat tried to look modest, and the woman bade us goodbye. She'd only taken a few steps when she paused, then turned back around. With a shy grin she said, "Mr. Conroy, your speech at the restaurant was one of the most stirring things I've ever heard, especially your praise for the good folks of Maine. But I have to tell you, after y'all left, we got to talking." She put a hand to her mouth, giggling. "And there wasn't a single Mainer eating at the restaurant that night. We were *all* tourists."

CHAPTER 12

A WRITER'S LIFE, HERE, THERE, AND EVERYWHERE

The first books Pat and I wrote during our years together were released within a few months of each other in 2002, *The Sunday Wife* and *My Losing Season*, and our crazy-busy life got even crazier and even busier. We were ships passing in the night. I returned after weeks on book tour just in time to say goodbye to Pat, whose own tour was starting. Each of us published five books during our eighteen-plus years together; thankfully it wasn't until 2013 that two others came out the same year, *The Death of Santini* and *Moonrise*. Even so, tours for paperback editions plus the speech circuit caused us to travel separately more than either of us liked. Although it got easier over time, initially I was totally unprepared.

Because my first book had been published by a small press with a limited publicity budget, I'd done very little touring. Seems like the farthest I went was southeast Texas. But everything was different with my second novel and the ones to follow, where I toured for several weeks. At first I was excited. A rookie writer imagines a book tour to be glamorous, pictures the paparazzi swarming with flashbulbs flashing as soon as you land. A limousine awaits to escort you to a five-star hotel where champagne chills as you freshen up before your appearance on *Good Morning America*. Your bodyguard (to clear a path through your adoring fans) is a dead ringer for Kevin Costner.

Maybe it happens that way with other writers, I don't know. A veteran at such things, Pat tried to prepare me. "The best thing about touring is meeting your readers," he told me. Otherwise, it was much more grueling than glamorous—much more. As I packed, he cautioned me to write my room number on the key flap. "But that's not safe!" I protested. "Just wait," he said with a knowing look. "You're not only going to forget your room, you'll forget which city you're in."

I laughed him off until I'd been on the road about three weeks on tour for *The Sunday Wife*, and I found myself in a different place each night. One morning I woke up in a featureless hotel room sleep deprived and in a panic. I couldn't remember where I was. The bedside phone only had the hotel name and the number on it, which was useless because the area code was unfamiliar. The hotel booklet was missing. Even going over my pages-long schedule didn't help because I didn't know the date, and I couldn't remember where I'd been the night before. Had it been Nashville or Memphis? I always got those two mixed up. One had country music and the other the blues, but which one had the hotel with the ducks?

Too embarrassed to ask anyone at the front desk when I went down for breakfast, I tried eavesdropping on the folks at the nearest table. *Yankees!* Good Lord, was I in Cincinnati already? It was a left-over Charlotte newspaper I spotted that put my mind at ease, until I began fretting on the way back to my room. What if someone from Charlotte had been traveling and left it on the table? Might've been left over from yesterday, which would mean the date was wrong too. Oh well. My publicist would be checking in soon to see how things were going, and I'd ask her. Surely in her business she'd heard it all.

Because we were separated so much for book tours, Pat wanted us to travel together when we could. He was appalled that I'd traveled so little and was determined to remedy that. In between books, Pat did some writing for *Gourmet* magazine (for which he'd earn a coveted James Beard award), and he'd accepted an assignment from them to write about Umbria. He'd never been to Umbria, and I'd been nowhere except England. Even though we'd been married a couple of years, we decided the trip would be our honeymoon. The magazine required us to stay in a new hotel for a week before it opened and try out the food. Talk about a dream assignment! It was every bit as fabulous as it sounds, especially for me. Pat had to do the work while all I had to do was tag along and eat. When the week came to an end, I didn't want to leave. I had gained a few pounds and a rekindled yearning to travel.

Finding a time when the two of us could travel together, however, presented a problem, since our schedules were filled with either writing books or blabbering about them once they came out. Another concern nagged at me as well, the cost of travels abroad. To my surprise, Pat admitted to feeling the pinch too. From time to time his grasshopper lifestyle and extravagant generosity caught up with him, and our accountant would frantically tug on the rein. Although we'd talked a lot about living abroad, it just wasn't doable. Then Pat came up with a solution that neither the ant nor the accountant could argue with. A couple of times in the past, he'd been a guest lecturer on a fancy cruise ship, a gig that paid all expenses for two, first class all the way. But he'd turned down other offers because he'd been unable to write on the trips and couldn't afford to get further behind with his latest book. "But I think I could write this time," he told me earnestly, "because you don't need to be entertained. You'll be perfectly happy doing your own thing while I'm working, won't you?"

I readily agreed while hiding a smile. Thanks to family gossip, I knew that Pat had taken his former girlfriends on the previous cruises. The message was clear: girlfriends had to be paid attention to, but wives were on their own. Sounded right to me. So far, neither of us could complain about too much togetherness.

Although I was thrilled with the first trip Pat signed up for, a Mediterranean cruise, I couldn't help but fret about life on the ship. Taking a cruise had never interested me—actually, had appalled me—because I had a misguided idea of what they were like. I thought of cruise ships as floating adult camps with strictly scheduled activities, mealtimes, and parties: an introvert's nightmare. Pat's response made me realize how silly I'd been. "Can you see my fat ass doing all that shuffleboard shit?" he scoffed.

Then I had another worry. (As a charter member of the worriers' guild, I can always find something.) To prepare myself, I watched *Titanic*, admittedly not the smartest idea I ever had. Although I knew how the story ended, I told myself that Hollywood surely wouldn't show *that* part. Nobody would ever board a ship again if they did! Pat hadn't seen the movie either, so a few nights before we set sail, we cuddled up in front of the TV with a bowl of popcorn. "You *sure* you want to watch this?" Pat asked me with a smirk. I shushed him, eyes glued to the opening scene. When the movie ended with all those frozen bodies floating around to the mournful strains of "My Heart Will Go On," I hurried out before Pat could make fun of my unwise movie choice. His howls of laughter followed me down the hallway.

~~~~~~

I would learn a lot on our first trip abroad and the others to follow, but one thing stood out: grasshoppers live better than ants. I'd never flown first class. I didn't even know enough to envy first-class travelers, reading their *New York Times* and looking world-weary as the poor suckers in economy passed them by. I assumed they just got free drinks and more legroom. So when we boarded our flight to Europe, I was blissfully oblivious to the way first class would forever change my attitude toward flying.

The flight attendant welcomed us aboard with champagne then settled us into seats roughly the size of king-sized beds. Pat buried himself in a newspaper as I sipped champagne and people-watched. What I saw was not exactly comforting. Elegant in cashmere cardigans and slim trousers, with Hermès purses and low-heeled sandals, the women of first class had obviously been there before. In my comfortable jeans, oversized T-shirt, and Birkenstocks, I looked like Little Orphan Redneck Annie. Until the plane actually took off, I kept expecting the Imposter Police to burst on board and haul me off to the economy section.

Although I could've slept easily in the comfort of the fully reclined seat, I was too excited. I kept watching the map on the screen, our little plane a mere dot over the Atlantic. To board the good ship *Rotterdam*, we flew Swiss Air to Zurich, then to Cairo, where we would sightsee for a couple of days. Because my paternal grandmother's parents emigrated from Switzerland, I was disappointed not to see anything of the countryside except the Zurich airport. Many years later I'd come back to see the family home in St. Gallen, but sadly, it would be without Pat. Although he and I always planned to go together, he never made it.

In Cairo, the sheer chaos of the airport appalled Pat as much as it delighted me. Hawkers swarmed us to sell their wares, everything from washers, dryers, fridges, and stoves to souvenirs. ("How would you get a fridge into a taxi?" Pat wondered.) You literally had to fight your way through them. I had a new experience at the loo, which wouldn't be the last I'd have during our journey. Outside each stall stood a stern woman draped in black, hijab revealing only her face. She held a single roll of toilet paper. Thankfully I saw the woman in front of me hand over some money in exchange for a few sheets, so I forked out two dollars. The woman gave me two sheets.

Our driver was a colorful character named Ahab (I swear), a bearded giant of a man. He plowed through the vendors, swatting or even kicking at the most persistent of them. To my horror, he boomed, "Get out of my way, infidels!" Somehow we escaped unharmed, and Ahab drove us helter-skelter to a swank Swissôtel at the end of a long, hidden driveway. I was taken aback to find a barricaded fortress, protected by machine-gun-toting guards. It was hard not to feel a tad nervous.

Our guide in Cairo was a lovely and extremely pleasant woman named Halla, who led us out into the *khamsin*, a hot, dusty desert wind. She was a university professor dressed in Western clothes: dark skirt, classic long-sleeved blouse, heels, and a patterned scarf wrapped around her head rather than the hijab. The desert she drove us to was barren and windswept, with a blizzard of dust obstructing our first view of the pyramids. Suddenly, there they were, massive and awesome and so very *ancient*, with nothing remotely Disney about them. Colorfully costumed camel riders urged tourists to hop on for a ride, but Pat and I resisted. The camels scared me.

We went inside a pyramid that held what Halla called a solar ship (I have no idea *what* it was), centuries old and about the size of an eighteen-wheeler. The oars were so large they could've only been worked by a chain gang of slaves. Inside another tomb it felt so closed in and airless that I couldn't get out fast enough. Even a raging dust storm was preferable to the claustrophobia of the deeply buried tombs. Pat was a bit more game but not much. Problem was, there was no poking your head in the opening to look around. If you wanted to see anything, you either went in deep, or not at all.

A visit to the main Egyptian museum the following day was another surprise and not exactly a pleasant one. I expected something like the British Museum in London, but the Cairo museum wasn't particularly grand. The Egyptian artifacts in both London and New York are much more impressive, the rooms more spacious and elaborate. It made me sad for the Egyptian people that so few of their treasures remained in their country. The highlight was the King Tut exhibit, held in a cold and darkened room, the perfect ambiance for such a monumental display. Impressive as the exhibit was, I took care not to reveal my shock at its simplicity and spareness. Even though they had Ramses II, there were only eight mummies in all. I longed to ask Halla to tell me more about the history of the acquisitions, but I dared not, for fear of an implied insult.

Our lunch stop was on a quaint, slightly swaying café-boat on the Nile River. *I'm having lunch on the freaking* Nile, I kept thinking in amazement. I could even forgive their uninspired food, though Pat eyed his plate in dismay. There was no menu; our guide had apparently ordered ahead. When they proudly served us plates of hard-fried fish pieces, limp greasy french fries, and a serving of rice, we decided they'd set out to honor us with their version of common American dishes.

Egyptian drivers were worse than New Yorkers, and Cairo was insane. No traffic lights, and everyone ignored the painted lines separating the lanes or indicating turns. The streets were sectioned off into three lanes but the drivers formed at least five lanes of cars, trucks, taxis, buses, and donkey carts, all jammed together. Horns blasted and donkeys brayed. Pat grimaced and put his hands over his ears, but I enjoyed every wild minute.

Pat perked up for a trip through the City of the Dead, his favorite part of our visit. Those cemeteries were more like burial cities that stretched as far as the eye could see. The bodies were buried underground, but there were elaborate "garden" homes—more often huts of stone—built over the graves. We assumed they were monuments, but entire families lived in the huts atop the burial grounds of their loved ones. They were very poor, Halla explained, and were looked down on by others because of their poverty and place of residence. It was in this setting that I heard my very first call to prayer, late that afternoon. Eerily beautiful, the call stayed with me long after the sound floated away over the haunting City of the Dead.

One of my most cherished memories from our time in Egypt was the two-hour drive to Alexandria, where we would board the ship. "Get ready to see the *real* Egypt," Pat told me. We were both ready for it. The fortresslike hotel that the cruise line had put us in had shielded us from the exotic street life. On the ride out, I studied the housing that had previously only passed in a blur as we careened through the crowded city. Everywhere I looked was row after row of many-storied, stark apartment buildings made of brick or cement. Most of the windows were merely square cutouts with no visible panes or screens.

On the rest of our ride to Alexandria Pat and I craned our necks to take in the unfamiliar sights. Farmers worked the dusty land by hand, with strange, old-fashioned-looking tools, and used water buffalo or donkeys as beasts of burden. Despite sparse traffic, the farmers—or mostly their children—sold their harvest beside the road. One young man stood with a bunch of live turkeys (or something that looked like a turkey). When we passed by, the young man twirled one of the fowls around by its feet, holding the poor bird high over his head. "Now that's what I call a sales pitch," Pat quipped. Along the way we met sunbaked, white-robed men riding donkeys. Rather than saddles or blankets, the men sat atop huge bundles of straw that the donkeys carried on their backs. It was like seeing a page from a *National Geographic* magazine spring to life.

Once we boarded the *Rotterdam* and headed out to sea, Pat and I studied the itinerary for our upcoming stops along the Mediterranean. "There's a helluva lot to see," Pat noted as he peered over his reading glasses. "Turkey, Greece, Sicily, Venice, Spain, Croatia. Since I've been to most of those places, I'll stay on the ship and work while you're sightseeing. Sure you'll be okay with that?"

I responded that somehow I'd manage to explore on my own, then added with a sly smile, "The family will be disappointed, though." At his puzzled look, I explained. "I'm sure they're hoping the grasshopper would buy their gifts."

Pat sighed in exasperation. "Promise me you won't buy them a bunch of cheap shit, okay?" At my amused expression, he threw his hands up in defeat. "Okay, okay. I'll come along for a couple of hours."

"Whatever you say, Babezee." (Embarrassingly, "Baby" had become my favored nickname for him; even more embarrassing, the way I cooed it made it "Babe-zee" over time.)

"What are you planning on doing besides sightseeing and shopping?" Pat demanded.

"Eating."

Pat mulled that over. "Then I'll have to come. Without me to show you where to get the best food, no telling where the tour guides will take you."

~~~~

Istanbul was a kaleidoscope of sensual images—beautiful people, lush landscapes, dazzling architecture, fragrant gardens, exotic dishes. Pat was so taken with it that he gave up his writing time to explore with me. Our guide was a sweet young man named Jem who declared he wanted to be a writer. We were touched that so many of the Turks asked what we did, then told us they wanted to be writers too. Always the cynic, Pat claimed they would've said pig farmers if that'd been our occupation, but I didn't agree. I found the Turkish people warm and lovely, and never felt a moment's fear during our stay.

Before lunch, Jem took us to the Topkapi Palace where we wandered through mosaic hallways and were followed by peacocks trailing their tail feathers. In the flamboyant gardens were sights I never could've imagined. Marble gazebos, with embroidered cushions on the floor and silk hangings fluttering in the warm breeze, looked like something out of an erotic dream. "The perfect place for a forbidden tryst," I whispered to Pat. Jem said we could go in the harem for an extra seven dollars, and Pat eagerly grabbed for his wallet. "No kidding? The harem's here now?"

Jem shook his head. "No, no. No one is there." Then his face brightened. "But you get to see the room."

Pat put his wallet back. "Forget it. What's the point of a harem room without a harem?"

We went to lunch instead. Pat instructed Jem to take us to a place where only the locals go. The outdoor café was everything we hoped for, except we were disappointed that Jem wouldn't join us. He had to go to his mosque to pray but would be back soon, he promised. Without his guidance, we played it safe and traditional with our orders. I already admired the Turks, but when I heard that every meal included sweets, they earned my undying devotion as well. Members of the sweet-tooth tribe always appreciate one another. I ordered by simply pointing to a luscious-looking dessert en route to a nearby table.

After lunch Jem took us to the Blue Mosque, his place of worship, then to the Grand Bazaar, which he said was a must-see in Istanbul. The beauty of the fabled Blue Mosque stunned me, and Pat and I tiptoed through it in reverent silence. Being in the Blue Mosque with so many devout followers prostrate in prayer was a holy experience for me. Because I make an effort to honor cultural differences regardless of my personal feelings, I tried not to get my feminist feathers ruffled at the sight of the women praying around the walls because they weren't allowed to enter the main area where the men prayed. *All prayer rugs face Mecca*, I reminded myself.

The Grand Bazaar was a welcome respite after the solemnity of the Blue Mosque. Rather than the lovely apple tea we'd had in other places, the bazaar shopkeepers greeted us with delicate glasses of a slightly sweet white wine. Jem warned us that refusing to drink it was considered an insult to the hospitality of the Turkish people. Since any self-respecting southerner would get shit-faced rather than insult a host, I gamely raised my glass time and time again.

Pat took me aside when we first entered the Grand Bazaar, and Jem looked away discreetly. "Listen to me, Alabama girl," Pat said in a low voice. "These folks are masters at selling, and we can only use one more rug. Keep your mouth shut and let me handle this. They know a rube when they see one, and you'll be putty in their hands. It's not about the money, it's about getting what we want instead of being swayed by their sales pitch. Okay?"

"Whatever you say, dear," I replied with a straight face, and he groaned. "Just leave it up to me is all I'm asking," he whispered conspiratorially, and I nodded. We were lured into the very first shop. Immediately an elegant, smooth-talking salesman presented us with crystal glasses of wine in a Park Avenue–worthy showroom. The patriarch came out and seated us in a place of honor under photos of his family with "Papa" Bush and the rugs he and the First Lady bought during his presidency. There were photos of South Carolina's Senator Hollings and other notables with their purchases. Although I hid a knowing smile, I knew Pat was a goner. Sure enough, he and the patriarch ended up grinning into the camera in front of two exquisitely expensive rugs that the patriarch had declared perfect for the nice American writers.

"Don't you dare say a word," Pat hissed as we left after an hour of prolonged, heartfelt goodbyes.

"Not a word," I agreed. We walked in silence for a few minutes, oblivious to the hawkers. I imagine they were put off by Pat's shamefaced grimness and my self-righteous smirk. Finally Pat stopped and faced me. "Why don't we go to the jewelry stores now?" he said. "We can get some pieces for my girls. And your sisters would like jewelry too. Twenty-four-karat gold?"

I pretended to think on it before saying, "Sounds perfect. I'll stay quietly in the background. I'm sure you'll pick them out something pretty."

He wouldn't meet my eye. "Oh, you know more what they like than I do."

I couldn't help but grin. "You think we can find a store that waits on rubes?"

"Aw, shit," he groaned. "You'll never let me live that one down, will you?"

⌐∾∾∾⌐

Our final day on the cruise, before our departure in Lisbon, was on Easter Sunday, which seemed oddly fitting to me. I'd set the alarm for dawn to keep from sleeping through my very favorite thing about cruising, entering a new port of call. A few days before, we had sailed into Venice at sunrise, a sight I'll remember till my dying day. I can only hope heaven is half as beautiful. Most mornings Pat asked me to wake him, then he'd turn over and keep snoring. But when I pulled back the curtains on our final morning, I had to wake him.

"Pat, you've *got* to see this," I cried as I stepped out on the balcony. "Holy Mother of God!"

I heard him stumbling out of bed, then he appeared next to me bleary-eyed and disoriented. Wearing nothing but his drawers, he stood blinking for a full minute in the cold morning breeze before saying, "What the fuck is it?"

I laughed but kept staring through the binoculars even though they were hardly necessary. As the ship drew nearer, I discarded the binoculars and took a couple of steps backward in amazement. Pat put an arm around my shoulders and we shivered together as the Rock of Gibraltar loomed over us, a monolithic message of hope on an Easter morning. "I didn't want you to miss this," I whispered to Pat.

"Be pretty hard to do, darling."

If our early-morning entry into a new port of call was an exciting, joy-filled way to greet the morning, our departures were bittersweet. It was traditional for the passengers to gather on the top decks of the ship and raise a glass of champagne as a toast to our departing city. Then, as the gigantic ship pulled away from the port, loudspeakers played a farewell song, Louis Armstrong singing "What a Wonderful World." I couldn't help myself; I cried every single time and still get choked up on hearing that song again, with the memories it brings.

Pat, of course, made fun of me being so sentimental about our departures, so I smiled bravely as I raised my glass to toast each departing port. Pat knew I'd be crying my eyes out when we got back to the room, so he tried to cheer me up. When Louis Armstrong sang the chorus, "And I say to myself, what a wonderful world," Pat would sidle up next to me and sing his version in my ear, which made me laugh through my tears. In an imitation of Armstrong's gravelly voice, he'd pull me close and croon, "And I say to myself, what a shitty world."

It wasn't all champagne and lullabies. Before we landed in LaGuardia on our way home, an inevitable snafu brought us down from our romantic high and we hit hard. Although Pat had showed me over and over how to fill out the customs card, I screwed up so many times he lost patience. Yanking the card and pencil out of my hand, he snarled, "Give it here, goddammit!"

I glared furiously until his head was bent over the card, then I waved my middle finger under his nose and hissed, "Jackass." The flight attendant, a lovely middle-aged woman whom I'd chatted with earlier, caught my eye. Chagrined, I mouthed, *Too much togetherness*, and she nodded with a knowing smile. On our way out, she touched my arm. "No trip is complete without at least one blowup. All the best to both of you."

God knows we'll need it, I thought, but once we were back on American soil, everything was forgiven. As much as I'd loved the cruise, I had missed Fripp Island and couldn't wait to get back. Since the fateful day I decided to pull up stakes and move there, Fripp had become my home.

CHAPTER 13

THE BOTTOM FALLS OUT

Pat and I had been married almost ten years when the bottom fell out. For once in our lives, it was literal and not metaphorical. The house on Fripp had been remodeled shortly before I came on the scene, but evidently the contractor didn't do the best job in the world, nor would he fix his mistakes. I heard a joke: What's the difference between a contractor and a criminal? At least a criminal returns to the scene of the crime.

We suspected trouble when the deck began to separate from the back of the house. To go out the back door onto the deck required a leap of faith. I knew nothing about home repairs but figured the deck falling away from the house couldn't be a good sign. Then the chimney began to leak when it rained, and leak *bad*. Pat must've gotten drunk during the remodeling process and thought he was in outer Siberia instead of on an island off the coast of South Carolina, because he'd decided he wanted a fireplace in the master bedroom. Needless to say, we never built a fire, except one cold winter night when we planned a romantic evening in. When the fire got going, we had to open a window to keep from passing out from the heat.

Poor Pat had always been teased about his lack of mechanical skills. He swore that in high school he scored low enough on the mechanical reasoning part of the standard achievement tests to be classified mentally challenged. No one argued with him or claimed it was another of his exaggerated tales. The man who could turn out some of the most beautiful prose in the world didn't know one end of a hammer from another. One night, I'd been away for a few days and returned home much later than I expected. I hurried back to our bedroom to surprise Pat but ended up being the one surprised. Propped in bed reading, Pat was in the dark. Or almost; the only light he had to read by came from the lamp on the table on my side of the bed.

"Pat! How come you're in the dark?" I asked in greeting.

He got up to hug me, then shook his head in exasperation. "Aw, my damn lamp's broken. Broke right after you left."

"Why didn't you sleep on my side of the bed? Or move my lamp to your side?"

He looked sheepish. "Oh. Didn't think of that."

I unplugged his lamp, which was one of our favorites, with an antique brass base. "Don't worry. I'll take it to Bobby Joe tomorrow." Pat's sister Kathy's husband, Bobby, was a whiz at fixing things, and had already repaired a couple of other lamps for me. In preparation, I wrapped the cord around the base and unscrewed the bulb, which rattled suspiciously. "Ah, Babezee? You checked the lightbulb, right?"

He gave me the sheepish look again. "Thought I did," he mumbled, not meeting my eye.

I replaced the blown-out bulb, turned on the lamp, and saved myself a trip to town. But the next time, I went to the local hardware store and bought myself a tool set. My daddy had taught me to hammer a nail in straight and had once taken a motor apart to show me how it worked. Every girl needs to know how to fix stuff, he'd said. I loved my new toolbox so much that I bought a book on home repairs and started taking on some of our repairs myself. I figured that one mentally deficient mechanic in the family was enough.

Our falling-apart house was beyond my meager skills, however. Try as I might, I couldn't get the deck back onto the house or stop the copious leaking around the chimney. Even more alarming, it was impossible not to notice that the downstairs commodes were wobbly. I kept expecting to find myself in nether regions whenever I made use of one. Finally I turned to Pat in desperation. "We've got to get a contractor here before the whole blamed house caves in."

Pat decided to ask a former student, Mike Sargent, to look at it. Mike was who he'd wanted for the original work, but he hadn't been available. "Mike was one of the biggest pain-in-the-ass students I ever had," Pat told me, "and I'm pretty sure he failed my course. But he's a great guy."

I adored Mike on sight, an old hippie with a long gray ponytail. Pat had been twenty-three years old when he taught at Beaufort High School his first year out of The Citadel, so Mike was only a few years younger than us. He took Pat's ribbing with a good-natured laugh. "You couldn't keep your damn mouth shut during my class, Mike," Pat reminded him. "I threatened to beat your ass more times than one. I hope I failed you."

"No, sir," Mike said with a grin. "You gave me a D if I promised not to take your class again."

Mike was less jovial about the state of the house. He showed us the problem with the chimney and said we were lucky it'd been too warm for fires because we could've easily burned the house down. Even without a fire, we could've perished because the wiring was so bad. And, as the separated deck and wobbly commodes proved, the foundation had shifted and fallen in. After cussing enough to condemn his soul to hellfire and damnation forever, Pat settled down and asked Mike if he could fix it. Mike's frown wasn't exactly reassuring.

"Yessir," he said finally. "I can. But it'll take some time. Y'all will have to move out."

Pat's eyes bulged and his florid face turned even redder. "Have to do *what*?"

Mike lowered his head. "I'm really sorry, Mr. Conroy. But the foundation's got to be rebuilt from the bottom up. It's the only way."

"How long?" I asked weakly.

Mike grimaced. "As soon as I finish the job I'm on now, I'll devote full time to getting y'all back in. Maybe two or three months?"

It was early fall. Both of us let that statement sink in, then I dared to ask, "But . . . we'll definitely be here for Christmas, right?"

Mike avoided my eyes. "I can't promise, but I'll do my best."

Pat was more furious than I'd ever seen him. We both had books to finish, and an extended time away from home was not in the plans. If we could've stayed in part of the house while the work was going on, we would've gladly done so. But Mike said with all the noise and construction, it would be extremely difficult for us to get any work done—especially Pat, since his writing space was square in the demolition zone. And there wouldn't be any floors.

That's how we ended up spending several months in Highlands, North Carolina. It was not a new experience for Pat; in the 1980s he'd hidden away in a friend's cabin in Highlands for several weeks to work on *The Prince of Tides*. He and I had spent some time there in the previous summers as well. I loved Maine and would've gladly returned every summer, but it would've been without Pat. As much as he loved the Siddonses, he wouldn't go back. It was just too far for him.

I couldn't argue the point and wouldn't have anyway, because I saw how hard the trip had become for him. During our years together, I'd learned much about the kind, generous, and fascinating man I'd married and loved deeply, none of which caused me to have second thoughts or love him any less. But many of his habits caused me great concern and plenty of sleepless nights. Pat was careless with his health to a degree that bordered on self-destructive. From the first he'd been honest with me about his drinking, but it took a while to make a believer out of me. And not because of denial (though I'm certainly guilty of that in every aspect of my life). Instead, Pat Conroy could hold his liquor better than anyone I've ever seen. Friends of his told me if they drank one-tenth of what he did, they'd be on the floor; but Pat could consume a copious amount of the hard stuff without showing it. Maybe it was genetic. Another cringeworthy joke I heard: Why did God make whiskey? Answer: To keep the Irish from ruling the world.

Pat was equally careless about diet and exercise. He'd get on different kicks, as he did with his drinking, and straighten up for several months at a time. I'd cook healthy (which he seemed incapable of doing), and he'd swear to eat right from then on. And he did—until he didn't. His doctors would lecture him or he'd have a health scare, and then he'd vow to give up his bad habits. He'd go on the wagon, start exercising or walking every afternoon, and soon feel better than he'd felt in years. About the time I relaxed and decided that he'd finally reformed, he'd be back to his old habits again. His weight was up and down, mostly up, which caused even more problems. So when he told me he couldn't do long road trips anymore, I didn't argue. Fickle by nature anyway, I easily transferred my love of Maine to Highlands, a lovely little town high in the mountains of western North Carolina. Best of all, we could drive it in half a day.

~~~

We went into exile in October, when the lavish leaves of the Blue Ridge Mountain forests turned into brilliant shades of red, orange, and gold. Highlands certainly wasn't the worst place to retreat to; on the contrary, it was magnificent, though neither Pat nor I was particularly happy about having to be there. We would've been a helluva lot unhappier if we'd known it would be April before we made it back to Fripp.

We rented a cottage across the street from Lake Sequoia, a serene body of water a mile or so from town. There were only two places in the house where the lake could be seen, one the small back deck and the other an upstairs bedroom window. Binoculars in hand, I spent many happy hours peering at the scenery through the bright, fluttering leaves of the trees encircling the lake. The locals, descendants of the early settlers, fascinated me, as did the well-to-do summer people who had second homes there. I had no doubt they came with many intriguing stories, great material for a new book. After the book tours were done for my fourth novel, *Queen of Broken Hearts*, I promised myself the next one would be about Highlands. And I felt the same surge of excitement that always came over me when the inspiration for a new book hit.

Pat was still disgruntled over our living situation, but with admirable resilience, he made the best of it. He often said he might not always like the things life threw at him, but if he didn't have a choice, no point bitching and moaning about them. Personally I enjoyed bitching and moaning too much to give up either one, but I commended his attitude. Part of his frustration was the lack of a good writing space. The desk in our rental was a ladylike one ill-suited to his bulky frame. Set up in the spare room, it provided him the necessary privacy, however, so he approached it gamely, toting his yellow pad and pen.

After doing the two nonfiction books about basketball and cooking, Pat had gone back to fiction. *South of Broad* was set in Charleston and almost as vast in scope as the last novel he'd published, *Beach Music*. Ever since Pat's days as a cadet at The Citadel, which is located in Charleston, the charming old city had held a fascination for him so strong it bordered on obsession. Charleston had appeared in some form or other in all his books and would be the setting for the last one he worked on.

The writing of *South of Broad*, however, caused Pat almost as much anguish as *Beach Music* had. Its storylines and themes were so heavy and depressing that I had to wonder: With Pat, was suffering so intertwined with creativity that he couldn't work without it? For the first time in his tumultuous life, Pat claimed to have found some serenity and peace. Lacking the chaos and turmoil he'd become accustomed to, would he have to create it elsewhere? When I raised the question with him, he looked startled as understanding began to dawn. "Good God," he said finally. "I think you're right. Chaos is my siren song and always has been. I've never gone this long without it." To my surprise he grabbed both my hands in a death grip and said, "Don't let me fuck up what we have like I've done everything else in my pathetic life. Promise me!"

I tried to reassure him that it wouldn't happen, but my words felt insubstantial, like snowflakes that melt on touch. I could only hope that our bond was strong enough to ward off the demons that would always call his name.

Although Fripp Island offered all the isolation any writer could want, Pat and I were in a totally different mode of solitude during our exile in Highlands that fall, winter, and early spring. The house was hidden from the road with no neighbors in sight. We were more completely alone with each other than we'd ever been, sometimes going weeks without seeing another living soul. The friends we'd made there were either weekenders from Atlanta or had closed down their houses after Labor Day and wouldn't be back till May. Most folks with any sense stayed away from Highlands's notoriously icy winters. Restaurants and stores closed and roads were impassable. But we figured that we'd be long gone before winter came.

By mid-November, Mike Sargent had let us know that we wouldn't be back in our Fripp house by Thanksgiving. Pat's buddy from Atlanta days, Jim Landon (whose cabin Pat had used to work on *The Prince of Tides*), took pity on us. Jim invited us to have

Thanksgiving dinner with him and his friends. His invitation turned out to be a happy one for us because we made new friends, the Sullivans and Mannings, and Pat reconnected with another Atlanta friend, George Lanier. Fortunately for our budding friendship, none of them knew that I'd one day use the whole lot of them as characters in my Highlands novel. Pat had written about Jim and George before, so they were used to his treachery, but mine would take them by surprise.

We had such a great time and great food at the Thanksgiving feast that we invited ourselves to continue the tradition from that year forth. I knew I was with kindred spirits the following year when the very elegant Jim Landon (whom I would base an equally elegant character on in my book) showed up in a turkey costume. To surprise us, Jim cut through the wooded path from his cottage to the Sullivans' house up the mountain, velvet tail feathers dragging behind him. He was lucky not to encounter an overzealous hunter; he would've either been shot or the hunter would've keeled over at the sight of such a large turkey coming his way.

Good thing we enjoyed Thanksgiving and the in-state rivalry football games on TV that weekend because reality hit us hard afterward. With December came the realization that we wouldn't be back in our house for Christmas. Pat's mood dipped, and even I, who'd come to love Highlands so passionately, didn't take the news well. Not being able to get into our house—by this time the floors were nonexistent—upset me not only because I loved Christmas on Fripp, but also because of the gifts I'd stashed in my gift closet. And what about the decorations? I wondered. We had so many at home that it would've been foolish to buy anything else. Brooding, I decided to go Little House on the Prairie and decorate with greenery from the woods. For a Christmas tree, I'd put a cedar branch in a large vase and drape it with strung popcorn and cranberries. *It'd be fun*, I told Pat. Holly grew in the dense woods behind the house and we might even find mistletoe. "C'mon!" I said to him, excited. I found a hedge clipper in the garage for cutting the greenery and waved it in front of him, ready for our adventure.

Pat gave me a look over his newspaper. "You're shitting me," he said. When I assured him I wasn't, he groaned. "In case you didn't get the memo," he said, "they have bears here. They live in the woods."

"They hibernate," I told him.

"How do you know?"

"Because they're bears."

"That might be a rumor they put out to lure folks into their lairs. Dummies like you go traipsing around looking for holly and mistletoe, then bam!—they're never seen again. Bear's got him a tasty treat." He lowered the paper and his eyes twinkled with mischief. "Maybe you're right. Once they get their bellies full, they hibernate until they get hungry again."

I glared at him unamused, but he got in a last word before disappearing behind his paper. "Stay out of the woods, Alabama girl."

~~~~~~

Bad as I hated to admit it, Pat had a point about bears. I'd seen a total of four during my previous visits, much to the envy of some of my friends who said that they'd been coming for decades and never even seen *one*. Pat and I shared a love of bear-sighting stories, which are plentiful in the mountains. My first bear sighting was a couple of years after we'd started coming to Highlands in the summer. I'd gone ahead to our rental, an isolated cabin in the middle of the woods. Pat was to join me in a few days. I was alone and standing in the kitchen as I washed dishes, occasionally glancing out the window over the sink. It was midmorning. When I looked up and saw the bear loping along the driveway a few feet from the open window, I thought it was a black dog. I realized my mistake and shouted like a fool, "Oh my God—a *bear*!" The poor thing reared up on its hind legs then hauled ass like a scared rabbit. Like an even bigger fool, I took off after him, but he disappeared into the thick forest.

The next bear encounter, Pat was with me. A different summer, a different rental, and our friend Janis Owens was visiting us. Although a native Floridian who'd never seen a bear in the wild, Janis handled her first sighting much better than I'd done mine, thankfully, and we got pictures. She'd just stepped onto the front porch of our rented cabin when a mother and two cubs came by, actually cutting across our low-slung porch on their way to wherever they were headed. Without taking her eyes off them, Janis stepped back into the house and instructed me to come quickly, and to bring Pat and her camera. She took photos and I videotaped the bears' progress across our porch and yard while Pat watched in sheer delight.

The bears were footloose. Later in the afternoon Janis and I were headed into town when we rounded a curve at the exact moment the same mother bear and two cubs (had to be!) started to cross the highway. Janis yelled for me to stop. She leapt out of the car and held up her hand to halt the oncoming traffic until the bears crossed safely to the other side. Cars in both lanes screeched to a stop and folks began popping out with cameras. The mother and little cubs made their leisurely way across and meandered back into the woods.

It's unusual to go to any kind of social gathering in Highlands and not hear bear stories. Most of the adventures are hilarious rather than scary, tales of bears coming into kitchens and helping themselves, or getting into unlocked cars as though going for a spin. A woman who lived near us reported that a bear broke into her house and rearranged the furniture.

But my favorite tale is about a new resident, a very proper and well-to-do matron, in one of the upscale golfing communities. One evening she frantically called security when she discovered that something had raided her trash can. The security officer arrived and tried to calm the poor woman down. "Ma'am," the officer said, "please don't worry. It was just a bear."

Instead of calming down, the woman was highly indignant. "How did a bear get in here?" she demanded. "This is a *gated* community!"

~~~~~~

A couple of weeks before our Christmas in exile, Highlands had its first snowfall of the year. I ran outside like a kid to twirl around in the steadily falling flakes. Having grown up a few miles from the Florida Panhandle, I'd only seen snow a half-dozen times in my life. Scrooge was less impressed and his demeanor darkened even more. Instead of frolicking in the snow, he looked through the fridge to make sure we wouldn't starve if we got snowed in. First he'd ordered me out of the woods; now he was forbidding me to drive in the snow. I reacted to his unusual bossiness with a childish retort. "Excuse me, Pat Conroy," I snapped, hands on hips, "who died and made you the boss of me?"

I got even madder when he pretended to tremble in fear of my temper, but I soon found myself giggling. Pat and I had some kind of strange alchemy and could never stay snappish with each other for long, no matter how badly one of us irritated the other. I don't know what it was, but if I could bottle and sell it, I would. Every time we tried to have a fight like all normal couples do, we'd end up laughing at how ridiculous we sounded. Guess at our age fighting just took too much energy.

Pat, much more of a people person than I am, came to terms with our isolation by suggesting we visit family during the holidays. He had a long-standing tradition that both impressed and touched me. He always spent some time after Christmas with his daughters Jessica, Melissa, and Megan at their mother's house in Atlanta. Unlike a lot of divorced couples, Pat and his first wife, Barbara, had remained close friends since they parted ways in the late '70s. Even so, I was still somewhat anxious the first time I went to Barbara's for the Christmas visit. How could it not be weird and awkward? I wondered. My girlfriends were incredulous and said they'd rather have a root canal than share a meal with their husband's ex-wife. But Barbara has such a kind and generous spirit that she always made me feel welcome, and over the years she and I became friends.

What I enjoyed most during the Christmas visit was the comfortable relationship between Pat and the mother of three of his daughters. It was bittersweet, since it appeared unlikely he and his second wife would ever be that cordial. I wished they could've been; I'd been in both places and cordiality was so much better. After my ex and I got over our animosity, the boys could enjoy both their parents equally without having to choose. Pat had heard that Susannah still lived with her mother in San Francisco, but no one ever heard from any of them. It remained a heartbreaking situation for all concerned.

In contrast, Pat and Barbara were easy and relaxed with each other, laughing together as they reminisced about their daughters growing up. Unwrapping gifts from his girls, Pat pretended to be disappointed and asked in mock dismay if that was all they'd gotten him. I can hear him now: "This is *it*? Sure didn't break the bank, did you?" Obviously, he'd add, Barbara's gifts were much more expensive than his and proved who they loved most. Everyone smiled indulgently, used to his well-worn jokes.

Watching Pat with his former wife and their daughters, I wondered why all our complicated past relationships couldn't be as congenial, though I suspect the answer's obvious. We refuse to let go of our grievances long after they have the power to affect our day-to-day lives. Some wounds never completely heal, of course, and stay buried in a tender place within us. It's the ones that we don't let go of that eat us alive, a cancer in the darkest region of the soul. And what does that get us? Nothing that I can see but the self-satisfaction of having been right, or wronged, or whatever it was that got us to such a bad spot in the first place.

The letter Pat wrote me that Christmas was a good reminder of the importance of nurturing the loving relationships of our lives. It pains me to admit that he was better at doing so than I was. My notes to him were nothing more than reminders: don't forget your interview; pick up a roast; call your publisher. By that point we'd been married several years, which shouldn't have made it easier to take our love for granted, yet did. Reading his letter, I vowed not to let it happen. The letter read: *This is the time of year I write you a love letter and thank you once again for finding me at a party in Birmingham and rescuing me out of a life I should not have been living. Until I met you, I did not know I could love this deeply; in fact, was not sure I could love at all. Now, I feel it rushing out of me every time you enter a room or come into my line of sight. Merry Christmas, darling—Pat Conroy.*

~~~~

Although our return to Fripp Island in April was a joyous occasion at the time, it will be always marred by a tragedy that occurred after we'd settled back in. Mike Sargent came out often, not just to show off his handiwork and touch up final details, but also to visit. I'd liked Mike from the first and liked seeing him and Pat become closer. Pat'd told me of Mike's background as a military brat with an abusive father, and I saw that Mike had come to regard Pat as a father figure. Mike never called him anything but Mr. Conroy, and at first he was shy and overly polite with me. But I treated him like one of my boys, and he relaxed. One day when Pat wasn't home, Mike asked if he could speak to me, a troubled look darkening his expression.

"I'm worried about Mr. Conroy," he said earnestly, and I told him I worried about him all the time. Mike explained that when he was tearing down stuff, he found several empty vodka bottles. "I'm afraid he has a drinking problem," he said.

Instead of saying "You *think*?" I told Mike I appreciated that he felt comfortable enough to share his concerns with me. I assured him I'd talk with Pat, which I did. To give Pat credit, I can only think of once or twice when we talked about his drinking that he was defensive. Otherwise he readily admitted it was a problem he would always struggle with, and he vowed each time to do better. And he would, for a while.

Several weeks later I was at a book festival in Fort Lauderdale, speaking about *Queen of Broken Hearts*, when Pat called me. Mike Sargent, he reported, was in a bad way. Things had not gone well for him recently. His wife had left him, and he was terribly depressed. Pat, as always, had tried to tease him out of it. It was the bad Conroy vibes from our house, he told Mike—you absorbed all of them because you failed my psychology course. Mike had laughed, and Pat felt somewhat cheered. "When will you be home?" Pat asked me abruptly, and I heard something in his voice that disturbed me.

I cut my trip short but didn't make it home soon enough. After his call to me, Pat checked on Mike, and Mike's son answered. His son was in the military but had come home to see about his father, because he sounded so bad. Pat knew that Mike'd been seeing a doctor for the depression, but not that he'd been stockpiling pills. His dad had tried to overdose, the son told Pat, but they'd gotten to him in time and he was okay. Pat asked if he should come stay with Mike. The son said no, that his father was safe now and Mr. Conroy wasn't to worry. Pat ordered him to put Mike on the phone. "I'm coming to stay with you," Pat said, but Mike was adamant. His son was there and it'd scare him more to see Pat so worried.

Pat had been right to worry. That night Mike had to be taken to the hospital, where he was put on suicide watch in the psych ward. The thing was, Mike had been a contractor for a long time and knew his business. Left alone in his barred room for barely a minute, he took down a panel in the bathroom ceiling and used a sheet to hang himself from a beam. Pat took Mike's death hard. If only he'd gone to see him as his instinct had urged him! Maybe he could've gotten through to him. He would never make that mistake again, Pat told me through his tears. From that day forward if his heart told him that someone was in trouble, he'd listen.

If only it were that easy, I thought as I took him in my arms. The problem was, we don't always know when those we love are in danger. Even though I still had the crystal ball Pat gave me in New Orleans, I had yet to see the heartbreak that lay ahead.

CHAPTER 14

REAL CHARACTERS, IN LIFE AND FICTION

Pat and I would return to Highlands many times in the years to come. The book I set there, *Moonrise*, was released in 2013, after several false starts and frustrations with capturing what felt like the essence of the place I'd come to love. Reading my first draft, I realized with both amusement and dismay that I'd relied a tad heavily on some of our real-life experiences. In many cases I hadn't even bothered to change names. I'm not sure if other writers would say this (certainly not Pat!), but I'm not always conscious of putting autobiographical information into my fiction. If something that actually happened fits into the plot of whatever book I'm writing, I have no problem using it. I especially like to excavate conversations to ferret out good dialogue, and I have shamelessly given a lot of my and Pat's pillow talk to my lovestruck characters. In *Queen of Broken Hearts*, I based a character on Pat but made him a Maine sea captain. My idea had been to portray a complicated man who hides his deepest feelings behind a devil-may-care demeanor, just as Pat always did.

I wondered how Pat'd react to seeing himself in a book for a change, but fortunately the sea captain amused him. Anne Siddons had gotten him good in *Hill Towns*, the novel she wrote after visiting Pat and Lenore in Rome for the wedding of Cliff and Cynthia Graubart. I think the character Anne based on Pat tickled him as well, though he pretended otherwise. "Annie made me a lecherous old fart who never bathes," he told folks. "Naturally, the character she based on herself is a beautiful, nubile young woman my character tries to seduce. But the poor fool can't even get it up."

Even my most autobiographical novel, *The Sunday Wife*, is mostly fiction. When I base a character on myself, I make her as different from my true self as possible. She's always drop-dead gorgeous, oozes charm and sex appeal, and has dozens of men desperately in love with her. I give her an angst-ridden or tragic childhood, unlike my decidedly ordinary one. And she's likely to be a brazen floozie who has numerous flirtations and affairs with my hottest male characters. I used to read for vicarious experiences; now I write for them.

Guess I learned from observing a master. Pat's family teased him endlessly about the protagonists of his novels, who are always him. The characters who Pat based on himself are saintly, heroic, godlike men of flawless character and integrity. And because he based his villains on real people who've wronged him, they're always the most vile and despicable of characters. I joined in the teasing until I found myself doing the same thing in a couple of my books. The temptation to take a stab at the villains of our life is just too great to resist.

We were in Highlands when I finished the final draft of *Moonrise* and Pat asked if he could read it. I hesitated. Since I'd made the novel's protagonist a cookbook author and her husband a well-known journalist, Pat might think that hit a little too close to home. One might even say the journalist-husband shared certain characteristics with Pat—and this time, I went for the gruffer, darker side of him. Not only that, I'd fictionalized some of our personal experiences that he was bound to recognize.

Sure enough, a few hours later Pat sought me out with several pages of the manuscript clutched in his hand. "Is this guy me?" he demanded. "He's an asshole."

I tried to reassure him. "Of course he's not you. And I don't think he's an asshole. He's tough, true, but he has a tender side too. Keep reading. You'll see."

An hour later he was back. "You used real names, Helen Keller. You can't do that."

I stared at him incredulously. "Is this the author of *The Great Santini* speaking? Remind me—what was your father's nickname in the Marine Corps?"

I thought I'd shut him up but he returned when finished, looking a bit abashed. He didn't meet my eyes when he said, "Ah, Sandra? I liked the way you used the eavesdropping incident. Worked out well. Good book, kiddo."

Pat patted my shoulder and walked out quickly, so he probably didn't hear my thanks. It was just as well. By my use of the incident he'd referred to, I'd taken a page out of his book (so to speak). He'd taught me that all personal experience is fodder for fiction, and the more unpleasant the better—for dramatic purposes, of course. One of the few bad rifts of our marriage had taken place a few years back in Highlands, and in a way similar to a scene I'd put in my book. I took the essence of the incident, a misunderstanding caused by something overheard, then spun it to fit the plot. It shames me (but only a little bit) at how excited I was to see how

I could use it as a pivotal point of my story. Sometimes, once in a blue moon, a writer gets to spin straw into gold.

We were in Highlands the year it happened, and both of us were working on books in rooms at opposite ends of the house. The whole thing came about when I went to retrieve something from the room next to where Pat worked. The room was so stuffy that I opened a window. Pat, sitting by an open window in the room next door, was on the phone with Doug Marlette. A benign conversation, and no big deal—or so I assumed until I mentioned it to Pat later. (He was often on the phone in bed so I'd been privy to many of his conversations as I dozed off next to him.) Over dinner that night I said, "So Doug's still feuding with those former friends of his, huh? Thought they'd worked things out."

I could tell by Pat's expression that something I said irritated him. His response was quick and sharp. "Who told you such a thing? Don't repeat stuff like that unless you know it's true."

I was taken aback by his reaction. "No one told me, Pat. I heard you and Doug talking this afternoon."

Pat's eyes narrowed and he snapped, "What d'you mean, you heard us? Are you telling me that you eavesdropped on our conversation?"

Of course not, I told him indignantly. I'd overheard them by accident and explained about opening the window. Things quickly went from bad to worse.

So you're an eavesdropper, huh? Pat said, ignoring my explanation. If I wanted to know what was going on with him, how about just asking instead of putting my ear to the door? He and Doug often talked about things that were highly personal and not intended for anyone else to hear. He never imagined I'd be lurking around listening to them.

I'd been too furious and insulted to respond. Instead I jumped up from the table and left the room. My sulky, infuriated silence only made things worse. Pat reacted to our first real fight as he always did to stress, by retreating into his shell and increasing his intake of booze. For the rest of our stay, things were extremely tense, with both of us miserable but too stubborn to clear the air. We never really did; it just sort of dissipated after we returned home. Without referring directly to our argument, Pat did apologize, in the uneasy, roundabout way he had of apologizing. If he'd said or done anything to hurt me, he said in an offhanded way without meeting my eye, then he was sorry and would never do it again.

Although I never found out what set him off or why he reacted the way he did to the incident, I let it go. Over time it was forgotten but I can't say regretted. Pat had been right about one thing: as painful as it was, our fight inspired a crucial scene in my book and I used it with no compunction whatsoever. When it comes to gathering material for a story, writers have no shame.

~~~~~

I never told Pat what else I did to put that unpleasant rift behind me. The owners of the house we'd rented where our fight happened were friends of mine, a young gay couple. The following summer we were staying in a different part of Highlands when one of them, Steve, gave me a call. Because he and I had discussed a mutual interest in spirituality, mysticism, and the afterlife (and other weird stuff that Pat referred to as New Agey bullshit), Steve had called with exciting news. A wiccan witch from the famed Cassadaga spiritual community in Florida was coming to visit them, and I was invited to meet her. We would gather at their house, the very one that Pat and I had occupied the previous summer. Then we'd go to a nearby clearing for a rite to celebrate the full moon. Was I interested?

Was I ever! I could hardly wait. Not only would I get to be with a real witch, I asked Steve if she'd meet with me in private beforehand, and he said sure. I didn't tell him the whole story, only that Pat and I'd had a nasty spat when we were staying in his house. Maybe the witch could exorcise the bad spirits? Steve assured me that was right up her alley. She never traveled without her white sage for just such purposes. (I never travel without white sage either. You never know when you'll end up in a haunted hotel.)

When the time came, I couldn't decide what to tell Pat about my disappearance that evening. He already teased me mercilessly about my interest in New Age stuff. If I told him I was meeting with a witch for a full-moon ceremony, he'd be convinced that I'd finally gone off the deep end. But I could hardly say I was going to dinner with a friend, because the ceremony didn't start until midnight. I had to either flat out lie or sneak out after he went to bed. The latter would be difficult since Pat read almost every night until one A.M. or so. I finally decided on a variation of the former. Maybe I could get by with just being vague.

It didn't go quite as well as I'd hoped. We were in the kitchen fixing dinner, with him doing the salad as I sautéed chicken breasts for piccata, when I said nonchalantly, "Babezee? After dinner I'm going over to Steve's. It'll be late when I get back so don't wait up for me."

Pat's curiosity was understandably aroused since neither of us ever went anywhere that late. Plus we were staying at the top of an unpaved, winding mountain road that wasn't easy driving in daylight. At night it'd be treacherous. "What'd you mean, after dinner?" he asked sharply. Normally he didn't question my comings and goings, but this wasn't a normal outing.

"Ah . . . closer to midnight. But don't worry. If you're asleep, I'll slip out quietly."

"To Steve's?" His eyes narrowed. "You running around on me, girl?"

"Yeah, right. You and Steve's partner both have a lot to worry about."

"Then what the hell's going on?"

I busied myself squeezing a lemon over the chicken. I knew with a sinking heart that Pat would prefer I had a lover than hear what I was really doing. Suddenly I had an inspiration. "Well, Steve and Rick have a visitor from Cassadaga they want me to meet. She's a . . . er . . . spiritualist. I was thinking I could interview her and maybe do an article."

Proud of myself, I wondered why I hadn't thought of that before. If there's anything a writer understood, it was a work assignment. But Pat was too smart for me. He stopped chopping tomatoes and said, "Is that right? And this so-called *spiritualist* only does interviews at midnight, huh?"

"Well. You know how spiritualists are," I said lamely. "Salad ready? I'm about to dish up the chicken."

Pat dropped the interrogation but knew good and well that I was up to something. I'd catch him eyeing me with a knowing smirk. I hoped by some miracle he'd be asleep when I left, but no such luck. At our bedroom door I threw him a kiss and he threw one back with a mischievous grin. "Full moon tonight," he said.

"Is it? I haven't noticed."

"Watch out for werewolves!" he called out. I heard him chuckling as I closed the door behind me.

~~~~

In the past I'd attended séances, met with mediums, and had my fortune told numerous times. Even after my marriage to Pat I'd kept it up as research for the psychic Madame Celeste, a character in *The Sunday Wife*. But I'd never attended a full-moon celebration nor met a real live witch, "white" or otherwise. Sudie was the real deal with residence in Cassadaga, the acclaimed "Psychic Capital of the World," as her credentials. I was a bit taken aback when I met Sudie at Steve's house that night. She looked really ordinary—a middle-aged postal clerk, maybe. At least she was dressed somewhat appropriately in a long floral muumuu like a lot of older women in Florida wear. Sudie was primping when we met in the guest room before the other guests arrived, getting dolled up for the moon-gazing ceremony. She sat in front of a mirror and penciled in her eyebrows while I perched on the daybed and told her my story. Without going into the gory details, I explained that my husband and I'd had a bad spate here, which had probably left bad spirits hanging around.

After applying rose-colored lipstick and blotting it with a tissue, she turned her attention to me. Her eyes held mine in the mirror and she nodded as I jabbered on and on. "Bad spirits *are* here," Sudie said when I'd finished. "I sensed it as soon as I arrived. I already told the boys the house needed cleansing."

Which she did, going through the darkened house waving a smoking bundle of white sage and chanting something that sounded like someone speaking in tongues. I trailed behind and truly felt as if something heavy had lifted from my heart when she finished cleansing the room where I'd unwittingly raised the window that prompted our fight. By then the others had arrived, about a dozen of us in all. We gathered outside then marched single file down the dark streets of the neighborhood with only the moonlight and Sudie lighting our way. In our hands we carried the candles that she'd given us, but only hers was lit. I hoped and prayed that the neighbors were safely asleep, especially since Sudie chanted in a singsong voice as we walked. The candle sent flickering shadows over her face and I figured if anyone saw us, they'd call the police for sure.

We reached the wooded, vacant lot and I breathed a sigh of relief. It was not only a safe distance from the neighboring houses but also enclosed by tall, dense rhododendron bushes. Once we were hidden away, Sudie directed us to form a circle. She lit the candle of the person next to her, who then turned to light the candle of the person standing by him, until we had formed a circle of candlelight.

No longer distracted by my nervousness I began to feel strangely elated. The clearing was eerily beautiful in the white light of the moon and the flickering of candles. I knew no one but Steve and Rick and no introductions had been made, yet I felt a kinship with those in the circle. Looking different now than she'd appeared seated at a dresser with eyebrow pencil in hand, Sudie stood tall and commanding in her muumuu, which rippled like a priest's robe in the cool breeze. Fittingly enough, the moon hung right above her. It was a sharply defined and absolutely perfect night without a cloud in the ink-black sky.

In a low but clear voice, Sudie spoke about the spiritual phases of the Goddess Moon, the mythic cycle of death and rebirth. Her eyes traveled around the circle and lingered on each of us for a moment as she spoke. She told us that the "Queen of the Night" was a powerful source of creative energy in all phases but especially when full. Every month we should celebrate the full moon, and we'd learn how meaningful its energy could be. Then she explained the ritual. First we were instructed to blow out the candles so we could rely solely on celestial light. Then we should stand facing the moon and taking in her power. We were to hold our arms over our heads and open them up in a bowl shape to channel the energy of the moon. Either silently or aloud, whichever worked best for us, we should call on the essence of the divine light to come down and fill us up, as though filling a bowl.

Sudie instructed us to focus fully on the ritual rather than looking to see how others were doing it. Keep our face and arms open and turned upward. Once we were filled with the divine light, she said, it was appropriate to thank the goddess for empowering us. That could be done in any form that felt right: folding our arms around our body to hold in the energy, bowing to the goddess, saying a prayer, crying, laughing, dancing—there was no right or wrong way. We would only know when it happened.

Sudie urged us not to break the spell afterward but to depart the circle quietly, making our way back to our lives renewed by the divine source of all life.

Following her example, we did as she instructed by blowing out our candles and placing them on the ground by our feet. I felt self-conscious and a little foolish until I raised my face to the moon and lifted my arms over my head.

I can't explain it except to say that something magical happened. It was as Sudie had said: I felt a flow—a jolt, even—of a strange energy flowing through me. I lost myself in it and became totally unaware of my surroundings. It was just the Goddess Moon, me, and the Divine. Although I could hear the voices of others offering up their praises, they didn't intrude on my moment of connection with the universe. For me, it felt right to bow in gratitude and to say a prayer of praise. Not a simple bow of my head as I did in church when approaching the altar or when the acolytes passed by holding the cross aloft; this was a full-fledged, from-the-waist bow that I was barely conscious of doing. It came naturally because I was so filled with gratitude for the powerful experience.

Walking back in silence to reconnect with my life outside the circle, renewed by the divine source, I didn't break the spell. The reverence stayed with me much as it did in church after I left the communion altar having partaken of the body and blood of the Lord. It was only as I drove away that a niggling image played in my mind. Try as I might, I couldn't summon enough of the celestial energy I'd just filled up with to shoo it away. Now that I was back on earth, I could picture myself standing there so earnestly in the midst of the circle with my arms raised above my head in a bowl shape, waiting to be filled with celestial energy. And I knew without question that if Pat had seen me, he would've had me hauled off to a mental hospital in a heartbeat.

I'd learned a lot about fictionalizing some of the real people in my life when I wrote *The Same Sweet Girls* a few years back. After I had plotted out the book, I'd mulled over my talk with Anne Siddons, when she'd advised me to tread carefully. To my surprise, even Pat warned me about the peril of turning close friends into characters. He wasn't hypocrite enough to tell me not to; he just wanted to make sure I knew what I was getting into. I didn't, but I hoped that following my heart and my instincts would carry me through the dilemma. By taking bits and pieces of the stories the Same Sweet Girls told one another over the years, I ended up making a collage of fiction, fantasy, and fact.

The real-life group of women that the book's based on have been friends of mine for decades (longer than any of us like to think about). We met in college, formed our bond, and have called ourselves the Same Sweet Girls ever since. Because we had such a special and unique friendship, I wanted to tell our story. It was one I thought that readers would find meaningful, and that's proven to be the case. I still hear from readers who have similar friendships, and from groups who call themselves the Same Sweet Girls in tribute.

The Same Sweet Girls' annual beach get-together was coming up not long after I signed a contract to write the book, so I decided to wait until then to break the news. The whole get-together I was a nervous wreck, wondering how I'd tell such dear friends that Judas Iscariot lurked among them, having sold the story of our friendship for thirty pieces of silver. I put it off until our last night together. With everyone gathered around the dinner table, I blurted out that my next book would be *The Same Sweet Girls*. After a startled silence, everyone burst into applause. I could've wept in relief. Giddy at their response, I promised to disguise everyone so they wouldn't be recognized. Fortunately they knew me well enough not to believe it. (Writers don't make the most trustworthy of friends.) For my next birthday one of the SSGs mailed me a T-shirt: BEHAVE OR YOU MIGHT FIND YOURSELF IN MY NEXT NOVEL.

In truth, I probably would've written the book regardless because I felt it was a story worth telling. Our group had met in the

1960s, when we were freshmen at Alabama College, a picturesque campus founded in the 1890s as an all-girls school. Although it had just gone coed, the college was still run as a girls' finishing school, a bastion of idealized southern womanhood (something I hadn't realized when I applied). There was a strict dress code and even stricter rules of decorum. In public we had to wear modest dresses or skirts, no slacks or jeans. I had no idea what I was getting myself into when I entered through the school's ornate iron gates. I found out quickly, and to my dismay. Unless we wanted to be sent home in disgrace, female students were expected to toe the line. Even though it was the '60s and revolution was brewing elsewhere, the times were far from a-changing in Alabama.

The stirring of something I'd later recognize as feminism was buried deep within me, but I had no way of articulating it then. All I knew was, I was miserable and lonely my first few months at school, away from home for the first time and not knowing anyone. I didn't fit in with the southern belles and debutantes who filled the dorms of my college but had no idea where I belonged instead. My bohemian dreams were dashed by the strict decorum of campus life, which couldn't have pleased my mother more. There I was, yet again trapped in a pattern I seemed destined to repeat—torn between my true self and the role society (and my mother) expected me to play.

To my great surprise, an incident at a student convocation drew me into the group of like-minded young women who would become lifelong friends. On that day, the convocation speaker was a senior who told us about her reign as a national beauty queen, when she'd represented the US as an ambassador of goodwill all over the globe. She was stunningly beautiful, poised, and a gifted speaker, but it was her parting words that got my attention. She assured her audience that although she'd traveled the world, met kings and queens and heads of state, she was still the *same sweet girl* she'd always been.

I stifled a giggle and lowered my head to keep from laughing out loud. That remark summed up my whole dilemma. No matter what else I might be, how educated or well traveled I might become, I'd better stay *sweet* and ladylike, as my mama had raised me to be, or there would be hell to pay. Then I noticed that I wasn't the only one struggling to keep her composure. Some of the girls seated around me elbowed each other, shoulders shaking in mirth. Even more surprising, they were the beauty queens, the campus leaders, the sorority girls—all of whom I thought of as the prim and proper ladies I could never be. Yet there they were, the same as me, trying not to laugh at a remark that struck us as both sad and funny. All of us, like generations of southern women before us, had been taught to take more pride in our sweet, ladylike behavior than in our accomplishments.

It was the moment that we dared to laugh at ourselves and one another that I realized kindred spirits had surrounded me the whole time. Unknowingly, I'd been in the midst of irreverent soul mates, disguised as demure southern belles, and they were as unfit for the role as I was, and as eager to break free. From that day forth we joined forces, and we became—and remain—the Same Sweet Girls.

When Pat and I had first started seeing each other, he met a couple of the girls, which made him eager to meet the rest. One was Loretta, who'd introduced me to Pat at the party the night we met. Pat said if the rest of the SSGs were anything like the luscious Loretta, then he couldn't wait to see the whole crew. So I invited another of the girls, Floozie, for a visit not long after I moved to

Fripp. She and her husband were the only friends of mine to meet the Great Santini, who totally charmed them. (I made sure to introduce Flooz to the colonel by her real name, Carol.)

On my and Pat's first road trip to New Orleans, I'd introduced him to my take on the fabulous term *floozie*, one of the many buzzwords of the Same Sweet Girls. We'd stopped for lunch and I mentioned that our waitress was such a great floozie. "You know her?" he asked in surprise. I said no, I didn't have to. He looked bewildered and I explained.

"It's like this, Pat. A floozie isn't a fallen woman or a hussy with a bad reputation. She can be, but that's not the thing. *Floozie* is an attitude. It's a way of carrying yourself, and the way you look at the world." I thought about it a minute. "Well, sort of. Something about a floozie has to *look* floozie. You know, flirty, with a certain twinkle in her eyes. There's usually one little thing about her appearance that gives her away—jeans a tad tight, or a bit of cleavage showing. Some floozies are more subtle than others."

Pat gave me a knowing smile. "You're the one who made this up, weren't you?"

"Maybe. But wait and see—once you get it, you'll notice floozies everywhere."

"You're talking about a certain kind of southern girl, right? As you call it, prissy."

I shook my head. "Not really. Matter of fact, most prissy girls aren't floozies. And it's not just a southern thing either. New York has some of the greatest floozies in the world."

He mulled it over. "And I'm guessing that Maine has the fewest?"

"See, you're catching on! New Orleans will be crawling with them. I'll help you figure out which is which. Let me give you a test to see if you're ready. Think about the women we know, and name the best floozie among them."

He didn't have to think long. "Melinda?"

"Perfect! Anyone else?"

"Your friend Loretta?"

"You're a natural at this, Pat. Trust me, it's going to enrich your people-watching immensely. You'll be coming up to me at parties with floozie alerts, like the SSGs and I do."

"Is your friend Floozie one?"

I pondered that. "Well, yeah, Flooz is definitely a floozie, but she's a bit too girl-next-door to be one a hundred percent. She's more like three-quarters. But wait until you meet the rest of the Same Sweet Girls, and you'll see all varieties. And I've got two cousins you'll meet called the Floozie Cousins."

Pat raised his glass of tea in a salute. "You've added much to my pathetic life, King-Ray, and now you've done it again." We clinked tea glasses and he said, "Why don't you invite the Same Sweet Girls to have a get-together on Fripp Island? Think they'd like that?"

"Are you kidding me? They'd love it," I responded, and Pat's eyes lit up in anticipation.

As I predicted, Pat got a kick out of floozie-watching and spent many happy hours at it. During a low point of one of his hospital stays years later, I'd brought him books, read him volumes of poetry, and retold our old stories, all to no avail. Understandably glum and depressed, he couldn't be distracted. It was easy to tell how sick Pat was; when he didn't interact with the staff, I worried. Gloomy myself, I was pacing when the shift changed. Pat's new doctor came in, looking so young I wondered if she was there to sell Girl Scout cookies. But when her long, tanned legs flashed beneath the white coat and stethoscope, I had her number. She got no response from prodding and questioning her patient until I positioned myself so she couldn't see me. Catching Pat's eye, I mouthed, *Pat! Floozie alert.*

Pat blinked and turned his head slowly like a turtle peering out of a shell. When he looked up at the pretty young doctor, I saw the old Pat for the first time that day. "Hey, Doc," he said. "Where're you from?" Before she left the room, he'd gotten her life story. She gave him a little wave as she closed the door behind her, and Pat pointed toward the yellow legal pad he always had with him. "Hand me my pen and paper, would you? Maybe I can use that story about how she got into med school somewhere."

I fetched the tools of his trade with relief. I'll never know whether it was the floozie doctor or the story she told, just that one or the other had greatly brightened his day.

CHAPTER 15

ONLY LOVE CAN BREAK A HEART

When I look back on my life with Pat, I try to concentrate on the good times. It's easy to do because they by far outnumber the bad. Pat had so many admirable qualities: compassion, generosity, kindness, and unselfishness. He hated injustice and never sacrificed his principles or backed down from a fight. He'd literally give you the shirt off his back, and he would always go to bat for you. He was brilliant but never snobbish or patronizing. But if I had to pick one thing about him that I cherished above all else, it'd have to be his sense of humor. He was every bit as funny on a day-to-day basis as he is in his books. That was what I first loved about reading him, how I could be laughing out loud on one page and crying on the next. Pat and I spent most of our days together sharing funny stories and making fun of ourselves or the foibles of human nature. But there were still plenty of times when things turned too dark for any light to shine through. As all of us do, he and I had our share of sorrow and loss.

In 2004, Pat lost his beloved high school English teacher and mentor, Gene Norris. Pat's written extensively about his admiration for Gene, and the profound influence Gene had on his life. Like everyone who knew him, I came to adore Gene as well, and we entertained him often at the Fripp house. He was always included in family gatherings or when we invited writer friends for a to-do. I loved it when he joined us because it was an excuse to put on the dog. Gene was an elegant southern gentleman of the old school and also a bit of a snob. Entertaining him called for the best china and silver.

Which, in my case, was something of a challenge. Fancy dinnerware was slim pickings with me, a failed southern belle. At my mother's insistence, I had a china pattern (Staffordshire Indian Tree), silver settings (Chantilly, of course, which I came to detest), crystal glasses, silver-plated serving dishes and trays, ornate gravy bowls, and embroidered tablecloths with matching napkins, including a set my mother embroidered herself. I love an elegantly set table as much as any other belle and made good use of my finery in my former role as a Sunday Wife. But when I left that life behind, I left the adornments as well. Instead I collected pottery and artisan utensils and wooden serving trays.

But no self-respecting belle, failed or otherwise, would serve Gene Norris on a pottery plate. I'd gotten back a few pieces of my fancy stuff from my ex; the rest I hunted up at estate sales and the Salvation Army store. It'd been a pleasant surprise to find that Gene was also an aficionado of thrift stores, and he joined me on many of my treasure hunts. Predictably, Pat teased us. "Norris," Pat'd say to Gene, "you and my bride go to the Goodwill because you're both cheap. She can't help it because she's an Alabama hick. And with your Scottish blood, neither can you."

Pat knew better than anyone how to get Gene's goat, and he never tired of doing so. Gene would draw himself up indignantly. No matter how often he heard Pat's bull, Gene always took the bait. "I beg your pardon, Irish scumbag. I'm *English*, as you well know, and on both sides. There's not a drop of Scottish blood in my family."

Having succeeded in getting poor Gene riled up, Pat's impish smile would light up his face. "My, my, looks like I hit a nerve. Someone's awfully touchy about his heritage."

Pat's other favorite thing to tease Gene about was his religion, and he could kill two birds with one stone by including me as well. Gene and I being Episcopalian, Pat often said, and members of the hoity-toity old church in town that was founded in 1720, proved to him that we were social climbers. "Naturally, Sir John Eugene Norris would belong to the Church of England," Pat said, eyes twinkling.

When Gene retorted, "By the grace of God, I'm not a papist," Pat upped the ante, as he was prone to do.

"My church was founded by St. Peter" was Pat's response, "while yours was launched by Henry the Eighth's dick."

Gene got back at Pat for the slights on his pedigree and religion by saying he wouldn't eat with us unless I did the cooking. Health conscious, Gene was appalled by Pat's extravagance with meals. Once when Gene was visiting, he became apoplectic watching Pat pour bacon drippings over an otherwise healthy dish of winter vegetables before roasting them. "I won't eat those," Gene sputtered furiously. "You can just go ahead and throw my portion out." Another time, when Pat doused a bowl of fresh peaches with heavy cream, Gene almost fainted. "Are you trying to kill us?" he squawked. "Lord God, keep that man out of the kitchen!"

Pat took it with his usual good humor but readily turned over the task of cooking for Gene to me. Gene and I bonded over the southern tradition of comparing stories about our mothers' and grandmothers' cooking. Pat enjoyed listening to them even though he had none of his own to contribute. According to him, the only cook in his family worse than his mother was his grandmother.

A lifelong bachelor, Gene was a private person with great dignity. He was our sole dinner guest the night he broke the news to us. He'd been diagnosed with leukemia. But his doctor assured him that the treatment should put him in remission. Pat put up a brave front but he was devastated. Watching his mother die from leukemia in her late fifties had been a traumatic experience that he never got over. I tried to tell Pat that the treatment was much improved since then. I had no idea if that were true or not but would've said anything to help him get through what I feared was coming.

Gene did well for a while. He celebrated his seventieth birthday and was otherwise healthy. Whenever and wherever he was hospitalized, Pat went, despite doing final edits for the cookbook at the time. Gene made an appearance in that book as well, but he would not live to see it published.

The summer before the release of *The Pat Conroy Cookbook*, Pat and I spent a few weeks in Lake Lure, North Carolina, where a friend had offered us the use of her cabin on a creek thick with lily pads. Taking the canoe out, we paddled through lilies and dragonflies. Pat had wanted to take me to Lake Lure for a long time. It was the setting for one of his favorite movies, *Dirty Dancing*, and he could do a mean imitation of the song-and-dance number "I Had the Time of My Life." But his attachment to the area was more sentimental. When Pat was a boy, his grandmother had a house there where his family often went. Since those visits took place when his father was deployed, Lake Lure held only happy memories for the Conroy clan. The house had long since been torn down but Pat showed me the site, on a high bluff overlooking the lake. He'd adored his colorful grandmother, Stannie, and wrote about her often. I remembered her best as the grandmother Ginny Penn in *Beach Music*.

During our stay at Lake Lure, Gene was hospitalized several times in Columbia, South Carolina, and Pat dutifully made the three-hour drive south to visit him. He returned chuckling because Gene had tried to run him off by insisting that Pat should be working instead of playing nursemaid. To calm him, Pat read aloud from *Look Homeward, Angel* and reminded Gene how he'd introduced him to the book when Pat was a high school junior.

"Worst thing I ever did," Gene snapped. "You've copied Wolfe's overwrought style ever since." Pat told me that he'd given Gene's oncologist our number at the cabin with instructions to call him immediately if Gene needed him. No cell service where we were staying, so the landline was the only way to reach us.

It was the first week in July. We'd spent a glorious Fourth on the lake with friends and stayed up late to watch the fireworks. Originally we'd planned to return home at the end of the month; but the following day Pat went to see Gene in Columbia and our plans changed. Gene was doing well enough to be released in a day or so. Figuring that he'd need help when he got home, Pat and I began to pack. Matter of fact, we decided, no reason why we couldn't pick Gene up on our way. "And once he gets home," Pat told me as he stuffed papers into his briefcase, "you can cook his favorites and I'll pester him as always. That'll keep him from fretting."

Later that day I was surprised to answer the phone and hear an unfamiliar female voice asking for Pat. Because we both needed privacy to work, we had only given out the number to family and our closest friends. I didn't disturb Pat when he was writing unless I had to, and he was trying desperately to finish editing before we left. I hesitated.

"I'm Eugene Norris's doctor," the woman said, and I told her to hang on and I'd get Pat. I took the phone to him, where he sat propped up on our bed with a legal pad in his lap. I sat beside him, waiting to hear that Gene would be released sooner than expected and we needed to head that way.

Pat took the phone with a frown, listened for a few minutes, then closed his eyes. "Thank you for letting me know, Doctor," he said in a tight voice. He hung up and handed the phone to me without a word, his eyes still closed. I'll never forget his face and the tears rolling down his cheeks. No need for me to ask if Gene had taken a turn for the worse. Pat's expression told me the terrible truth. Gene was gone.

~~~~~

All our losses didn't come in the month of July, but the next one did. Three years later, Pat and I were spending a month in Highlands. It was 2007, the year following our difficult time there, and a few days after I'd met with the witch for exorcism. Both of us were working on new books that summer (*South of Broad* for him, *Moonrise* for me) and were busy and happy, even though we'd just returned from a sad occasion. We had driven to Charlotte for the funeral of Doug Marlette's father, whom I'd met a couple of times and whom Pat knew well. Even though Doug had told us not to make the five-hour drive to Charlotte for the funeral, his face lit up when he saw us coming into the church.

An odd thing happened after the funeral that haunts me to this day. We were the last to leave because we wanted to spend a few minutes alone with Doug and Melinda. Their son, Jackson, was attending college in France and had just gotten in, jet-lagged and teary-eyed. Jackson hugged Pat long and hard and thanked us over and over for coming. We'd parked across from Doug and Melinda, and the five of us walked together to our cars. In the parking lot we hugged each other again, saying our goodbyes. I'd come to love Doug and Melinda. Doug would sometimes call me to talk about his concerns about Pat's health, particularly during the times Pat was hitting the bottle too hard. "Don't tell him I called!" Doug would always say, which tickled me.

Standing by Doug's car, Pat asked if Doug's trip to Mississippi was still on. Ole Miss was doing a student production of the musical based on Doug's syndicated cartoon, *Kudzu*. Several years back, Pat and I had gone to Chapel Hill to see it performed. In a few days Doug was supposed to travel to Oxford to meet the cast and see it onstage again. "Some happy news, then," Pat said, clapping Doug's shoulder. "Ole Miss is one of my favorite colleges. You'll have a great time."

Pat and I were walking to our car and something—I'll never know what—told me to turn around. I looked back and Doug, too, had stopped beside his car and was looking at us. The early afternoon sun outlined him in a dazzling glow, so bright I put a hand up to shield my face. My eyes met Doug's and held for a moment before his gaze shifted to Pat, where it lingered for an even longer time. Getting into the driver's seat, Pat didn't see him. Then both Doug and I lifted a hand for a wave of goodbye and got in our cars.

"That was odd," I said as I buckled myself in and Pat pulled out of the parking lot.

"The funeral?" he asked in confusion, and I shook my head.

"No. Something about Doug."

"He just buried his father," Pat reminded me, but I shook my head again.

"No, this was something different." I let it drop because I couldn't explain it. I almost said, *Doug was looking at me and you like he'd never see us again.* But I knew Pat would demand to know what that meant and I couldn't tell him. In the years to come I'd remember that moment, the golden glow of the sun and Doug's strange expression, but I'd never know what to make of it.

It was only a couple of days later when we got the call. Doug had flown into Memphis where an Ole Miss student picked him up for the drive down to Oxford. He was to talk to the cast of *Kudzu* before the production and a big hoopla was planned. Melinda hadn't gone with him because Jackson was about to return to school. It was a stormy day, and on the drive to the university, the student lost control of his vehicle, left the road, and slammed into a tree. Fortunately the student got out with minor injuries. Doug was killed instantly.

———

It seemed as though someone had pushed the domino that started the fall. Pat and I would remind ourselves many times that this was what happened as you grew older. You lost people you loved. I didn't handle any of them well. It was as though each one tore off the barely healing scab of the last wound. In 2014, we lost another dear friend, Barbara Warley. I'd become friends with Barbara, the wife of one of Pat's close buddies from The Citadel, John, after the Warleys relocated to Beaufort from Virginia. Barbara was a radiant, dark-haired beauty of Native American descent; otherwise, she and I had a lot in common. We shared the same political views and dark sense of humor. We'd both raised three sons and had plenty of war stories. Whenever our husbands got together, we were subjected to the same old Citadel stories. They hooted and hollered as though they'd never heard them before, while Barbara and I smiled indulgently and rolled our eyes.

Barbara differed from me in one crucial way, or so I thought. She was perpetually sunny and cheerful. A breast cancer survivor, she suffered the aftereffects of prolonged treatment and had to rely on pain medication to even move around comfortably, but she never let on or complained. She refused to talk about it or let it get her down. As time went on her suffering became more apparent, no matter how hard she gritted her teeth. But she kept up a good front. It pissed Pat off and he didn't hesitate to say so. "Dammit, Barbara, stop being so brave," he said to her. "Just because you're an Apache from Idaho—or wherever the hell your tribe is—you don't have to be the old Indian who goes off to suffer alone. Scream and yell and curse your fate like a normal person would."

Barbara laughed and took Pat's face in her hands, as I'd seen her do a hundred times. "You're so cute when you're mad," she said. Pat melted, as he always did, but he had to have the last word. "If it were me, I'd be whining and crying like a big baby."

"Amen to that," her husband, John, said.

I had gone to Florida for a speaking engagement when I got the call about Barbara's death. Stoic to the very end, Barbara hadn't told anyone that the pain had become unbearable. Hearing that she was gone, I flung myself on the bed and buried my face in the pillow. It brought to mind the last time I was in a hotel in Florida, and Pat had called about Mike Sargent. I couldn't help but wonder if I should ever schedule another event in the Sunshine State.

I returned home to find that Barbara's memorial service in Virginia was scheduled for a time when Pat and I both had speaking engagements. Mine couldn't be rescheduled, a ticketed event in Alabama that had been sold out for months. Pat's couldn't be postponed either; it was some hotshot award at USC that the university president was presenting to him at a fancy shindig. But his event wasn't until the day after Barbara's memorial service, so he could drive to Virginia first.

Before I left for Alabama, I baked a loaf of bread for the Warleys, my go-to for grieving families because sometimes a piece of bread is all we can manage when we're sick with grief. After packing for both Pat and myself, I put the bread in the passenger seat of Pat's car, along with a sympathy letter to John and the kids. Due to Pat's notorious absentmindedness, I'd learned the hard way to tape notes on the steering wheel, front door, mirror, or wherever to get his attention. I also learned not to trust him to pack for himself, as embarrassing as it is to admit. It was less trouble to pack for him than to get wherever we were going and have to shop for shoes, a dress shirt, or even underwear. The man was pathetic. I had no choice but to take things into my own hands after we'd been married a couple of years and Pat was set to address the student body of Queens College in Charlotte. An hour before the talk, he buttoned the obviously too-loose pants to his suit and said to me, "Where's my belt?"

"What d'ya mean where's your belt? Didn't you pack it?" I screeched.

He wouldn't meet my eye. "Doesn't look like it. And I'm afraid these pants will fall down."

"Well, at least you'll wake up the students." I sighed. "But don't worry; I always have a safety pin in my suitcase."

Except when I didn't. Pat and I eyed each other in a panic until I said, "We passed a mall on the way in. Hang tight and I'll be right back." It was rush hour in Charlotte, a nightmare in the best of times, but I flew to the mall, grabbed a belt at Penney's, then sped back. We were five nerve-racking minutes late to the auditorium, and it took me twice that long to catch my breath. But Pat's britches stayed up.

Driving straight to Barbara's memorial, Pat wore his docksiders, baggy khakis with a navy shirt, and a rumpled navy blazer. The other Citadel guys would be in respectable dark suits, I knew, but also knew that Barbara would've held Pat's face in her hands and laughed at him for being his usual rumpled, unstylish self. The big USC event the following day was my main concern, but I'd taken care of that. In the trunk next to his overnight bag I'd put his good suit in a hanging bag with a dress shirt, tie, and shoes. Then I'd taped a big piece of paper on it: USC AWARDS CEREMONY!

I'd just gotten in from my trip to Alabama when Pat returned home. Seeing the car I ran out to meet him, anxious to hear about the memorial service. We hugged and wept for Barbara and the family, then Pat hobbled into the house toting his overnight bag. Driving for eight hours for two days in a row had hurt his back, as long drives had done since his back surgery in the early '90s. I told him not to worry, I'd get the rest of his stuff.

My heart sank as soon as I opened the trunk. There was the hanging bag I'd packed him with the sign still on it. The paper was taped over the zipper so the bag couldn't have been opened. Unbelievably, Pat had appeared at the hoity-toity awards ceremony in the same thing he'd worn for *two days*. I closed my eyes and sighed at the futility of my efforts to keep such a thing from happening. Then a dreadful suspicion hit me and I stomped over to the passenger side of the car and flung open the door. Sure enough, both the bread and my letter were still on the seat, exactly where I'd put them.

~~~~~

Sorrow wasn't done with us, and never is done with any of us, regardless of how blessed our lives may seem. During those years, Pat and I would lose many friends and family members, each blow seeming to come while we were still reeling from the previous one. If we'd learned anything from our losses, it should've been that no matter how bad the heartache, the next one is just around the bend. One afternoon in 2010 Pat came in from a trip into town and found me huddled on our bed in a fetal position. Even though I heard him come in, heard the door close behind him, I couldn't make myself move. It took him by surprise; I was rarely in our room late afternoon and certainly not catatonic on the bed. Proceeding cautiously, he put a hand on my shoulder and leaned over me. "Sweetheart? Anything wrong?"

My response was "Yeah. Everything's wrong."

Pat thought a minute before saying, "Is it me?"

Normally I would've laughed. Instead I said, "I can't do this without you."

"I'm not going anywhere." Pat moved me over and sat beside me with his hand caressing my shoulder. I scooted myself upright and leaned into him. "You want to tell me about it?" he asked.

I took a deep breath, wishing I didn't have to put it into words. Otherwise, maybe it wouldn't be real. Finally I said, "Do you remember a few weeks ago when Nancy Jane had her gallbladder removed? She was perfectly fine one day; sick and in severe pain the next. They figured it must be gallstones. But it wasn't, so they've been running more tests. She just called to tell me that the test results came back, and she's scheduled for more surgery next week. Turns out, it's not her gallbladder."

"What is it?"

I could tell by his tone that he knew the answer, knew the reason he'd found me in such a state. "It's cancer," I told him.

Pat closed his eyes. "Oh dear God," he said finally. "How old is Nancy Jane, fifty?"

"Fifty-two. It makes no sense! *I'm* the one who's always having problems, not her. She and Beckie tease me about my delicate constitution."

It was true, I'd drawn the short stick in a family of hearty and healthy stock. Beckie and Nancy liked to boast that they never got so much as a cold or a stomach bug, despite kindergarten kids sneezing in their faces or barfing on their feet. Another factor occurred to me, however, one that was hard to ignore. Only a couple of years before, Nancy Jane had gone through an extremely stressful and painful divorce (*Is there any other kind?* Pat would ask). Not for the first time, I questioned the relationship between stress and illness. As a therapist told me once, your biography becomes your biology. When I'd repeated that troublesome thought to Pat, his response had been typical of him: "I'm a dead man, then."

I appreciated that Pat didn't try to make me feel better with platitudes, he just took my hand in his and sat with me. He knew better than anybody how close Nancy Jane and I were. She and

I thought so much alike that we practically finished each other's sentences. We shared the same irreverent humor, same politics, and same spirituality. I'd always been protective of her and knew that was a big part of my despair. I couldn't protect her from this. No one could. We might say we'd take a bullet for those we love and mean it sincerely, but all the sincerity in the world can't alter the course of the bullet. The only thing we can do for those we love who are in pain is to be with them and hold their hand.

By the time I traveled to Birmingham for Nancy Jane's surgery, I'd fallen back on the comfort of platitudes and had force-fed myself every single one I could think of. An even better metaphor, I grabbed each one that floated by and held on to it like a life preserver. Sitting in the waiting room of St. Vincent's Hospital with the rest of the family and my sister's teacher friends, we repeated platitudes to one another ad nauseam, trying to convince ourselves that everything would be fine. After all, they didn't know for sure it was cancer, right? Lab tests could be wrong. We told stories of false diagnoses or miraculous healing.

Several hours later than expected, Nancy Jane's surgeon came out grim faced. They'd found widespread cancer, a rare endocrine kind that no one saw very often. Because the treatment options were so limited, the surgeon had taken out as much of it as he could. Unfortunately the only way to save her had been to remove two-thirds of her intestines. Nancy would survive, the surgeon told the family, maybe even for a few years. But her life would be greatly altered. It would be an ongoing struggle to keep her well.

I'd learn later that her surgeon, a soft-spoken, exceedingly compassionate young man, had taken pity on the family and friends who had to hear such a difficult prognosis and had softened it as much as possible. I'll always appreciate that he broke it to us gently and left us with a glimmer of hope. Several years earlier when my mother had been diagnosed with cancer, her oncologist had walked in and with no preliminary, informed her that nothing could be done. She had six months to live if she was lucky, he added briskly, then walked out. He didn't get far. I stormed after him and suggested he change either his bedside manner or his profession. (I heard later that he did the latter.)

My sister lived in a small town about an hour from Birmingham where she had a wonderful support group. She returned home after a month's stay in St. Vincent's, and her friends went into full swing. Nancy Jane was spunky and hardheaded, as I well knew, traits that would serve her well in her recovery. She was already planning her return to teaching, as soon as the doctors gave her the go-ahead. Knowing my sister was in good hands, I understood it was time for me to go home. I'd spent most of July at the hospital, sleeping on a plastic bench a few feet from her bed. I was determined to put up a brave front when I left, but I caved in as we hugged goodbye. She felt so fragile.

"I wish to God it'd been me," I told her in a choked voice. The old Nancy Jane would've said, "Me too," and we would've laughed together. Instead she blinked back tears to say, "It would've killed me, either way."

It's so true, I thought as I walked to my car. Watching someone you love suffer is a killing thing.

CHAPTER 16

LOCATION, LOCATION, LOCATION

In 2012, five years after our exile in Highlands and return to a solid foundation, Pat and I left Fripp Island and moved into Beaufort. Our decision to move involved mixed emotions for both of us. Because he and Lenore had bought the Fripp house, he'd insisted from the start that I needed a place to fix up the way I liked. Lenore had great taste, so I hadn't gotten rid of any of her stuff. My preference was for neutrals and earth tones, but I learned to live with the bold patterns and colors of my predecessor. Besides, I told Pat, if he kept buying houses for his wives, he'd end up poor as Job's turkey.

Mainly I was so happy to get back into our house after exile that I had no desire to go anywhere. But our lives were changing in ways that neither of us could continue to ignore. Pat's years of hard living and hard drinking began to catch up with him, causing more problems. He'd been in the hospital a couple of times and had just gotten out when I had to leave for Nancy Jane's surgery. After my return, he and I found ourselves driving into town to see

Dr. Laffitte often. Every couple of months Pat traveled to the diabetics clinic in Charleston—though I don't know why he bothered since he ignored their advice. Nevertheless, change was in the air.

I was more torn about the move to Beaufort than Pat was. Fripp Island, and our small cozy house, had been my refuge and my safe harbor. It was odd; Pat'd always been averse to change, no doubt stemming from his childhood of constant moves. When he saw that change was inevitable, however, he didn't look back. I too adjusted easily to the move into town once we were there, but a part of me will always remain on Fripp Island.

Pat was the one who found our Beaufort house. At the time we still had the *Grasshopper*, but we rarely took the boat out. After the Warleys relocated to Beaufort, John, Pat, and our friend and attorney Scott Graber would occasionally take the boat and cruise up and down the Beaufort River. On one such occasion, a crisp, late fall day of sun and sparkling waters, they took the boat down Battery Creek, a deepwater tributary of the Beaufort River, which is the body of water that Beaufort's on. Scott pointed out a house high on the banks and told Pat that we should look at it. A friend of his was selling.

Pat liked what he saw, I could tell. As soon as he returned to Fripp, he told me about the place that Scott's friend was selling. "You might want to call our realtor," Pat added casually, but his voice held a telltale note of excitement, which surprised me. He was a master of the poker face, a trait I envied; and I still believe it to be one of the reasons he was such a great storyteller. I do okay at relaying a sad tale—unless it's so sad I burst into tears—but when I try to tell something funny, I crack myself up. As Pat always reminded me, I enjoy my humor more than anyone else does.

The house on Battery Creek spoke to me when we drove into

the yard with its moss-hung oaks and heirloom camellia bushes, many of them tall as trees. Inside, the voice was loud and clear: *Conroys, I am your house.* It wasn't fancy, but vastly comfortable with space for two offices and an expansive view of the beautiful, marsh-edged Battery Creek. We'd found our new home. Later that spring, we moved in. I decorated it in my own funky, eclectic style, with furnishings from consignment shops or thrift stores. Gene Norris would've been proud.

"You don't have to tell everybody that you got our stuff at the Habitat store," Pat groused one day.

"Why not?" I cried. "The Habitat store has great stuff. Especially the one on Hilton Head. You wouldn't believe what rich people get rid of. Besides, I'm recycling. You're all for that, aren't you?"

He wasn't impressed. "Always the same with you ants—so proud of your miserly little selves."

I eyed him smugly. "I might be an ant, Babezee, but I have grasshopper taste. You like your office, don't you?"

He admitted that he did, and I hid a smile. Mr. Poker Face had given himself away. The truth was, he loved his new office and couldn't hide his pleasure. The house had given me the opportunity to repay Pat's gift to me, when he'd insisted years before that I have a room of my own. This time, I made sure that *he* did. And I'd surprised him with it. By a stroke of luck (for me and him both), Pat had been away speaking about his latest book, *My Reading Life*, when the moving van came to Fripp to pack us up. By the time he returned, we were moved in, and he had his own space.

The layout of the new house had been a major selling point for me. There were plenty of rooms for me to choose an office from, and no one had to urge me to claim one. I picked out a choice one with windows overlooking the creek. But I'd been determined that Pat'd have an equally fine one, plus his own library with plenty of shelves. Cost be damned; before we moved in I hired a master woodworker to make him a special desk and to add plenty of bookshelves. One whole room, down the hall from his office, was dedicated to Pat's books, with library-style shelves that could be accessed from either side. When Pat walked into the room for the first time, he stared in disbelief, then his face lit up like a kid on Christmas morning. From then on he spent endless hours in his library arranging and rearranging his beloved books. I've never known anyone, before or since, who loved books the way he did.

I loved my new office too, but never with the same devotion I felt for my first one. For one thing, it was harder to work in the Beaufort location. I soon discovered the danger of too much distraction. The vista from the back windows was so stunning it mesmerized me. Because Battery Creek is tidal, it ebbs and flows, either flooding the marsh on the horizon until water and sky merge, or pulling itself away, baring the mudflats and exposing the oyster beds beneath. Boats traverse the wide waters, leaving a glorious wake of waves behind them. Constantly moving, constantly beautiful, the ebb and flow of life itself, the creek is hypnotic to watch. Sometimes I can't tear myself away.

My room here is different too, smarter and more stylish. The wicker tray's gone, having been replaced by a utilitarian number from the office supply store, especially designed for laptops. I'm pretty sure neither Goodwill nor the Habitat store have anything like it. I can't imagine I'd find an antique Chinese screen there either, like the one I use to block off even further distraction from the door. My first painting still hangs on the wall, the one Pat gave me of the woman reading in the chaise, as do my beloved bird prints. But they're joined by posters from signings and framed covers of my six books, something unimaginable to me all those years ago when I decorated my first writing room.

With the move into town, so much changed for us, as things always have and always will. I couldn't wait for the family to see the house and our new location on Battery Creek. I never told Pat, but I harbored a foolish hope that being in town would make us more accessible, and one day Susannah might show up. We'd heard that she'd moved to Atlanta with her mother to be near Gregory, who'd relocated to Savannah. Maybe during a visit to Savannah, only an hour away from Beaufort, Pat's estranged daughter would look up the father she hadn't seen in thirteen years and show up at our door. It was a pipe dream that never happened.

Pat made one thing clear from the start—Camp Fripp wasn't moving with us. At first he'd agreed with our accountant that we couldn't afford both places, and the Fripp house would have to go. But to my surprise, he reneged on the agreement. "Are you *kidding* me?" was his response when I questioned his reversal. Pat was usually as good as his word. "I would've agreed to anything to get this house," he said. "But hear me loud and clear: Camp Fripp is staying on Fripp. We're too old to run Battery Creek Camp. When family comes, our guesthouse is located twenty miles from here and that's where they go. Period. End of discussion."

I didn't say a word. One thing I knew, Big Boss Man might talk a tough line, but hospitality had always been a part of his makeup. Sure enough, he was horrified when our first visitor, Nancy Jane, said her goodbyes after a tour of the new house. Pat looked at her in disbelief. He'd been so relieved that she'd done well enough after her surgery the summer before to return to teaching and was going about her life as best she could. Stubborn as ever, she'd shrugged off her doctor's advice not to drive to Beaufort alone and had hit the road the day school let out.

"Where do you think you're going?" Pat squawked. Why, to Fripp, Nancy Jane responded, and she wanted to get there before dark.

"The hell you are," Pat snapped, then turned to point an accusing finger at me. "Are you going to let your little sister go all the way out there? That's the most ridiculous thing I've ever heard."

"I'm not going to impose on you and Tanna," Nancy Jane told him. "I'll be perfectly happy at the Fripp house."

Pat stuck out his hand and demanded her car key. "I'll put your suitcase in the guest room. And I better not hear another word about you going anywhere."

He snatched up her key and stormed out the door, muttering to himself about Helen Keller doing such an awful thing to her poor sick sister. Nancy Jane and I looked at each other and giggled, taking care to rearrange our amused expressions when Pat reappeared. After putting her suitcase down, he wrapped Nancy Jane in a big hug. "I'm so glad you're here, kiddo," he said, and his voice caught. "Don't you dare leave us, you hear?"

I looked away quickly and swallowed hard. I knew he wasn't referring to Fripp Island.

~~~

It wasn't long before the new house was flooded with guests. Shortly after we got settled in, we had a housewarming that my sister Beckie still talks about. Unlike Nancy Jane and me, Beckie's down to earth and has always been suspicious of anything she considers weird or offbeat. Pat had brought in Father Mike Jones, an old friend of Pat's and a retired Episcopal priest, to conduct a house-blessing ceremony. Even as a staunch Methodist, Beckie was impressed with the lovely, joyous ceremony. But afterward, she pulled me aside to whisper, "Tanna, what on *earth* was that girl doing?"

Puzzled, I looked around at the gathering of our friends, neighbors, and family. "What girl?" I asked.

"Shh—she'll hear you!" Beckie hissed. She nodded her head toward Maggie Schein. "*That* girl. Don't look now or she'll know I'm talking about her."

Maggie, a tall, black-haired beauty, was the daughter of our friends Bernie and Martha Schein. After completing a doctorate in Chicago, she'd settled in Beaufort with her Yankee boyfriend, Jonathan. Although Maggie was a lot younger than many of our guests, I wouldn't call her a girl. But to Beckie I said, "Right now she's having a glass of wine and talking to Pat. What was she doing *when*?"

My obtuseness exasperated Beckie. "When do you think? During the blessing of the house! She lit a joint and followed the priest around waving it in the air. I can still smell it."

I was dumbfounded until it hit me what she meant, and I burst out laughing. "That wasn't a joint, Beckie. It was the white sage I gave her to cleanse the house with."

Beckie looked at me as if I'd dropped down from another planet, then her eyes narrowed. "Does Pat know that you're not right in the head?"

"If he doesn't know it by now, then he never will."

Later I saw Beckie bending Pat's ear and wondered if she was sharing her astute observation about my mental state. "So what did Beckie want?" I asked him that night as we readied for bed.

"Oh, just to tell me how much she likes the house. I told her you did everything." He patted my shoulder. "Great job, sweetheart."

I turned off the lamp and smiled to myself as I crawled into bed. Say what you will about sisters, when push comes to shove we have each other's back. Beckie hadn't outed me after all.

———

Once Pat and I got settled in, we decided to celebrate. Late spring in the Lowcountry, it had been a sun-bright day of clear blue perfection. "Let's take the boat out at sunset," Pat proposed. "I want to show you Battery Creek."

"Just us?" I tried not to sound skeptical. The *Grasshopper* was now tied to our very own dock, but Pat and I had wondered if the two of us would be able to take it out alone. As we often lamented, we were old coots now, in our midsixties, and not as dexterous as we once were. Pat was overweight with some neuropathy, and I was just flat out of shape. Not long ago, I'd stayed lithe and agile by religiously practicing yoga, swimming, and biking. But now I spent most of the time sitting on my butt at the computer. I still did yoga, but half-heartedly.

"If we can't do it," Pat warned, "no need for us to have a boat."

It was an effective threat. I loved the *Grasshopper* and would have even if it never moved from the dock. I was content to sit in it while it was tied to the dock, or stretch out and take a nap as it bobbled on the tidal waters like a gently rocking cradle. "I'll pack us a picnic," I said.

Late afternoon, I carried chilled champagne in a cooler as we walked down to the dock. A few steps ahead and carrying the picnic basket, Pat stopped and I almost ran into him. "You're gonna love this, bird woman," he said with a grin.

I looked up to see a great blue heron perched on one of the tall pier-pilings by the boat, and gasped in delight. Another bonus of the new house, the abundance of sea birds. Even while trying to keep my balance as I climbed on board, I kept my eyes on the heron. Of all the birds, the great blue was a special favorite of mine and Pat's. To my astonishment the heron not only stayed put but also seemed to be eyeing me back. "It's a sign," I told Pat in a hushed tone.

Pat snorted. "Could've fooled me," he said as he too climbed on board, much more nimbly than I dared hope. "Looks like a bird to me."

When he got behind the wheel, Pat turned his head my way, eyebrows raised. I sat perched on one of the cushioned seats, looking around blissfully as I awaited our maiden voyage into our new life. "Ah, sweetheart? I need a second mate here."

I looked at him puzzled before it hit me what he meant. I jumped up red-faced, climbed off the boat quickly, untied us from the posts, then jumped back in. Balanced on the side of the boat, I stretched out my leg to give us a push away from the dock. The motor purred, the *Grasshopper* lunged, and off we went.

It could not have been more beautiful, the weather more perfect, nor the creek more welcoming. Pat steered the boat deftly through the steel-blue, rippling waterways edged in marsh as I perched on a cushion in the strong salty breeze and took it all in. I was enchanted, entranced, spellbound by the marshes lining the creek, the earthy smell of pluff mud, the foam-tipped wake created as the boat parted the silvery waters. Soon we lost sight of the house. Finding the most isolated spot near a low-hanging oak on the bank, Pat dropped anchor so we could enjoy the sunset. There the boat swayed back and forth, the only sound the swishing slap of waves against its sides.

The sun was low on the horizon, hanging just over the top of the marshes across the creek. Neither of us said a word as we reveled in the glory of the place we'd landed. As the sun disappeared into the marsh, the ripples of the slowly moving creek went from soft blue to deep gold to burnished pink. Darkness fell, but neither of us could move, or break the silence. I had no doubt we were thinking the same thing: *This is as close to heaven as either of us sinners might ever get.*

In the afterglow of sunset, Pat opened the champagne. We toasted our good fortune at living in one of the most beautiful places on earth. I pulled out the picnic basket and we feasted on deviled eggs and boiled shrimp. In a celebratory mood when I'd prepared the picnic earlier, I'd even made cookies. I told myself that a few treats from time to time would help ease us into the healthy new lifestyle I hoped to instigate now that we'd settled in.

Our picnic had been a simple one and hadn't taken long, but darkness crept in faster than we expected. "Guess we'd best start back," Pat said as he reluctantly pulled himself up to return to the wheel. I was equally reluctant but packed the remains of the picnic so we could be on our way.

It was only when Pat steered us away from the embankment that we discovered the boat lights weren't working. Our moods shifted quickly. The night was black as sin, and there we were, two old codgers who had no business staying out so late, on a dark river with only a quarter moon to lead us home. We dared not look at each other in case our apprehension turned to fear. I climbed onto the bow to see if the meager glow from our flashlight could guide the way. And it might have, had we thought to check the batteries before we left. There was nothing to do but creep along through the black waters and pray we wouldn't hit a sandbar. Now that darkness had fallen, the warmth of the day had faded as well. From my perch on the bow of the boat, I shivered violently in the strong night wind.

When the lights of Beaufort came into view, I turned to Pat in alarm. Not only had we passed our dock, unfamiliar in the darkness, we had come way too far. We were on the Beaufort River, not Battery Creek. Before I could suggest that we dock in Beaufort and call someone to come get us, Pat had turned the boat around. *The Water Is Wide*, I reminded myself, the book where Pat wrote about the time in his life when he made the journey to Daufuskie Island by boat five days a week, twice a day. Never mind that he was a young man then; he was still an experienced boater. I kept telling myself there was no need to panic.

With the quarter moon and the lights of Beaufort now at our back, Pat steered the boat through increasing darkness to retrace his steps. But my fear increased when I saw that all the docks we approached looked exactly alike. How would we ever find ours? Then we rounded a bend and I saw a familiar sight in the distance. My heart pounding, I yelled out, "It's our dock, Pat! Pull in."

And the great blue heron was there waiting for us, I swear he was. I saw him plain as day, perched exactly as he had been when we first spotted him on the piling. As we neared the dock, he lifted his magnificent wings and flew off, a shadow etched in the darkness of the night. It's not possible, Pat scoffed when I told him how I recognized our dock. We were gone too long. I only imagined that the heron was waiting for us to return, he said. But I knew better. The great blue heron had stayed to guide us home.

Often a new environment inspires new resolve. The move to Battery Creek would be a fresh beginning for us, I decided, and I was hell-bent on sticking to my guns. The time had come for us to get serious about health issues. In the new Conroy house, there would be no more rich food, lavish spreads, or overindulging. I debated about the best time to discuss my plans for a lifestyle change with Pat, but it had to be soon because *The Death of Santini* was coming out. It wasn't just being on the road that made book tours hazardous to one's well-being. Pat rarely got a chance to eat at events because he was always surrounded by eager fans. His book signings would go on for hours, and he refused to take a break or have a snack.

In truth, I worried more about Pat when *I* was the one traveling than when he was. When I wasn't home to give him the evil eye, Pat ate whatever he pleased, as I'd find out. My oldest grandson lived in Beaufort for a few years and worked as a line cook in a local restaurant. Pat not only encouraged his interest in cooking but loved to loan him cookbooks. Tyler told me what happened one night when I was out of town, and he'd stopped by after work to return a cookbook. My grandson stuck his head in the door and saw Pat sitting in his recliner in front of the TV watching a ball game. Spotting Tyler, Pat motioned for him to come in. "You would've *died*, Gram," Tyler told me later, laughing. "There sat Pat in his boxer shorts. He had a half-gallon of ice cream in one hand and a big serving spoon in the other, and I swear, he ate the whole thing."

To my surprise, Pat agreed wholeheartedly that things had to change and swore on the rosary to mend his wicked ways. As much as I wanted to believe him, I couldn't help being skeptical, but I didn't want to police his behavior. Not only was it a no-win situation, it was bound to cause trouble between us. I had to let go.

I should've learned that after my one bold attempt at intervention, which had been a spectacular failure. It happened a few weeks before we moved into town and preceded the worst health scare Pat'd had to that point. We were still on Fripp and just beginning to pack up for the move. For days I'd been concerned about Pat and had tried in vain to persuade him to go to the doctor. Something just wasn't right. He wasn't himself. He had no energy and his coloring was waxen.

Then one day it hit me that he hadn't been out of our bedroom all morning, and I went to check on him. He appeared to be sleeping, but it was two o'clock in the afternoon and he'd never slept that late. When I tried to rouse him and couldn't, I panicked, sure he'd gone into a diabetic coma. I called the Fripp paramedics then paced the floor waiting for them. Two young men arrived, super nice and professional, but they were hesitant to follow me into our bedroom. Why didn't I try to wake him one more time, they said. If he agreed, they'd go back and check his vitals. If he *agreed*? That seemed overly cautious to me, but I figured they had their reasons, most likely Fripp regulations. When I went back to try again, Pat's eyes finally opened and he looked dazed. I explained that the paramedics were there to check him out, and he pulled himself up.

"Okay," he mumbled, obviously confused. "I'll be out as soon as I go to the bathroom."

I tried to make him stay put, but he insisted on getting up. After I'd helped him to his feet and into the bathroom, I hurried back to report to the young men in the entrance hall that Pat'd be right out. One of them had a pad and began to write down Pat's history while I tried to keep myself from hyperventilating.

Suddenly the bedroom door flung open and Pat came out with a smile on his face and his hand extended. He'd pulled on a pair of sweats and a T-shirt and looked chipper for someone who'd been unconscious only minutes before. "Hey, guys!" he called out. "Thanks for coming by to check on me. Want to sit at the table?" Turning to me, he added, "Sweetheart, why don't you get us a glass of tea? Or maybe a Coke. You guys want a Coke?"

I was too stunned to do anything but watch in disbelief as they made their way to the table. Somehow I managed to serve tea over their joking and laughing as the paramedics checked Pat's vitals. I never found out what they were, since Pat asked me to run back to the room and get the guys a book. While signing their books, he pumped them for their life stories like he always did. After they'd gone, following much backslapping and promises to visit again, I stood over Pat with my hands on my hips, staring at him dumbfounded. "What?" he said innocently. No longer putting up a big front, he looked as ghastly as before. I knew he'd been faking it, the whole thing.

"I'm not believing this!" I yelped. "You're on death's door until those guys come in, then you get up to play the Prince of Tides? Gimme a break."

His eyes narrowed. "You didn't call them, did you? Tell me you didn't call them."

"I did call them, but here's the good thing. They'll spread the word that Pat Conroy's wife is a hysteric, so you won't have to worry about them coming back." I stopped my tirade long enough to rub my face in exasperation. "Lord God in heaven—you're going to drive me insane before this is over."

A few days later when Pat got so sick he started throwing up blood, I didn't take time to test my theory about the paramedics.

Instead I led Pat to my car, buckled him in, and handed him a towel in case of more bleeding. His head lolled and he appeared to be only semiconscious. I turned on the flashers, put the pedal to the metal, then hit Dr. Laffitte's home number on the Bluetooth. When he answered, I told him calmly, "I'm taking Pat to the ER. Could you arrange for the gastro guy to meet us there? We're going to need him."

Even though Dr. Stewart, our gastro doctor, did a magnificent job of patching Pat up temporarily, he sent him by ambulance to the Medical University of South Carolina (MUSC), the hospital in Charleston, and ICU. Thankfully no one had asked why I drove Pat to Beaufort Memorial rather than calling for an ambulance. If they had, I would've had to think fast to come up with a plausible reason. Nobody would believe the truth, that I couldn't trust the silver-tongued devil not to charm the drivers and talk his way out of what was obviously a very real emergency.

~~~~~

After we'd lived in town a couple of months, somehow a miracle occurred and the change happened. Whether it was the health scares, the more nutritious meals, or the influence of Pat's friends now that we saw them more, I'll never know. Whatever it was, I watched it unfold with gratitude. Pat's old friend from high school, Bernie Schein, had recently retired from years of teaching in Atlanta and moved back to Beaufort, so he kept Pat company when I was on the road. Bernie was hardly a good influence on Pat since he had most of the same problems, but at least they entertained each other. It helped that both were tattletales: Pat couldn't wait to tell Martha when Bernie got out of line, and Bernie loved tattling on Pat to me or anyone else who'd listen. Fortunately, Pat was also friends with Bernie's brother, Aaron. A retired banker, Aaron's as different from the zany, free-spirited Bernie as night is from day. I enlisted Aaron in my campaign for a better and healthier Pat, which we hoped would rub off on Bernie too.

It was Aaron who urged Pat to work with a personal trainer that he'd discovered at the YMCA, a young Japanese woman named Mina. When Aaron told us about her, I held my breath, afraid to get my hopes up.

To my great relief, Pat adored Mina. He joined the Y and started going three or four times a week. After all the years of hoping and praying, it seemed too good to be true. No one else could've worked with Pat like Mina did. She had just the right touch and knew instinctively when to push him and when to ease up. She was considerate of his bad back, the neuropathy, and other problems, and she never pushed beyond what he was able to do. When Pat asked me to come to the Y to meet Mina, I eagerly complied.

I too loved Mina, but their workout was hard for me to watch from the sidelines. It wasn't because Mina was pushing Pat too hard. Instead, it took all I could do to keep a straight face. Poor Mina didn't know what to make of Pat's never-ending patter of jokes and just plain bull. If I'd been her, I would've taped his mouth shut. The first workout I witnessed went something like this:

"Mr. Pat, how are you today?" Mina said politely, with a little bow.

"Don't call me Mr. Pat," he said. "Makes me feel like an old man."

"In my culture we respect our elders, Mr. Pat."

"See? You're saying I'm old."

"But how are you feeling?"

"You've almost killed me, Mina. I need an ambulance."

Mina grew alarmed. "An ambulance? Are you sick, Mr. Pat?"

"Yeah. I'm sick of exercising."

"But exercising makes you feel better!"

"I know what you're up to, Mina. You're paying me back for Hiroshima."

Mina became agitated, then caught on. "I think I understand now. My English is not too good. You are trying to be funny. Are you trying to be funny, Mr. Pat? Like, ha ha ha?"

"No, Mina. I'm perfectly serious. I'm dying. You're killing me."

Aaron was nearby, and I appealed to him. "Mina's not going to thank you for getting her into this, Aaron. Go tell her it's okay to make Pat shut up."

"Oh, don't worry," Aaron said with a grin. "Mina's more than capable of handling him. Wait till the workout starts. He'll quieten down then."

He was right. To this day, Mina remains the only person I've ever known who could make Pat Conroy shut his wisecracking mouth and get down to business.

CHAPTER 17

WHEN EVERYTHING WE DO ISN'T ENOUGH

Little did I know when I launched my plan for healthier living that I'd end up having not just one opponent but two, and both would go into it fighting me every step of the way. No sooner had Pat gotten on the path toward better health than I turned my attention to Nancy Jane, as if she didn't have enough to worry about. For two years after Nancy's diagnosis, I made the trip to Alabama on a fairly regular basis, often to pick my sister up and head somewhere looking for a new treatment approach.

Nancy Jane had survived her first year much better than anyone could've imagined, and her doctors were cautiously optimistic. I constantly researched doctors and clinics in order to find help. We'd go to any that offered a shred of hope: specialists at the Mayo as well as clinics in Mobile, Atlanta, Baton Rouge, and Lexington. Each trip, Nancy Jane and I drove along singing "We're off to see the wizard, the wonderful wizard of Oz." There's no cure for carcinoid, the kind of cancer she had, but it's manageable.

Slow growing, it doesn't respond to conventional treatment. Good news, she wouldn't lose her hair; bad news, chemo doesn't work. My sister's only hope was to stay alive long enough for a treatment to be found.

Nancy Jane was always up for a trip, and we'd traveled together a lot before she got sick. (Neither the Mayo Clinic nor Emory Cancer Center had ever made our list of go-to places, however.) One of our most memorable adventures had been at my oldest son's wedding in the British Virgin Islands. We swam with dolphins one day then found ourselves swimming with a shark the next—though not for long. No one's ever seen a crowd of swimmers clear a beach like we did at the appearance of that dark, finned shape, at least five feet long, in the turquoise waters of St. Thomas. The shark wasn't our only scary adventure in the islands. On a lark, Nancy Jane and I had decided to go native one evening and hired a car to take us to an isolated nightclub, high atop a mountain, that only the locals knew about. Some kind of festival was going on with dancing, drinking, and a pig roast. We hadn't told anyone in the wedding party, so they wouldn't talk us out of it. When the car we'd hired broke down on the way back, the driver disappeared to look for help and didn't return for an hour. Suddenly two southern girls found themselves up the proverbial creek without a paddle, and we realized our foolishness.

"Think we took immersing ourselves in the local culture a tad too far?" Nancy Jane drawled as we peered out of the rattletrap, broken-down car with only a sliver of moon illuminating the vast darkness outside.

"Looks that way," I said. "Mainly I feel bad for Jim and Liz, having their wedding ruined by the disappearance of the groom's mother and aunt."

"Jim'll forgive you because you're his mama," Nancy Jane offered helpfully. "But Pat won't. He'll call us dumb Alabama hicks for getting ourselves into this mess."

"He's *not* doing my eulogy. No telling what he'll say."

Nancy Jane was more pragmatic. "He won't get the chance. They'll never find our bodies."

An isolated mountaintop on St. Thomas would've been preferable to the Mayo Clinic in Jacksonville, Florida, where we found ourselves on our first stop at Adventures in Cancer-Land (Nancy Jane's humor, not mine; I like to think I'm not quite that morbid). Although we always started out full of hope and good cheer, we rarely returned that way. Nancy Jane was so determinedly upbeat that it shamed me when each disappointment hit me so hard. So many times, I'd rave to her about a new clinic, how great they were and how much hope they'd offered, only to dissolve in helpless tears as soon as I got back to South Carolina. I knew it wasn't her I was trying to convince; it was me. Every time I returned home from one of the quests, I'd find Pat waiting for me, hoping to hear that we'd finally found the Wizard. He'd take one look at my face and hold out his arms. During those times, a shoulder to cry on was the only thing he or anyone else could offer.

Although Nancy Jane was willing to keep looking for the elusive wizard, she was less cooperative when it came to the other aspect of her well-being, nutrition. After my struggles with Pat, it was déjà vu. Every doctor we saw had stressed the importance of nutrition and set her up with a dietician. With her digestive system so compromised, it'd take a lot of trial and error to see what she could tolerate. The problem was, despite her dire situation, my sister was as resistant to healthy eating as my husband had been. Not being much of a cook, she was fine with fast foods or takeout.

But now, nutrition had literally become a matter of life and death. Processed food, I told her, was full of preservatives that she could no longer tolerate. Nancy Jane just groaned and rolled her eyes.

Over time the situation became even worse. Eventually, it wasn't my sister's resistance to healthy choices that caused the biggest problem. Because her weight loss and compromised digestion made nutrition impossible to ignore, she finally listened. But it's one thing not to *want* to eat a certain thing and altogether another not to be *able* to. Finding food that she could tolerate was an ongoing battle, one I never gave up on. Things had gone so well the first year that we weren't prepared for the decline in the second year. Nancy'd gone back to teaching, but it'd become more difficult and she'd reluctantly applied for disability. The only thing that kept her going was her faith and determination. She fought every day just to be able to live a normal life, something the healthy take for granted. Whenever I was with her, I came away with a different perspective on my petty gripes and complaints.

Pat was a great help in keeping Nancy Jane's spirits up. He'd call and sing some ridiculous song he'd make up to make her laugh. "Don't cry for me, Argentina," became "Don't cry for me, Alabama. The truth is, I never loved you. You lost to Auburn, you lost to Notre Dame; you'll never win another football game." He sang equally ridiculous songs about her ex-husband, as well as the principal at her school who was giving her a hard time. Instead of supporting a career teacher determined to return to teaching despite a major illness, Nancy Jane's principal seemed equally determined to force her to quit. I only saw my sister cry twice during her long battle, and the first came after a call from the principal.

A few days after school started, the principal called to express her fears that parents might complain about their kids having a sick teacher. Since Nancy Jane had been named Teacher of the Year more than once, the woman's concern was not only ludicrous, it was the worst kind of insult to throw at a dedicated professional. Nancy assured the principal that the minute her illness affected her teaching, she'd leave. Putting down the phone, she covered her face and tears rolled down her cheeks. Maybe she should just give up, she said. Beckie and I were visiting that day, and our reaction was fast and furious. The only thing that kept us from storming the principal's office was Nancy Jane's pleas not to make things worse.

When I told Pat what had happened, he called Nancy immediately. "If you need me to go to battle with your principal, just say the word," he told her. "I wrote the book on it." Nancy laughed, but Pat was dead serious. After hanging up, he asked me to contact my sister's teacher friends. He'd met them several times and declared them the sassiest bunch of good old girls he'd ever seen. "Nancy Jane won't tell me if she's harassed again," he said, "but those girls will. Tell them to call me if anything else happens."

From the first time they met, Nancy Jane had been a great source of story for Pat, the obsessive story collector. She had a self-deprecating wit that he appreciated, and he'd egg her on to tell even more tales of the myriad ways she'd embarrassed herself in all sorts of social situations. The story he loved best, though, was when *I'd* been the one embarrassed, not her. When Nancy Jane was four years old, I'd been charged with making her behave one Sunday during morning worship service at our church. Daddy was home sick, my sister Beckie was at a friend's, and Mother was in the choir. We had communion that Sunday, and Mother had forgotten to give me instructions on what to do with my little sister. Sure enough, the call to communion came and Nancy Jane tagged along with me to kneel at the altar. In the

Methodist church, children were supposed to stay in their pew. When the preacher got to me with the tray of tiny communion cups, Nancy Jane grabbed one before he could stop her. After slurping it down and smacking her lips, she stuck her tongue in to lick out all the grape juice. Because I glanced up to see if anyone had noticed, I missed the moment when she snatched a wafer from the tray in the preacher's other hand. When we got back to our pew, I saw to my horror that she still held the wafer. *Oh God*, I thought. *The body of Christ—my sister's holding the body of Christ in her grubby little hand.*

"Nancy Jane!" I whispered. "What are you doing with that?"

"I'm not gonna eat *paper*," she said loud enough for the whole church to hear. "What'd you think I am, a billy goat?" When the congregation tittered, Nancy laughed with them, and from the choir loft my mother gave me a you're-in-big-trouble-missy look. I not only got an earful when I got home, I also got a punishment Mother found even more fitting. Her missionary society took turns cleaning the church, and Mother made me do it in her place. Hopefully, she said, it'd give me time to think about the importance of showing proper reverence in a house of worship. All that, while the true culprit got off scot-free, the little imp.

The third year of Nancy Jane's illness brought so many setbacks with her health that I began to lose hope. Although she'd tried to start the school year, she'd simply been too weak; and true to her word, she took a medical leave of absence. I feared that giving up teaching would crush her, but again, I'd underestimated my sister's zest for life, and her determination to make whatever time she had left meaningful. Her willpower was strong as ever, and she remained active not only in church and community activities but also with her work as an advocate for other cancer victims. *If sheer determination can keep that girl alive*, I thought, *then she'll outlive us all.*

As the illness progressed, dietary concerns were still the main challenge Nancy Jane faced. The extreme blandness of her daily fare began to take a toll on her normally ebullient spirits. Because so much of what she ate couldn't be digested, she was always hungry. In truth, my sister was literally starving to death. Despite everyone's best efforts, she simply wasn't able to get enough nutrients through either diet or supplements. She was wasting away before our eyes, her weight less than ninety pounds. It was during this time, and a couple of years later with Pat's illness, that I became a fierce advocate of medical marijuana. It seems like the worst kind of sin that if my sister had lived in another state, her suffering could've been lessened. It's a slap in the face that something that could've helped her, or others like her, is denied—and not simply denied but something people are punished for. I can only assume that legislators who vote against relieving the pain of sick people have never watched anyone they love die. I'll go to my grave bitter at the injustice done to cancer victims by denying them a chance to try anything that might help.

The third October after Nancy's surgery, I took her to Louisville to see another wizard my research had turned up, who held the hope of a clinical trial. The Louisville doctor couldn't have been kinder or more compassionate, but he wasn't able to offer any miracles. Nancy Jane's cancer was too advanced for her to be eligible for the clinical trial. Looking at her chart, the doctor noted that her birthday was a couple of days away. "Get your sister to take you somewhere fun for your birthday," he told her with a forced note of gaiety. "Kick up your heels and do whatever you want for a change. You deserve it."

I adopted the same tone as we started the drive back home, though it took all the effort I could muster. "You heard the doctor," I said brightly. "I'll take you anywhere you want to go. Just name the place. New York? Miami? Las Vegas? We'll even go to Switzerland!" It was one of the places we'd been promising ourselves for years that we'd visit.

Gamely, Nancy played along. Her answer surprised and touched me, and I had to blink back tears to keep up the forced cheeriness. "There's only one place I really want to go," she said finally. "And we can do it on our way home. I want to go to the Atlanta zoo one more time to see the pandas." She laughed, sounding for a brief moment like her old self again. "Guess you could say I'm just dying to see those pandas."

Because she was too weak to walk around, I pushed my sister in a wheelchair and perched her in front of the panda exhibit. To our amazement, on a sunstruck late October day, the exhibit wasn't the least bit crowded, although normally people waited in long lines to catch a glimpse of the youngest of Lun Lun and Yang Yang's offspring, two-year-old Po. To our further delight, Po was in full view and cavorted around for almost an hour. For a suspended moment of time, Nancy Jane lost herself in the simple joy of watching the roly-poly little panda play. A group of schoolkids arrived, and Nancy motioned for me to wheel her out of the way so they could see better. We paused for a minute to witness the kids squeal at the sight of the panda cub, and I watched Nancy Jane watch them wistfully. I knew she was thinking of her own students that she'd had to give up. Her eyes shone bright with unshed tears when she motioned for me to push her out, and she waved goodbye to the happy horde of kids, who waved back enthusiastically.

"You up for one more thing, Tanna?" she asked, and I assured her that I was up for anything. Pointing, she directed me to a place farther back in the zoo where I'd never been. It'd been years since I'd gone to the zoo, and there was tons of new stuff. "The pandas were for me," Nancy Jane told me, "but this is a surprise for you."

I started to protest that it was her birthday, not mine, but decided to keep my mouth shut for once. She fretted about me having to push her, and I retorted that it was much-needed exercise for my lazy butt. When we got to the walk-through aviary, I stopped in my tracks and Nancy Jane grinned at my reaction. The aviary, a spacious, screened landscape of rainforest, was full of pastel-colored parakeets who flitted through the trees like winged flashes of light. We purchased a handful of birdseed-tipped sticks and entered expectantly. Suddenly both of us found ourselves laughing in sheer surprise as the parakeets descended on us. They perched on our shoulders, arms, and outstretched hands, and eagerly nibbled our proffered treats. It was a blessed moment of magic that I'll never forget, and I mouthed *Thank you* when I caught Nancy Jane's eye. Despite the deafening chatter of birds, the squeals and giggles of kids, and the constant swoosh of wings, my sister and I maintained a reverent silence as we exited the aviary and started our journey home. Neither of us was ready to break the spell.

~~~~~~

Christmas was on us before we knew it. After much conferring, the family decided to gather at Nancy's house the day after Christmas for our usual get-together. Her son, Will, having just completed a graduate degree and gotten his first job as a physical therapist, was the perfect one to be with his mother during the holidays. Our October trip to the zoo had been a foretaste of what was to come, and my sister'd been confined to a wheelchair ever since. She couldn't be left alone, so I planned to stay when Will returned to work. Pat was coming to help out too, after his visit with the girls in Atlanta.

Despite Nancy Jane's obvious decline, the Christmas get-together was a festive occasion, which she enjoyed without a smidgen of self-pity. Everyone had made an effort to be there. Jake had flown in from California, with Jim and Liz driving up from south Florida and Jason from Birmingham. Nancy Jane was a beloved aunt who never forgot anyone's birthday.

When the holidays were over and everyone went back to their regular routine, Nancy put me to work. With Ziploc bags, note-cards, and pen in hand, we spread out all her jewelry for her to decide who'd get what. It could've been a morbid task; instead we joked around as we always did. The uglier the jewelry, the more fun we had deciding who'd get it. Pat came down with a bad cold and had to postpone his visit, but he checked in. He asked his sister-in-law what she'd gotten him for Christmas, although he knew full well what the answer was. It'd become a running joke between them. She always gave him the tackiest Bama souvenir she could find, just to hear him groan and carry on about what godawful cheap relatives he had.

I planned to stay with my sister as long as she needed me, though I knew she'd balk. Nancy had pleaded with me to spend New Year's Eve with Pat but I refused, using his cold as an excuse. So she turned to the national championship football game, Alabama versus Notre Dame, as her trump card. She insisted I go home and watch it with Pat. Knowing I'd protest, she enlisted the help of her friends, and they worked out a schedule to stay with her while I was gone. I agreed to go home for a few days but told her to get used to it: I'd be coming back. I was the only one among the family and friends without a nine-to-five job, and, by God, I'd be back to stay with her whether she wanted me to or not. At the time, I was in the final edits of *Moonrise* and could work from her house as easily as mine.

I got home January third, exhausted but upbeat. I'd left Nancy Jane in good hands and high spirits. Her teacher friends came to her house with nachos, margaritas, and a movie, then piled on the sofa and floor to eat, drink, and be merry. I called her to say I'd gotten home fine, and that Pat was better and would be with me when I returned after the big game. The three of us would celebrate Bama's almost certain victory, I said cheerily. In the background I could hear her friends laughing and cutting up, so I cut my call short. My last words to her were "Glad to know that those rowdy friends of yours haven't settled down. Love you, and I'll check in tomorrow." I hung up smiling.

An old friend of my sister's, Jan, spent the night with her; at home in my own bed I slept soundly, cuddled up to my sweet husband on a cold winter night. Jan was as solid and reliable as they come. About noon the following day when Jan called me, her voice was even and composed. She hadn't been able to rouse Nancy Jane, she reported, so she'd phoned the hospice nurse. For an hour or so, I paced the floor and waited to hear what the nurse said. I was anxious but not fearful; after all, I'd talked to my sister just the night before, and she'd been fine. She'd been in good spirits so there was no reason for alarm, right?

As usual I was in denial, refusing to hear what I knew to be true. Nancy Jane was in a coma, the nurse said. By nightfall, she was gone. It was January 4, 2013, and freezing cold in Alabama.

～～～

I headed out early the next morning, after telling Pat that I'd get us a place to stay and let him know where, soon as I worked everything out. He'd been upset that I wouldn't let him drive me, but I made him see that we needed to travel in separate cars. As the executor of my sister's will, I'd have to stay afterward, and who knew for how long. I was on the road when my daughter-in-law, Liz, called. Efficient as ever, Liz had gone online and gotten everyone a place to stay. I told myself to remember that. In times of grief, someone has to do the practical things. We tend to forget that grieving families need more than condolences and casseroles.

The next day when Pat drove up to the VRBO house that Liz had arranged for us, I met him in the driveway, eager for his comforting presence. We held on to each other, then he went in to greet the family. My nephew came outside to fetch Pat's suitcase.

"Where are Uncle Pat's hanging clothes, Aunt Tanna?" Will asked me. When I stared at the empty trunk, I couldn't help but smile and shake my head. Big surprise—Pat hadn't brought anything to wear to the funeral. Nothing would've tickled Nancy Jane more.

CHAPTER 18

THE BEST-LAID PLANS OF MICE AND MEN

In the weeks following my sister's death, I turned my attention back to the final edits of *Moonrise*, which was scheduled for release in the early fall. Editing was a much-needed distraction from my crippling grief, and I threw myself into it. It could not have come at a better time. For the past few years I'd focused almost all my attention on the health of my husband and my sister, and in a way that couldn't have been healthy for me or them, either one. My nearest and dearest are quick to point out my tendency to obsess. My obsessiveness is a by-product of a decidedly unpleasant character trait that my father called being just plain bullheaded. Bulldoggish is a better description. My sister Beckie has a big fat bulldog who'll sink his teeth into a discarded sock and clamp down on it for dear life. You can drag him all over the house with it, but, by God, he won't let go. I can identify.

After Nancy Jane's death, I struggled to regain my equilibrium. Losing someone I loved so deeply had thrown everything in my life off-kilter, it seemed. For one thing, I'd lost the joy I once took not only in entertaining but also in planning and preparing meals. With my obsessiveness over food as fuel, food as enemy, food as a power to be reined in or conquered, I'd gotten off track and lost perspective. My appetite was poor, and for a while, I lost my appetite for life as well. Thankfully I'd finished the rewrites of *Moonrise* and was only editing; otherwise my heart wouldn't have been in writing either, something that had always carried me through dark times. It took some time before things leveled out and the Conroy household began to get back to normal (whatever that was).

Healthwise, Pat was doing better than I could've ever hoped for. He grew accustomed to our new lifestyle of exercise and healthier eating. Oh, he still cheated occasionally with the latter. He would be proud of himself for buying a power salad on his way home from exercising, but neglect to mention the chocolate-chip cookies he picked up as well. His daily routine of working out with Mina helped to counteract backsliding. On his own, Pat gave up alcohol completely. He told me he'd drunk enough in the past to last him a lifetime, and I didn't doubt it. Exercising, eating right, and forgoing booze, he lost weight and looked great. Always ruddy-faced, even his complexion cleared. His eyes sparkled and glowed with pride when folks commented on how well he looked. For the first time in years, he had a bounce to his step and energy to spare.

I'd been so focused on Pat and Nancy Jane that the next health scare to come along caught me off guard. This time, it was *me* who got blindsided. In the summer of 2013 the stress, grief, and worry of the past years caught up with me, and I got thrown for a loop. One thing I should've known by then: if we don't listen to our bodies, they have a way of getting our attention. And it's never pretty.

June came, and Pat stood his ground about Camp Fripp remaining on Fripp. No one argued with him; on the contrary, the grandkids preferred staying at the beach. "Imagine that," Pat said, glancing my way with a smug grin. I conceded that he'd been right but hoped he didn't get too full of himself for such a rarity. In our sixteen years together, the tally was a million or so for me, one for Conroy.

One miserably hot day in June, everybody was at the beach but me. I hadn't gone because I'd had one of those horrific commode-hugging nights we've all suffered through at one time or another, usually courtesy of a stomach virus (the puke bug, as the kids call it). That morning I still couldn't keep anything down, so I called Dr. Laffitte for some nausea meds. He insisted on admitting me to the hospital and running tests. For a couple of days I went through a battery of medical tests that would make a medieval torture chamber envious. After a diagnosis of diverticulitis, IBS, and a highly inflamed stomach—the usual suspects—I came home to life as usual. Or sort of. Things still weren't quite right, I knew, but I told myself I'd be back to normal in no time. As always, I knew better than my doctors. I could manage my own health, thank you very much. I'd dealt with the same issues all my life. The Princess and the Pea, Pat and I called my hypersensitive constitution. Dr. Laffitte took a wait-and-see stance, not quite as convinced. I was the worst kind of stubborn, know-it-all patient, but he was too gentlemanly to point that out.

For the rest of June and July our summer went on as planned, and I either felt okay or faked it well enough to fool everyone (including myself). Just as Pat had hoped, Camp Fripp had morphed into a different animal after our move into Beaufort, but it was still all-consuming. With the grandkids getting older and involved in their own activities, our families' visits became even more erratic and spread out. Even so, things were decidedly easier on me and Pat. For our family togetherness time, we scheduled communal lunches or dinners either at the Beaufort house or on Fripp. Late one afternoon Pat and I were gathering up the ingredients for a Lowcountry Boil to take out to Fripp. I shucked corn as he peeled shrimp when he turned to glare at me. "Hey! Why are we doing this? Didn't we move into town to get away from Camp Fripp?"

I asked how he'd spent his day. Hadn't he been writing without grandkids coming into his office to pester him? He conceded that he had indeed. "Well, then," I said. "Camp Fripp can come here, or we can go to them when we please. Which do you prefer?"

"I prefer we get the hell out of here," he retorted. "When do we go to Highlands?"

"I told you, in August after everyone leaves."

Pat groaned dramatically. "I was afraid you'd say that." Before turning his attention back to the shrimp, he narrowed his eyes to study me. "Helen Keller? You're okay, aren't you? You better *not* be holding out on me. Dr. Laffitte says that everything's fine now, right?"

"He did," I said, then added, "but he told me not to buy any green bananas."

My flippancy didn't amuse Pat, so I assured him that all was well. His concern for my well-being moved me, though, and I told him so. His response was "I just don't want anything to delay our departure." He dodged my swat with the dishtowel, grinning.

I too was anxious to get away from the brutal heat of a Low-country summer and could hardly wait until August, when we'd head for the hills. Because *Moonrise* is set in Highlands the launch would be there, a big, hoity-toity affair at the Old Edwards Inn.

I'd rented an isolated house by a waterfall, a perfect place for Pat to work and for me to prepare for my grueling tour schedule. Since Pat's upcoming book, *The Death of Santini*, wouldn't be released until late fall, his own travels were a few months away. And blessedly so, now that he'd started to map out a new novel and needed some alone time to write. That was our plan.

~~~~~

When the last of the kids were packing up to return to their respective homes, Pat decided to give his daughter Melissa his car and get a new one for himself. He was overdue, and Melissa was happy to have his hand-me-down. The grasshopper never traded in cars when he got ready for a change, he simply gave the old one away. Whoever was around at the time and in need of a car became the lucky recipient. It was a random gesture of generosity that amused me. He dispensed with his cars in the same way I might say, *You're cold? Here—take my coat. I need a new one anyway.* This time, though, there was a catch. Pat claimed he could only get a new car if *I'd* be the one to shop for it. His argument was, I'd finished my book but he was busy at work on a new one. Besides, he always got ripped off at car dealerships. I was a much better negotiator than he was, he added slyly.

Melissa and family took off for Philly in Pat's five-year-old car, and I went to the dealership and bought her dad another old-man Buick, exactly like the one he had. Or rather, as close to it as I could, considering they didn't make the exact car anymore. I'd wanted to upgrade him to a roomier model but decided not to take any chances. Pat didn't like change, and he knew how to work everything on the old car. The problem was, the things he knew how to work were now obsolete and had been replaced. I worried momentarily about the fancy bells and whistles on the new one, then told myself to chill out. Before Pat drove the car, I'd take him out for a demo. He'd do fine.

I had no way of knowing that I wouldn't get the chance. The day the car was delivered, Pat balked at taking it out for a lesson. "It'll keep," he said with a shrug. I warned him not to drive it until I showed him some of the new features, which were high-tech even for me. I didn't remind him of the real reason he refused to drive my Prius (which I'd nicknamed Miss Priss; Pat called it the Pious). He couldn't even crank it because the starter's so different. Without knowing how to drive his car or mine, he was trapped. Again, he shrugged me off when I pointed that out. He'd learn to drive the new car in a day or two, he assured me, if I'd quit bugging him about it. What could possibly happen during that time? Never tempt the gods like that, he'd say later.

The following day started out like any other. Now that everyone was gone, I spent most of the morning getting the house back in order. Then I planned to pack for Highlands. It'd be a couple of days before the rental would be ready for us, but we were determined to pull into the driveway as the previous tenants pulled out.

It was around lunchtime when I felt something was a little off. I didn't feel sick, just a tad peculiar. A friend called to ask me to lunch, but I explained about the packing and asked for a rain check after our return to Beaufort (which wouldn't be until early October, though I didn't tell her that). We said our goodbyes, and it occurred to me that I wasn't the least bit hungry. *Odd*, I thought; I'd had no appetite at breakfast either.

I shrugged it off and brought out the slow cooker for the pot roast I'd bought for Pat. Later I'd add onions, carrots, and brussels sprouts. It was one of Pat's favorite suppers and worked for me because I could eat the veggies and be just as happy as he was with his beloved beef. I smiled to myself as I wedged the big roast into the cooker, recalling how I'd used pot roast to blackmail Pat into eating leftovers. Alas, I'd told him, I couldn't find a roast small enough for only one meal, so guess he'd have to forgo having one of his favorite dishes. He gave in and said okay, okay, he'd eat leftovers if I'd quit harping about it. Afterward he was forced to admit that the roast was just as good—if not better—the second time around.

Later that afternoon I added the vegetables to the roast and had started toward my office when Bernie Schein let himself in the front door. By then I was definitely feeling puny but still couldn't pinpoint anything specific, just an overall malaise. I feared I might be coming down with something but wouldn't let myself go there. Getting a bug before a book tour ranks high on the list of a writer's worst nightmares. Book tours are grueling enough in the best of health. Not only that, cancel a couple of gigs after all the advertising and planning involved, and you aren't likely to get invited back. The launch in Highlands was a ticketed luncheon, with a waiting list. I simply couldn't afford to be sick.

"Hey, baby!" Bernie called out when he closed the door behind him. "Pat upstairs?" Ever since Pat gave up his bad habits, he and Bernie had developed a new routine. Or rather, they'd traded one bad habit for another. Instead of cocktails at five, Bernie and Pat now smoked cigars, drank Diet Cokes, and shot the bull on our little porch off the master bedroom upstairs.

"You're early, Berns," I said. "Pat's still in his office working. Don't bother him, okay?"

"Wouldn't dream of it," Bernie assured me. He then meandered to the kitchen as he always did when he came over. Every day, he'd go through any pots, pans, or foil-covered containers I'd left out or had simmering on the stove. Bernie had no qualms about dipping a spoon into our supper, or cutting himself a slice of cake or pie, even if I'd planned it for a dinner party and tried to hide it from him. He poked around at the roast, tasted the broth, and nodded in satisfaction, then got a Diet Coke out of the fridge. "Boy, have I got some good gossip," he told me with a wicked grin. "You gonna join us on the porch?"

Maybe a little later, I told him, after I checked my email. I waved goodbye and went to my office without telling him that I felt a sudden need to lie down, and sooner rather than later. Just as I opened my door I heard Bernie yelling, "Hey, Pat! Get your fat ass out here—I know you're only pretending to work. Man, I've got some gossip you ain't gonna believe. And about some of your favorite Beaufortonians, too."

Ordinarily I would've chided Bernie for pestering Pat after I'd said clearly that he was at work. Over time, Bernie and I had developed a sort of brother-sister relationship, and neither of us had any qualms about going back and forth at the other. But it was always in fondness, and with good humor. I adored Bernie and had from the first time I met him. Once you got to know Bernie Schein, you found that his zaniness hid a great big heart and a sweet, gentle nature. If I'd fussed at him for bothering Pat at work, Bernie would've been remorseful and apologetic. But I wasn't up to it, so I hurried into my office. Pat might bitch and moan about being interrupted, but he'd gladly put his work aside for cigars and gossip.

In my office the daybed's under the double windows that face Battery Creek. My computer's there, making a bright and sunny spot to curl up in and work. But work was the last thing on my mind. Feeling more peculiar by the minute, I hurried over to the bed, moved my laptop stand off, and plopped down. Gone were my plans to check email. I was suddenly too dizzy and nauseated to stand upright. My mind went back to the Lyme disease I'd gotten soon after moving to Fripp. *Oh, great,* I thought. *All I need now, a recurrence.* It was always a fear with Lyme's. When I got the diagnosis, Pat had been upset with me because I'd ignored the angry red circles around the infected tick bite and had only asked him to take me to the doctor when I became almost delirious with fever.

But nothing like that would happen again, I told myself. Pat and Bernie were right upstairs, and all I had to do was holler if I needed them. For now, I needed a nap. If I could sleep for a few minutes, maybe the dizziness would go away and I'd wake up feeling back to normal.

The way the house is laid out, my office windows are almost directly underneath the upstairs porch. Stretched out on my daybed, I could hear Pat and Bernie upstairs laughing and talking, and I saw cigar smoke floating in the air. It was always like that during their cigar hour. On milder days when my windows were open, I'd end up closing them to block out the smoke and noise. Not only did Bernie have the biggest mouth in town, both he and Pat were about half deaf. As the hour wore on they got louder and louder.

If the conversation was especially good, cigar hour would stretch into two or three. I couldn't count the times I'd been in the kitchen when Bernie came running downstairs in a panic. "Martha's going to kill me," he'd yell as he banged out the front door. "I left our supper cooking." His wife, Martha, worked long hours as a psychologist and put him in charge of the evening meal. Most of the time Bernie either forgot to fix supper altogether or forgot that he'd started it and let it burn.

I tried to nap but closing my eyes made me dizzier, as if the daybed were a raft caught on the tidal surge of Battery Creek. I took several deep breaths to calm myself down. I'd had a couple of episodes of vertigo, several years apart, but vertigo was another thing no writer wanted to deal with before a book tour. A bug, Lyme disease, vertigo—none of those would be a problem if I had to miss the book tour because my publicist had put so much work into it that she'd kill me.

I caught motion outside and watched as our next-door neighbor, Liz, came to stand in the yard outside my window. She put her hands on her hips and glared up at Bernie and Pat on the porch above her. It was another song and dance that I'd seen often. Pat had recently hired Liz, a nutritionist, to help with his diet. Talk about a thankless job! Poor Liz came around with her handouts and readings on nutrition, which Pat pretended to peruse. As soon as Liz left, he tossed them. Sometimes she'd ask to see one of them to underscore some point, and Pat would pretend to look for it, knowing full well he'd thrown it away. But he soon found that Liz didn't take any bull from him.

"What are you drinking, Pat?" Liz demanded from her spot in the yard.

"Not vodka," I heard him tell her. "Come see for yourself if you don't believe me."

"It better not be Diet Coke either" was her response. "That stuff's as bad for you as liquor."

"It's unsweetened iced tea," the liar said. He hid his Diet Cokes from her, just like he used to hide his liquor bottles. I never really knew if Liz was fooled by him or not, but I stayed out of it.

"Come up and gossip with us, Lizzie-poo," Bernie called down.

Liz shook her head. "Gotta take the kids to soccer. I was just checking to make sure no one's drinking over here."

"Nobody but Cassandra," Bernie told her with his high-pitched hyena laugh. "Usually she's passed out drunk by now."

Waving them off with a groan, Liz left, and their laughter and yakking picked up again. Whatever Bernie's gossip was, it must have been good. I tried to get up to go to the bathroom and the room spun. It hit me that I was too dizzy to even sit up. Falling back on the bed, I could no longer deny that something was very wrong. My heart had started to race, really fast, but even worse, I began to sweat profusely. I never, ever sweated. When I had trouble catching my breath and began to gasp for air, that settled it. *Oh my God*, I thought—*I'm having a heart attack!*

That had to be it. As a woman in my late sixties, my age was a prime risk factor. A few years ago one of the SSGs had died of a heart attack, and another had survived one on a plane a year or so later. *What was it like?* the rest of us asked, and she'd described dizziness, nausea, pounding heart, and sweat. Lots of it. She had no history, was lean and fit—a health nut, actually—and was shocked to learn (from a doctor who happened to be on board her flight) that she was indeed having a heart attack that called for an emergency landing.

My problem was, I had a history. Nothing serious, just a congenital valve thing, but I'd be a fool to ignore the signs. Dr. Laffitte would still be in his office, and Pat could drive me over for a quick EKG. Ignoring the vertigo that even the slightest movement brought on, I banged on the window to see if I could get Pat's attention. When that didn't work, I managed to raise the window enough to call out to him. He and Bernie were making so much racket that my cries for help didn't get any farther than the windowsill. I fell back on the bed.

I tried to talk myself down, to take deep breaths and not move again until the dizziness went away, but nothing worked. Matter of fact, things were quickly going from bad to worse. When it hit me that I was actually struggling to remain conscious, I tried not to panic but could feel myself fading out. There was nothing to do but call 911 while I still could. Otherwise I was going to die, and poor Pat and Bernie would come downstairs to find my cold and lifeless body. I fumbled for my cell phone and made the call, then fell back on the bed. "Do not move," the dispatcher ordered. "Is your front door unlocked? Tell me exactly where you are in the house and they'll find you. I'll stay on the phone with you until they arrive. Then hang up, and the paramedics will take over."

The ambulance got there in a matter of minutes, a shrill siren alerting me to its arrival. By that time I was only half conscious, but I was aware that four muscle-bound men had suddenly filled my room, dragging their equipment behind them. They hooked me up to oxygen and started an EKG. The EMT's eyebrows shot up when he took my blood pressure. "Off the charts," he told the others, and I tried to tell him it wasn't possible. My blood pressure had always been perfect. I heard another one say that the EKG didn't look good either. Before moving me to a stretcher, one of the young men leaned over to ask, "Ma'am? Are you here alone?"

In a small voice, I managed to tell him that my husband was upstairs. I heard one of them clomping upstairs and calling out, but I don't remember a lot after that. They wheeled me out, loaded me up, and off went the ambulance to Beaufort Memorial, siren screaming. If I'd been in any condition to think about it, I would've assumed that Pat was right behind us. Our car situation never entered my mind, but neither did much of anything else. Everything that happened for the next few hours is a merciful blur.

The comedy of errors that followed I would only hear about

later. After I was taken away, Pat and Bernie's visit went on as it often did, much longer than either of them planned. Neither of them heard the EMT come upstairs or call out to see if anyone was there. We can only assume that the guy stuck his head in the bedroom door and failed to see them on the porch, which is not easily visible from the door. No doubt he'd figured it was more important to get a possible heart patient to the hospital quickly than to prolong a search for the husband. We'll never know for sure. We don't even know how long after I left that Bernie and Pat kept up their chatter and smoking, until Bernie suddenly remembered that he'd left something in the oven again.

The sun had set when Pat finally came downstairs. He turned on the kitchen lights, spotted the slow cooker with the roast in it, and decided I wouldn't mind if he didn't wait for me to have dinner. After all, I'd made the roast for him, right? It was time for the news, and occasionally we'd eat on a tray to watch the news or a ball game. It was not a practice I encouraged, as Pat well knew, but one he was more than happy with. He took advantage of the fact that I was working late (so he'd tell me later) to fix himself a tray and enjoy the news while feasting on roast beef, onions, carrots, and brussels sprouts. One of his favorite dinners, and his dear wife had fixed it just for him.

Not believing his good luck at getting to watch both the local and national news with as many refills as he wanted and no one to complain about his overindulgence, Pat enjoyed himself immensely. (At least he managed to look guilty when he related the story to me.) Afterward he took his plate in and cleared up his mess. Noticing that the living room had gotten dark, he turned on the lamps. *Strange*, he thought. His wife was a quiet little thing, but this was unusual even for her.

Finally, my prolonged absence struck him as odd. He called out to me, and when there was no answer, he went to look in my office. It was dark and deserted. Puzzled, he looked in the other rooms in the house, which were all dark and empty. Then he checked to see if my car was outside. Yep, in the garage, where it belonged. He thought I must've gone home with Bernie. I'd never done so before, but where else could I be?

Bernie answered Pat's call in disbelief. "Of course she's not here, you idiot!" Bernie yelled into the phone. "She's probably gone to the store or something." Hearing that my car was in the garage, Bernie grew alarmed. "I'll be right over," he said.

When Bernie arrived, he and Pat searched the house again and Bernie had to agree that I definitely wasn't there. They got flashlights and went outside in a gently falling rain, where they walked all around the dark yard looking and calling out for me. Neither of our neighbors were home, but they tried their yards anyway. Pat told me that they saved the worst for last.

"We've got to go to the dock and look in the water," Bernie told him.

Pat panicked. "No! She couldn't be in the water," he argued, but Bernie disagreed.

"It's finally happened, Pat," Bernie added helpfully. "Your biggest fear. Living with you has driven a woman to suicide."

By the time they shone their lights on the water, Pat was convinced that's what had happened. He was a terrible husband, as his previous wives had often pointed out. Bernie was right. Life with him had driven me to jump in the river rather than face another day.

When their search for a body floating in the water came up empty, Bernie declared there was nothing else to do. He was calling 911, he said, and Pat panicked again. "But—what can they do?" he asked Bernie fearfully.

"Pat, listen to me," Bernie said and shook his arm to calm him down. "She obviously ain't here. Something has happened to her, and we've *got* to get help."

To their surprise and relief, the dispatcher told Mr. Conroy that his wife had been taken to Beaufort Memorial a few hours earlier. At first, Pat argued. "But that's not possible," he said. "I've been here the whole time." Checking her records, the dispatcher confirmed the details and told them that the EMT had searched for the husband but not located him. Then she said the scary words, possible heart attack.

Pat hung up quickly, and he and Bernie rushed to his car. They'd gone a few blocks when Bernie yelled that the headlights weren't on. "I don't know how to turn them on," Pat yelled back. "I've never driven this car before."

"Then turn around and we'll get mine," Bernie said, stating the obvious.

"No way in hell," Pat said. "I've told you before I'm never riding with you again. You scare the shit out of me."

"Better scared than dead," Bernie retorted, but Pat didn't relent. Instead he started pushing any buttons he thought might work the headlights. Bernie joined in, hitting the things that Pat missed. After a few blocks, they'd pushed enough buttons that they finally got the headlights on. But just before they got to the hospital, the gentle rain turned into a downpour.

Pat didn't know how to turn on the windshield wipers. "You're a bigger idiot than I thought," Bernie cried, and Pat told him to shut the hell up. "We're going to die," Bernie yelled, "because you're too stupid to even drive a car."

After some wrangling, Pat figured out how to roll down his window, so he stuck his head out to see the road. When they pulled up to the covered entrance of the emergency room, Bernie ordered Pat to let him out while he parked the car. "The hell I will," Pat told him. "It's *my* wife in there."

"Yeah, but you're already soaking wet," Bernie said reasonably. "No point in me getting wet too. You park and I'll meet you in the waiting room."

Like a dummy, Pat did as Bernie suggested, and Bernie hopped out of the car and ran into the lobby of the ER. Soaked and shivering after finally finding a parking space, Pat rushed into the waiting room and ran to the security desk. "My wife!" he gasped. "Possible heart attack. Mrs. Conroy?"

The guard looked over the list then eyed Pat suspiciously. "Ah . . . Mr. Conroy's already with his wife. Sorry, sir, but family only."

"But *I'm* her husband," Pat yelled, then it hit him. "Little bitty Jewish guy claiming to be me?" he asked the guard. "I'm gonna kill the son of a bitch!"

About that time, Bernie stuck his head out the door. "Hey, Pat! Don't worry, she's okay. Some kind of arrhythmia going on, they said, but not a heart attack. You need to calm down or you'll have one yourself."

When Pat turned to the guard and yelled, "I've got to see my wife," Bernie walked out and put an arm around his shoulder.

"She needs her rest," Bernie, the model of serenity and compassion, said. "They're going to keep her for a couple of days, so why don't you go on home? Trust me, I've got everything under control here." The security guard demanded to know what was going on. Even though he'd forgotten to bring his wallet, Pat managed to convince the guard that he was the one who needed to be with me, not Bernie.

"Look at your records," Pat told the guard. "My wife is Mrs. *Conroy*, a very Irish name, right? Now, which one of us looks like a Conroy, me or this grinning jackass here?"

Bursting into my room, Pat stood there soaking wet and utterly befuddled. "My God!" he said. "I thought you'd drowned."

"Looks like you're the one who's been in Battery Creek," I said.

Pulling up a chair and grabbing my hand, he said, "You're not going to believe what happened."

"Is it about you and Bernie?" I asked, and Pat acknowledged that it was.

"Then I believe it," I told him with a sigh.

~~~~

Somehow I got back on my feet for the *Moonrise* tour, though barely. It had been a harrowing time. In the hospital I'd gotten a rather scary diagnosis and was sent to the medical university in Charleston for further treatment. Only a few days before the big launch in Highlands, I had a successful surgical procedure that made everything right again. Through it all, I put on a cheerful, optimistic facade but it took a lot of effort. Pat's barely concealed concern had been unsettling. *If Mister Cool was worried*, I thought, *then the rumors of my demise might not be exaggerated.*

It would've made me feel better if my husband had made jokes or teased me about my predicament, his usual way of showing concern, instead of hovering, bringing flowers and plants, and leaving sweet notes while I slept. Because it was impossible for Pat to stay serious for long, the love letters he wrote me always contained at least one sardonic or humorous twist. He might sign off as "one of your many, many husbands," or declare himself a mere substitute for my ex. A note from that time did neither: *The house you provided me is a constant joy and your company I don't want to live without. It astonishes me and makes me proud that I finally made such a fabulous choice in finding you to share the rest of my life with.*

It was only a day before the launch of my book when we finally got ourselves to Highlands. At first Pat was as solicitous as he'd been during my illness, and my apprehension flared up again. Had the doctor told him something they were keeping from me? *Be extra nice to her during the short time she has left*, maybe? I need not have worried. I'd soon see that the old Pat was back.

My friend Floozie and her husband, Tom, came to the launch party, driving over from their cabin in the scenic north Georgia mountains. After the luncheon and signing, Pat was helping me gather up my stuff when we spotted Flooz and Tom waiting for us. Delighted to see them, I called out, "Get your butts over here and give me a hug."

As we were hugging and greeting one another, I told them how much it meant to me that they'd come. They'd had their tickets for months, Tom said, but had been concerned that I might have to postpone. "Concerned! That's putting it mildly," Flooz interrupted. "I've been sick with worry. And K.B.'s so blamed stoic I was afraid she wasn't telling us everything."

"Helen Keller not telling everything?" Pat said dryly. "You know better than that."

"Yeah, right," Flooz said. Squinting her eyes, she studied me from head to toe. "But seeing you, I feel much better. I'll let the SSGs know that we can take you off our prayer list." She then turned to Pat and put her arm through his. "Bless your heart, Pat! I worried about you almost as much as I worried about K.B. I'm sure you were scared to death."

Pat nodded his head sadly. "Sure was. Matter of fact, I was so worried that I joined Christian Mingle. You know, in case she didn't make it."

Flooz and Tom tried not to laugh but couldn't help themselves. Flooz rolled her eyes and looked at me sympathetically. "Lord, K.B. How do you put up with this man?"

"Hopefully I'm earning a lot of stars in my crown," I said.

Flooz gave Pat a playful sock on the arm. "I swear, you're the craziest person I've ever met."

"You want crazy?" I said. "Let me introduce you to his friend Bernie. He makes Pat seem sane."

"I can't even imagine that," Flooz said.

I refrained from telling her that I didn't have to imagine it—I'd lived through it. But barely.

~~~~

After we'd said our goodbyes to Tom and Flooz and returned to the peaceful little house by the waterfall, Pat and I sat snuggled together on the porch, too tired to move. The hypnotic sound of the waterfall lulled us into silence and a sense of serenity I hadn't felt in a long time. I put my head on Pat's shoulder and he gave me a squeeze. "I forgot to tell you this morning, but you looked great today," he said softly. "I should remember to tell you that more often."

"I need to hear it. Did I tell you what my friend Joan told me last time I saw her?" When Pat shook his head, I told him the story that'd been at the back of my mind that morning when I dressed and primped for the luncheon. "She said I really needed to get my eyes fixed before the tour so I wouldn't look so tired."

"Fixed? What does that mean?"

I leaned toward him and tugged at my droopy eyelids with my fingertips. "You know. *Fixed*."

Pat scoffed. "Bullshit. I don't want you to look different. Can't we just let ourselves grow old?"

I told him not to worry, I was much too chicken to have anything done. All my droopy places would just have to stay droopy. "Anyway, it's too late," I added. "Ready or not, the tour starts tomorrow. First stop, Decatur, Georgia."

The Decatur Book Festival is held on Labor Day weekend, which seemed an odd time to me. Other writers had expressed similar reservations, but when it grew to be one of the biggest festivals in the country, the skeptics were silenced. The following day at the Downtown Decatur Marriott, I entered my room with a sigh of relief. It'd been touch-and-go for a while, but I'd made it! I sent up a prayer of gratitude to the good Lord and a special word of thanks to St. Raphael, the patron saint of the sick. In my suitcase I found a note from Pat and sat on the bed to read it. Before opening it, I sent up another prayer of gratitude for such a dear and supportive husband. Then I read what he'd written:

Dearest Sandra, I'm proud of the books you've written since you got your room with a view. Your talent as a writer is exalting to me and makes me proud to be along for the ride. Now, if you'll just do something about your f-g eyes. I adore you, Pat.

CHAPTER 19

BIRTHDAY BASH

A couple of years before his milestone seventieth birthday in 2015, Pat had plunged himself into a project that would bring him a lot of personal satisfaction despite the tremendous drain on his time. He'd always been in great demand not only as a speaker but also as a mentor to fledgling writers. Advising and encouraging new writers as well as writing blurbs or introductions for their books gave him immense gratification. Becoming editor-at-large for the University of South Carolina Press's fiction imprint, Story River Books, enabled Pat to do all those things, and he threw himself into it wholeheartedly. The excitement that came over him after reading a promising manuscript was contagious. He'd come out of his office waving a manuscript, his face aglow. "You've *got* to read this," he'd say to me, "and tell me if it's as good as I think it is."

The manuscripts almost always came with stories of the writer's disappointing foray into mainstream publishing. Many readers assumed that Story River only published first-time novelists, but that was far from true. Pat would read a wonderful manuscript by a published author who'd done quite well with previous books and be shocked to learn the book had been turned down by his or her New York publisher. So-called literary fiction doesn't always hit the bestseller list. It's a two-edged sword, of course; publishers have to sell books to survive. More and more, university presses are taking up the slack. During Pat's tenure and under the guidance of USC's gifted publisher, Jonathan Haupt, Story River published about twenty novels, many of them winners of prestigious literary awards.

It amused me to read in the paper that Pat was working for the USC Press. I held out my hand to him, palm up. "Hand it over, buddy," I teased. "Lemme see that big paycheck." His work for USC was strictly pro bono, and his payment came from the pride he took in his writers' successes. He sometimes groused that Jonathan was demanding too much of him, and that he'd never get his own book finished. Unfortunately, Pat had a valid point—there's just so much time in the day. As much as he loved doing it, his work with Story River threatened to consume him. I tried to help him find some middle ground.

"You've launched Story River," I argued. "You don't have to go to every signing with every author. They're doing well—let them fly on their own." Although he agreed with me, easing up proved difficult for him. He was fully invested and determined to see it through.

The thing was, Pat had started writing a new book that I'd read with great excitement. As much as I applauded Story River, I was ready for a new Conroy novel, and even more so after reading what he was working on. Some of my favorite stories Pat told me had to do with the two years he spent teaching at Beaufort High before going to Daufuskie. "You've *got* to write about that, Babezee," I'd said for years, and he'd promised to do so one day.

That day had finally come, and Pat had started the book about his first teaching job. Fresh out of college, he'd taught with three other young male teachers, and the stories of their bumbling through their first year in the classroom were both hilarious and heartwarming. After Pat wrote a chapter, he'd give it to me to proofread before sending it to Margaret, a local journalist who did some of his research. Margaret also offered to type his manuscripts because no one else but me could read his handwriting. I'd learned to decipher it over the years, but it'd gotten decidedly worse with age. (Like everything else does!) Often I had to consult with the man himself. Pat would scowl at his handwriting and was apt to say, with a dismissive wave of his hand, "Aw, hell I don't know what I meant. Just take the whole damn sentence out."

Each time he gave me a section to proof before giving it to Margaret, I'd get more excited. As the plot took form, I simply couldn't wait for the next installment. It was that good. One thing for sure, the new book was destined to be one of his best. I saw it as *The Lords of Discipline* meets *The Water Is Wide*, with elements of the Vietnam subplot in *The Prince of Tides*.

But Pat's schedule was stretched too thin for him to do much writing, no matter how I pleaded with him to make it top priority. And it was about to get even busier. One day he came in from having lunch with Jonathan Haupt, looking dour. "Jonathan's got this wild idea, and he's enlisted Bonnie Hargrove's help with it. But I've told him to forget it."

"What on earth?" I asked warily. Bonnie was director of USCB's Performing Arts Center, so I figured it'd be something big.

"They want to do a festival in Beaufort this October to celebrate my seventieth birthday."

"Pat! What a lovely idea."

He looked at me as though I'd suggested he take a plunge in Battery Creek butt naked. "You don't even acknowledge your birthday, Helen Keller. How'd you like it if we had your seventieth and invited the whole blamed town?"

"Too late," I replied. "I had mine last year. You married an older woman, remember?"

"Yeah and I'll be divorcing one if you encourage them in this."

"*Pat!* It'll be great."

Scowling, he stalked out of the room. Over his shoulder, he called out, "I ain't doing it. And you can tell Haupt to kiss my ass."

~~~~~~

Jonathan and Bonnie were brave souls. Ignoring Pat's protests, they went ahead with plans for a literary festival / birthday celebration as close to Pat's actual birthday, October 26, 2015, as they could schedule it. When various writer friends accepted their invitations to speak, along with some of the actors who'd been in Pat's movies, excitement began to build. Tickets went on sale and events quickly sold out. Pat kept up his grumbling, but I knew him well. Grousing aside, I could tell that the idea was growing on him. He'd never admit it, but it was obvious that he was even a little bit pleased.

One thing about the celebration filled Pat with both anxiety and excitement. He'd invited Susannah, his estranged daughter, to come, and she'd accepted. In August, Pat had seen her for the first time in sixteen years. We'd heard through a friend in Atlanta that Susannah was working in administration at Emory Cancer Center and had moved out of her mother's house. Megan did some sleuthing and found the address, so the next time Pat and I were in Atlanta, he left a note on her door. He'd left too many at her mother's Atlanta house to have any expectations, but this time Susannah responded, and they'd met for lunch near Emory. Afterward Pat returned to the waterfall house in Highlands to report to me and our friends Janis and Wendel Owens, who were visiting at the time, that the lunch hadn't gone well. It had been awkward and tense, but later Pat and Susannah began to correspond by email. And she agreed to come to Beaufort for the birthday celebration.

I reminded Pat that the love of a parent and child wasn't something that was easily destroyed, no matter what. "Huh! Could've fooled me," he said, but his pleasure in reuniting with his daughter was stronger than his anxiety.

The seventieth birthday celebration turned out to be a marvelous and unforgettable event, made even more so in the wake of what followed. The festivities went on for three days, with everyone in high spirits and enjoying themselves, even Pat. All the family who could make the trip were there, and for the first time in too many years, all four of Pat's daughters were together again. His sister Kathy made Pat a quilt from scraps of his old shirts that I'd supplied her. Embroidered with significant dates, the quilt squares were set off by the background of Citadel blue. When the quilt was unveiled in the lobby of the Performing Arts Center, Pat's jaw dropped. Kathy's gift was an amazing work of art, but more than that, an intense labor of love. "It's all too much," Pat said, and his voice broke. Among the special guests were Michael O'Keefe, who'd played a young Pat in *The Great Santini* movie, and David Keith, who played Will McLean, the character based on Pat in *The Lords of Discipline*.

The grand finale of the weekend came on the last evening when Pat got up to say a few words in closing, totally unplanned. Although he kept choking up, he gave a moving talk expressing gratitude for his readers and his career, which he said was beyond anything he could've ever imagined. For those few moments of his impromptu speech, the wry, sardonic Pat Conroy who'd always had trouble letting down his guard bared his soul. The prolonged standing ovation that followed almost brought Pat to his knees. I've never seen him so touched, or so humbled. It was later, after the heartbreak of the next few months, that it hit me like a punch in the gut. With the final words he gave at his birthday celebration, Pat had delivered his own eulogy.

Pat could never stay sappy for long, however. The old sarcastic guy who was more familiar to us quickly resurfaced. Offstage, Jonathan told Pat that the event had been such a success, he and Bonnie had decided to have a Pat Conroy Literary Festival the following year as well. Pat gave Jonathan his cold blue stare. "Over my dead body," he said.

I recoiled when Jonathan repeated the story to me the following year as they began to plan the next festival. "Oh God, Jonathan!" I said, wincing. "That's horrible. Please don't repeat it to anyone." Jonathan looked at me with a knowing smile. "Now tell me the truth," he said. "Who would laugh at the macabre irony more than Pat?" I had to admit he was right. One of the things I miss most about Pat is his dark, cringeworthy humor.

After the birthday celebration, Pat kept up his busy schedule of appearing at book signings for Story River authors. He looked so exhausted, however, that I talked him into going to Highlands earlier than we'd planned for our Thanksgiving visit. Getting away from Beaufort and the constant demands on his time was the only way he could get any rest. We couldn't stay as long as I would've liked because he had a trip after Thanksgiving, another event with one of his Story River authors. But both of us needed a break.

In Highlands, it became obvious that Pat was more exhausted than I'd realized. I persuaded him to use the time to catch up on his reading, the only thing that really relaxed him. He spent a lot of time in the recliner with a heating pad on his back. Because lower back pain was nothing new, I wasn't surprised that it'd flared up again, considering how hectic his schedule had been.

Neither did it surprise me that he wasn't as interested in the dishes we'd prepared for the Thanksgiving feast. I'm more of a traditionalist, happy to stick with turkey and the usual fixings, while Pat liked searching for new recipes. I'd packed some foodie magazines with his other reading material. And he half-heartedly flipped through a couple of mags then asked what I'd planned. The Mannings, our hosts that year, were doing the turkey while the rest of us would bring whatever side dishes we chose.

"Unless you come up with something more exciting," I told him, "then it'll be cornbread dressing, cranberry sauce, and sweet 'taters."

Pat put the magazines aside. "Let's stick with that, then."

I leaned over and nuzzled his neck. "You're still worn out, aren't you, Babezee?"

"Yeah," he said with a frown. "But I should be working on my book instead of lazing around reading."

"No, you should not!" I gave him a little shake. "You need to sit right here and do nothing. Don't worry about helping me with the food. I can do it with my eyes closed."

He thought a minute before saying, "It's all yours."

I got up to start supper without any alarm at Pat's unusual lethargy. Nor did I have any when he asked for soup instead of the steak he'd requested. "It's more of a soup night," he said casually, as he built a fire. We were staying at a friend's house, a wonderfully serene place with a native-stone fireplace and stunning mountain views. Although it was freezing-arse cold, we bundled up and went to the screen porch to watch the sun sink into the mountaintops. Later we sat in front of a crackling fire to eat vegetarian chili with homemade bread and Amish butter. Warm, cozy, and content, we agreed that life was good.

Things got even better at the Thanksgiving dinner, held at the Mannings' spectacular home high atop Kettle Rock Mountain. Pat was his usual jovial self, talking and joking with Jim Landon, George Lanier, and Claude Sullivan; hugging on and enjoying the company of their lovely wives and daughters. (After using the whole gang as characters in *Moonrise*, I was grateful they were still speaking to me.) I noted, and not for the first time, that Pat was particularly at ease with our Highlands friends. He loved each of them individually and as a congenial group when we got together. For whatever reason, he not only socialized more in Highlands but also seemed to enjoy himself more. At most social gatherings, I was trained to be on the lookout for the restless signals that he was ready to leave. That Thanksgiving, any niggling worries I had at the back of my mind about Pat's exhaustion dissipated, and we stayed late.

The feeling of well-being carried me through the rest of our time in the mountains. The weekend after Thanksgiving we spent watching football games on TV, always one of our favorite things to do. Rivalry weekend for the college teams, and we planned our time—and meals—accordingly. The big game for me was Auburn-Alabama, which Pat loved to tease me about. "Every year I pray that Bama wins," he'd tell folks with that impish twinkle in his eyes. "My bride goes into mourning if her team loses." My retort was always the same: "Fortunately that's a rare occurrence." To celebrate Bama's victory, I made Pat's favorite pumpkin pie to top off our turkey sandwiches. Later when I looked back on that time, I'd remember pumpkin pie as the last food Pat really enjoyed.

We left Highlands to go our separate ways, Pat to Florida for his next gig and me back to South Carolina. I'd gotten exasperated with Pat before I left, but my argument had fallen on deaf ears. He'd made up his mind to drive straight to Pensacola instead of breaking up the ten-hour trip by staying overnight on the way. Even I, who have no history of back problems, would be stiff and sore after such a long drive, I argued. He had *no* business doing anything to make his back worse. But would Mr. Stubborn listen to me? He called after his arrival late that night to say I'd been right. His back was killing him, and he should've heeded my advice. I felt no vindication, just regret that he'd been too stubborn to listen to reason. For the past week I'd witnessed his grimaces of pain with every movement, his jaw clenched in agony. I'd tried every rub the Highlands drugstore had to offer, but nothing helped to ease the pain.

Pat's trip, to help promote our friend Katherine Clark's latest book, began in Pensacola, expanded into the Mobile area, then culminated in New Orleans. When he called to suggest that I fly down to meet him in New Orleans, I hesitated. It was the first week of December, always one of our busiest months, and I had dozens of things to do. Pat knew the perfect bait to lure me, though. A friend of Katherine's had offered us their guesthouse in the Garden District. As icing on the cake, we could add a visit with our close friend Janis Owens on the way home. The Owenses had moved to Virginia but would be at their house in Florida then. Janis'd been on the program at the birthday celebration, but it'd been such a madhouse we'd spent very little time together. Pat knew how much I missed her, so with those enticements, I flew into New Orleans on Thursday.

That Friday night, after the event at the Garden District Bookstore, Pat and I joined Katherine; her husband, Brandon; and their extended New Orleans family for dinner at a restaurant that only the locals knew about. Since my arrival Pat and I had pretty much done our own thing. That day he'd spoken at a private school, so I'd taken a trolley to the museum. I'd been enthralled with the museum's unique sculpture garden and had shared my photos with Pat as we dressed for the evening. Instead of politely scrolling through them, he'd taken his time with each photo, asked questions, and seemed genuinely interested. Next time we came to New Orleans, he told me, he had to see the sculptures for himself. Next time, we said.

At dinner Pat and I were seated at opposite ends of the long table, where everyone seemed to be enjoying themselves, comparing orders, chatting away. After dinner we were saying our good-byes when Katherine pulled me aside and handed me Pat's dinner in a carryout box. "I'm worried about him," she said, her brow furrowed. She went on to tell me that he had not eaten one bite. "To tell you the truth, he hasn't been himself this whole time," she added. There was no mistaking the concern in her voice. She said that even Brandon, a doctor who usually kept his opinions to himself unless dealing with a patient, had commented on Pat's lethargy and lack of appetite. I tried to assure her that it was just exhaustion, but her frown deepened. "I hope that's all it is," she murmured ominously.

The next day proved that Katherine's concern was far from unwarranted. Her in-laws were hosting a shindig during the SEC championship game, Bama versus the Florida Gators. Another way Pat had lured me down, by saying we'd get to watch the big game together. I'd replied that he knew the way to my heart.

I was getting dressed for the party, jeans and a Bama shirt, when Pat told me to go without him. "No way!" I protested. "We're watching it together." I studied him carefully before saying, "You're not well, are you?" Pat shook his head and admitted he hadn't felt well lately, despite his assurances to the contrary. He asked me to call Katherine with our regrets, and to tell her we'd get together for breakfast the next day, on our way out of town.

He called off the breakfast get-together as well, which worried Katherine even more. "I *knew* he wasn't well," she cried, "but he wouldn't admit it." He and I left early to drive to Janis's place near Gainesville, another long trip. When Pat asked me to drive, I knew he had to be feeling bad. Janis confirmed my fears when she, like Katherine, pulled me aside to ask about him. "Pat looks like pure-dee shit," she whispered. "What on earth happened? He was doing so well! Everybody at the birthday party talked about how great he looked."

I sighed and rubbed my face wearily. "I kept thinking he was just tired from all the birthday stuff, but it's been over a month now."

"Think you can get him to the doctor when y'all get home?" Janis asked.

"If I have to hog-tie him," I promised.

Christmas was on us before we knew it. It hadn't been necessary to hog-tie Pat to get him to see Dr. Laffitte; he'd gone willingly, another worrisome sign. His appetite was off, and as my grandmother used to say, he felt peaked (pronounced pee-ked in the South). Whenever he went to Mina for exercise, she sent him home early with some vitamin concoction or tonic she'd prepared to perk him up. Dr. Laffitte took a more wait-and-see attitude, unable to find anything wrong. A blood test revealed nothing except inflammation. Most likely the reason for the back pain, Dr. Laffitte said. Because Pat had done so well for so long, none of us considered anything more serious.

Despite everything—including my protests—Pat stuck to his busy schedule. He dragged himself to a couple of events in nearby Bluffton and Savannah to help promote another Story River author, our friend Ellen Malphrus. Many of the authors had become close friends of ours, so Pat felt he was helping out friends as well as promoting books. He never would have put it this way, but the truth was, if he appeared with a newly published author, a crowd would turn up. Otherwise, it was hit or miss.

Bernie continued to come over for his late afternoon visits, and he and Pat took to the porch with their cigars regardless of the cold December breeze off Battery Creek. One afternoon Bernie forgot Pat had a signing, and I was the one to join him on the porch, bundled in a shawl and waving off the smoke from his cigar. "How do you think Pat's doing, Berns?" I asked.

"As big an asshole as ever," Bernie said. "Why?"

"Be serious for once in your life. You know he hasn't been feeling well."

Bernie was immediately suspicious. "That son of a bitch better *not* be drinking again."

At first I shook my head, then confessed that it'd crossed my mind too. It was hard to believe that Pat would jeopardize his newly restored health, though. He'd talked openly about it for the past couple of years—how getting off booze, eating healthy, and exercising regularly made him feel better than he'd ever felt. He'd sworn never to go back to his destructive old habits, and I'd seen no evidence of his backsliding.

Bernie thought it over. "Naw, I'd know if he had." He studied me for a long minute. "You'd know too, wouldn't you?"

I nodded. "Yeah, you're right. He's definitely not drinking. It's got to be something else."

"He's probably just tired, don't you think?"

I was eager to agree, even though tiredness was beginning to wear thin as an explanation. Bernie puffed on his cigar then said, "The idiot needs to stop catering to everybody by running to all those damn Story River signings. I'll remind him that I'm his only real friend. From now on, he needs to cater only to *me*."

Christmas Day with the Conroy clan was a merry occasion where we exchanged gifts before our communal feast. Whether the dinner was held at our house or Mike and Jean's place on Fripp, Pat usually did something with lamb; Mike and Jean brought a honey-baked ham; and I fixed turkey-and-dressing. Everyone contributed a side and dessert and departed as stuffed as the turkey.

That Christmas, however, Pat made a face when I asked how he planned to cook the lamb. "Don't think I will this year," he said, not meeting my eye. "Nobody really likes it but me. And I haven't had much of an appetite lately."

He repeated that at Mike and Jean's Christmas table after picking at his plate, then left early while I stayed to help with cleanup. Again, I got bombarded with questions: Is Pat okay? Is he going to Atlanta to see the girls? To Birmingham to see your family? I could only shake my head helplessly. I had no answers.

Pat didn't like the idea of canceling his visit with the girls in Atlanta, but he finally decided he had no choice. His back pain hadn't eased up despite heat, rubs, ice packs, and tons of Aleve. Though I was reluctant to leave him, he insisted I stick with my plans to see both families. While I was gone doing all that "family crap," he said, he'd double-lock the door and stay in bed the whole time. When I returned, he'd be back to his old frisky self, just wait and see.

⁓

Two thousand sixteen arrived on schedule, as those things are apt to do. Pat and I celebrated the new year, then a Bama victory in another national championship game. It would turn out to be our last happy moments together. I returned from the Christmas visits expecting (or more truthfully, hoping and praying) to find Pat rested and refreshed, as bright-eyed and robust as he'd been before the first of December and the downward spiral. He faked it when I first got home, peppering me with questions about the family as a way of deflecting mine about his health. He even insisted he felt better.

But it was no longer possible to pretend that things were as they used to be. He still had no appetite, and his pain had worsened. A note from that time, evidently written while I slept, verified how bad things were, and would be the last note I ever got from him. He wrote,

Dearest Sandra—been up all night throwing up. Overall, exhausted. I emailed Mina. Please let me just sleep until I'm a recognizable human again. I love you to pieces, your beloved second husband.

Pat not only agreed to see Dr. Laffitte again without putting up an argument, he let me drive him. Because he'd only allowed me to drive him to the doctor's in emergency situations in the past, I took that as a bad sign. When the receptionist beckoned Mr. Conroy into the exam room, I didn't ask if I could come along, I just went. Normally Pat would've given me a you've-got-to-be-kidding look if I'd even tried such a thing.

After the exam, Dr. Laffitte's furrowed brow told me more than I wanted to know. Suspecting pancreatitis because of the back pain and increased inflammation, he acted quickly to set up an appointment with Dr. Stewart, the GI specialist who'd patched up Pat's internal bleeding four years before, and to order a CAT scan. I went from being concerned to scared. I could hardly wait to get home to google pancreatitis. It sounded awful, and I prayed that wasn't what Pat had. Looking back, I can't understand why I didn't consider a more dire diagnosis. Instead I reverted to my old habit of denial and refused to see what was becoming more and more apparent. Something was terribly wrong.

Dr. Stewart was far from reassuring. One thing Pat revealed

during the examination startled me. Yeah, he'd lost a great deal of weight since his last visit, a routine checkup a year ago. "Even my fingers are getting skinny, Doc," Pat said with a grin, holding up his left hand. "My wedding ring won't stay on."

"Likely story," I said to the doctor with a wink, but fear clawed at my throat. Sudden weight loss was a red flag that I'd seen with both my mother and my sister. But I wouldn't let myself go there.

Pat nodded his head toward me. "My wife's been working her butt off cooking everything she can think of to get me to eat, but I can't hold anything down. Been living on smoothies."

A sharp knock at the door interrupted Dr. Stewart's questions. The results of the CAT scan had arrived, and I could tell by the doctor's face that it wasn't good. A shadow, or a mass, presented in the pancreas area, Dr. Stewart announced, then left abruptly to set up an appointment at the hospital for an MRI. After he left, Pat looked at me with a frown. "Remind me what a pancreas is?"

Pat wouldn't make it to the MRI appointment scheduled for the following week. Things went downhill fast. I had the sensation of being swept away, down a tumbling whitewater river, desperate to grab anything I could hold on to. But the current was too swift. It seemed that the more I struggled against it, the farther downstream it carried me.

Only a couple of days after the visit to the GI doctor, Pat got so sick and was in such severe pain that I called Dr. Laffitte in a panic. "Don't try to bring him here," said the doctor. "As soon as I finish with my last patient, I'll stop by and see what's going on."

I've never been so glad to see anyone. Dr. Laffitte arrived and quickly took charge. Pat'd been throwing up for two days, and the back pain had become excruciating. Even so, he pulled himself up in bed to greet his doctor in his usual playful manner. "Hey, Doc! It's beginning to look like you're not going to have Conroy to kick around anymore."

Dr. Laffitte, cool and composed as ever, was the perfect counterpart to Pat's ongoing blarney. But I could tell by his expression, or lack thereof, that things weren't good. "Let's get you to the hospital," he said before he calmly called for an ambulance. My face must've revealed my fears because he explained that we'd get him in quicker by ambulance. The hospital was always swamped in the winter, flu season, and Pat was in no condition to sit in the waiting room.

I nodded, forcing myself to stay calm too, and watched as Dr. Laffitte closed up his little black bag. *So doctors still carry those things*, I thought inanely. In previous scary situations I'd noted how the mind tends to flit from one mundane thing to another as a diversion from the crisis. My thoughts had become a jumble, a mess of tangled fears, bouncing off one wall before slamming into another.

In the emergency room, the MRI confirmed what the GI doctor had seen—a suspicious mass on the pancreas—and Dr. Laffitte began to search for an ambulance driver willing to transport Pat to Atlanta through a snowstorm heading that way, where he'd have a liver biopsy at Emory Hospital. Because Susannah worked at the cancer center, she'd been able to set her father up with a specialist there. I ran home frantically to grab our suitcases, praying the ambulance wouldn't be gone before I could get back. I planned on following it to Atlanta, snowstorm or not. At home I fixed Pat a smoothie, had a meltdown and fell on the floor crying, then pulled myself together to return to the hospital.

My fear of Pat being carted away before I got back almost came true. The cubicle in the emergency room was empty and a harried nurse waved me toward a back door. "They took him but the ambulance might still be here," she said. I ran outside cursing myself for not checking my phone; Mina had left me panicky messages to hurry.

I caught the ambulance just before they lifted Pat's stretcher into the back. In freezing weather, he was in a short-sleeved T-shirt, sweatpants, and bedroom shoes. Mina was on one side of him and Bernie the other, with Dr. Laffitte supervising. The ambulance driver and a woman EMT were doing the lifting. Despite Mina's English being quite good for someone who'd only been in the country a few years, she was having trouble communicating with the driver. Over his arguments, she kept trying to wrap her hoodie around Pat, although Mina wore a size four at best, and Pat an XXL. To add to the confusion, Bernie was joking as usual, helpfully telling the ambulance workers they'd never lift Pat's lard ass that far up. Maybe they should just tie the stretcher to the back and pull him along behind it.

"Wait!" I yelled. Everyone stopped when they saw me, but only for a moment. Since they'd already hoisted the stretcher, the EMTs completed their task and hopped in to secure their passenger for the journey. They wouldn't let me get in, so I crawled up far enough to grab hold of Pat's hand. He was surprisingly cheerful. "Hey, kiddo," he said with a weary smile. "Fun day, huh?"

"I feel really good about you going to Emory," I told him

in my fake-cheery voice. "They're the best. You'll be in good hands."

The ambulance driver hustled me out of the way and said gruffly that they had to get on the road. No time for lingering, so Bernie, Mina, and I told Pat goodbye as they closed the ambulance. "I'll be right behind you," I cried out just before the doors closed in my face. Pat waved bravely and blew kisses, but he looked so helpless with his strapping body on that little-bitty stretcher that my heart broke all over again.

I was standing behind the ambulance swallowing back tears when both the ambulance driver and Dr. Laffitte accosted me. "Listen to me, Mrs. Conroy," the driver growled. "That storm's coming in fast. No way in hell you're following me."

Dr. Laffitte took my arm. "You're not driving to Atlanta tonight, Cassandra. That's ridiculous. Wait and see how tomorrow looks. The snow will be gone in a day or two."

A *day* or two? Didn't they understand that I couldn't stand not being with Pat now? No one should go through something like this alone. When I started protesting, the driver walked off in disgust and cranked up the ambulance. It was Dr. Laffitte who had the final word. He knew exactly how to get through to me. "The last thing Pat needs is to worry about you." He was kind but firm. "He made me promise I wouldn't let you go tonight."

I was defeated, of course. There was nothing to do but get in my car, the suitcases and Pat's forgotten thermos in back, and drive home. Bernie and Mina pleaded to come with me but I wanted to be alone. If I wouldn't let him come with me, Bernie said, he'd send Martha as soon as she got home from work. I shook my head. I couldn't talk to anybody right then, not even my nearest and dearest. By the time I got home they'd spread the word, and friends and family called to ask what they could do. There were kind, heartwarming offers of drinks, supper, or just being with me. I told everyone I was going straight to bed. What I didn't tell them was, I'd be setting my alarm for six. I intended to drive to Atlanta come hell, high water, or a blizzard.

I awoke in the icy darkness of early morning, surprised to see that Pat had left a message on my phone only a couple minutes before. I called back immediately without listening to his message. When the phone in his room rang and rang with no answer, I figured they'd taken him out for more tests.

Listening to Pat's lengthy message, I was flooded with relief at how upbeat he sounded. Chuckling, he told me about the ambulance ride from hell. The attendants were great but the ambulance lacked toilet facilities. They stopped once to relieve themselves, but Pat was stuck with a bedpan as they sped along at top speed. "You can imagine how that turned out," he said. In spite of the horrific weather, the five-hour drive took them less than four. Just outside of Atlanta, the snowstorm hit hard, and the roads to the hospital were closed. That's when he found out that the crew had never been to Atlanta—they'd just moved to Beaufort from Michigan. Fortunately, Pat knew the area and was able to help them navigate through the backstreets.

They finally made it, and he got settled in a room a little after midnight. One of the nurses was a hoot, he told me. When she asked if he needed anything, Pat said yeah, a double martini extra dry. "Uh-huh. I'll bet that kind of shit has gotten you in trouble all your life," she retorted, which tickled him good. His final words to me were what I expected: "Now listen to me for once in your life. Do not even think about coming over here today. The roads are closed and you can't anyway, but I know how stubborn you are. I'm fine and they're taking good care of me. You hear me? Do *not* try to drive to Atlanta today."

His words of warning were wasted on me, as he knew they'd be. I was dressed and out the door before the sun came up. On the drive I played his message again, smiling at the story of the ambulance ride and the night nurse with a sassy comeback for his smart mouth. I had no way of knowing it'd be the last voice message I'd ever have from him. A year later an update wiped it out, and like the Rubaiyat's moving finger, no amount of tears or pleas to my cell provider could bring it back.

~~~~~~

I arrived midmorning to find Pat in good spirits and cutting up with the nurses. I had the utmost sympathy for any of them who had to put up with him. For pure aggravation, he'd pretend they were killing him whenever they drew blood and holler like a stuck pig. In response to how he was feeling, his eye-rolling answer was always the same: Oh, great. Just great. Having the time of his life. And heaven help the ones who asked if he needed anything. Why, yes, thank you. He'd take a double martini. Put it on his supper tray next to the caviar and filet mignon.

When Susannah came by for visits, Pat's face lit up. I couldn't imagine what it was like for her to see him so changed; when she'd seen him at the birthday bash just two and a half months before, he'd looked so well. Would the capricious god of chance deny them an opportunity to become reacquainted? The terrible irony of their reconciliation followed by his illness couldn't be lost on either of them. She'd returned to him after all the years apart; now it seemed that fate would snatch him away.

Susannah had pulled some strings and gotten her dad into a spacious room, with the unbelievable luxury of a pullout sofa for me to sleep on. When I'd stayed with Nancy Jane after her surgery, I'd made do with a plastic bench. (In Pat's hospital stays to come, I'd learn to sleep on even worse.) At Emory everything was top-notch. The nurses quickly caught on to Pat's teasing and gave it right back to him. He became a favorite patient, and it wasn't unusual for a nurse or doctor to pay him a visit after their shift, pulling up a chair and telling him their stories. When he was released five days later, the staff gathered around to hug him goodbye, and many of them wiped away tears.

The downside of Pat's time at Emory was the false sense of security and well-being I came away with. Why, he'd be fine, just fine! Even if the liver biopsy revealed cancer, the worst-case scenario, he could beat it, I knew. Pancreatic cancer was no match for Pat Conroy. Didn't his jovial manner and upbeat spirits prove that? A positive attitude was everything. And if he had one, by God, then so could I. Together, we'd get him through this. I ignored the taunting voice in my head that reminded me how well that had gone in the past. I'd said the same about both the Great Santini and Nancy Jane.

A few days after we returned home, the last week of January, the call from Emory came with the diagnosis of pancreatic cancer. By then, Pat had gotten so much worse that the confirmation was hardly necessary. His Emory doctors had made it clear that the biopsy would confirm what they already knew. They were straightforward and answered our questions without hedging. The palliative care staff was amazing, and I thanked God for all the new approaches to dealing with terminal patients. Things had changed in the three years since my sister's death when palliative care simply meant hospice at the end. Even so, I prayed that Pat wouldn't ask for a prognosis because I sure as hell wasn't about to. Neither of us did. As long as it wasn't put into words, we had hope. And one thing I came to believe during that time: false hope is better than no hope at all.

CHAPTER 20

DARK DAYS

As soon as we came home from the week at Emory, I began working on plans for treatment, making calls and filling out paperwork. At that stage of the illness, treatment was aimed at symptom relief, not a cure. We'd been impressed by the excellent care at Emory and could've returned there, but MD Anderson in Houston was a more obvious choice for us. My oldest son and his family had recently moved to Houston, where Jim would be heading up one of Anderson's new research clinics. If Pat went there, I'd have not only somewhere to stay but also insider help finding my way around. But getting a very sick patient there proved too much of a challenge. Pat was simply not able to make the trip. In a matter of mere days, he'd gone from joking around with nurses and visitors in his hospital room to barely being able to sit up. We had no choice but to stay as close to home as possible.

A new branch of MD Anderson was under construction in Jacksonville, Florida, which was a couple of hours closer than

Emory. Some of the medical offices had literally just opened, so off we went. Megan flew in from California to help me take her dad, with Jessica and Melissa planning to join us later if he had to stay. I don't know what I would've done if Megan hadn't been with me on the drive to Florida. Just that morning, a new phase of the illness caught us off guard. Pat had fallen and became extremely disoriented afterward. During the drive he started talking out of his head and didn't know where he was or who was in the car with him. Before Megan and I went into full-panic mode, he quieted down, and we made it without further incident.

Although Pat seemed okay once we got to the oncologist's office, the doctor took one look at him, then at the results of the blood tests, and admitted him to the hospital. Again, we would spend another week in yet another hospital. Pat had to be stabilized before receiving any kind of treatment, we were told. Although I had no idea what was going on—stabilized how?—there was nothing to do but accept it.

The trip to Jacksonville began a pattern that would be repeated throughout the month of February. It was unbelievable how fast the illness was progressing. If we chose to remain at Anderson for treatment, we were told before Pat's release, we should plan on relocating for the duration. No traveling back and forth in his condition. When I asked about MUSC in Charleston as an alternative, the team sprang into action. I'd looked into MUSC when I ruled out Houston, but to no avail. No one could tell me when anyone could see us, so I'd given up. The Jacksonville doctors got Pat in only a couple of days after our return to Beaufort, which reinforced the truth of that old adage: it's not what you know but who.

While in Jacksonville, another top-notch hospital with a wonderful palliative care team, Pat had a new nerve-block procedure to help ease the lower back pain. Although it didn't work for him, at least it offered hope of relief. His downward spiral had been so rapid that he wasn't yet on strong pain relievers; that would come next. Megan and I were foolishly optimistic when Pat was released and we started the drive back to Beaufort. Although there hadn't been any more episodes of disorientation, Jacksonville was still in the rearview mirror when it happened again. Pat insisted we were driving the wrong way before it hit him what was going on. "I'm talking nuts again, aren't I?" he asked in a voice of despair. I pulled over so Megan could retrieve the medicine they'd given us. Something about an imbalance of liver enzymes caused it, I explained to Pat. Later Megan and I would marvel at our willful ignorance. Our giddy relief that the disorientation wasn't caused by a brain metastasis masked the dreadful reality of the true cause, liver failure.

The same scenario played out again at MUSC, where Pat was admitted to the hospital as soon as the oncologist came in with his test results. His doctor turned out to be a lovely British woman who could match Pat's wry humor, though she'd have little opportunity during the two weeks he was under her care. Neither would any of us. As his condition worsened, Pat seemed to slip more and more between this world and the next. What little hope I'd clung to would soon be snatched away. It was obvious that he'd gotten much worse when I'd brought him to Charleston, yet I was shocked when his doctor told me that she hadn't expected him to live through his first night there. I honestly had no idea he was that near death. Only a couple of weeks ago he'd been laughing and cutting up with his visitors at Emory! For the disease to have progressed so rapidly didn't seem possible, too much for me to take in.

A strange thing happened the first night in the MUSC hospital that threw me for another loop. I got up from my makeshift recliner-bed in the corner of the room to make my way to the bathroom. Pat didn't stir when I paused to check on him. He was so out of it that I feared he might be slipping into a coma. But after I left the bathroom and tried to slip back to my perch without disturbing him, he stopped me in a loud, clear voice. "Did you hear that?"

I went over to whisper that it was just me, returning from the bathroom, but his eyes were fixed on a point beyond me. "Do you hear them singing?" he said, and his face lit up with something I can only describe as pure joy. When the singing stopped (or so I imagined), Pat grabbed my arm with such a strong grip that I sank down beside him. "Sweetheart?" His eyes, now perfectly focused, held mine and he said, "You know what? I killed myself yesterday."

I swallowed, hard, and managed to say, "It must've felt like that . . ." but he interrupted me with a shake of his head. "No. You don't understand. I did—I killed myself." Before I could stop myself, I fell on his shoulder, sobbing. I'd been so determined not to cry. He held me for a long time before saying, "It's okay. I did it and everything's okay now. You don't need to worry anymore. Go back to bed and I'll see you in the morning."

I never knew what to make of that strange conversation, and it took me a long time before I was able to share it with anyone. I can only assume it was his way of saying that he'd accepted his fate and had killed off the part of him that was still earthbound. The King family tells the story of my grandmother's final words, and I've heard similar stories from others. My grandmother had been in a deep coma for several days. Just before she died, she opened her eyes and focused on something beyond everyone else's line of vision. Her face aglow, she said in a strong, clear voice: "I can see the other side, and it's so beautiful." She smiled, closed her eyes, and passed over to it.

Only a couple of days later a visit from Bernie would break my heart even more. Plenty of visitors came and went, family and friends, staying briefly because Pat was so sick. He mostly slept, and I had the distinct feeling he was partly here and partly in the other world. Bernie paced the visitors' lounge, waiting for word that Pat could see him. Finally Bernie came in to say goodbye, even though Pat slept on. I'd almost reached the door to give them some time alone when Bernie lost it. He fell across Pat's bed and wept. "Pat, you can't leave me! I don't have anyone else to talk to. You're my only friend in Beaufort. Everybody else hates my guts."

His crying woke Pat, and Bernie quickly pulled himself together, forcing a smile. Like me, he didn't want Pat to witness him falling apart. I stepped outside the room but could hear them speaking softly to each other. In a few minutes the door flew open and Bernie came out, pale and trembling. Without a word to me, he fell against the wall and wept with the kind of grief that's painful to witness. I went over to help him make his way back to the waiting room, and he apologized for being such a baby. I told him to shut up. Walking down the hall and holding each other up like two very old people, we made our stumbling, silent way to the waiting room.

The next morning I'd just come out of the bathroom when Pat suddenly sat up in bed and swung his legs over the side. "Where are my shoes?" he demanded. Unlike the day before, he was wide awake and completely lucid.

"Whoa!" I rushed over to stop him from pulling himself up by the IV stand. "Where do you think you're going?" I cried.

"To Beaufort," Pat said. "I've got to see Bernie. Bernie needs me. He doesn't have anybody to talk to."

━━∿∿━━

Pat would live for two more weeks. After one round of chemo, then another trip to the ER in Beaufort, he was taken back to the MUSC Intensive Care Unit by helicopter, where once again he surprised everyone by reviving. "He has nine lives," Pat's brother Jim remarked, and I said, sighing, "Yeah, but the problem is, he's in his tenth one."

Even though his condition was much more dire, Pat appeared more lucid than he'd been during his stay the week before. He slept a lot but was aware of his surroundings, even chatting a bit with the staff. Not being allowed to stay overnight in the ICU, I made my weary way to Anne Siddons's house late every night. It was one of the most forlorn journeys I've ever made. I walked through the darkened, empty lobby toward the deserted parking garage, with my footsteps the only sound disturbing the eerie stillness.

On the second day, the girls arrived and Pat called them in to say his goodbyes. I don't know how they endured the deathbed scene, or his final words to them. I'm ashamed to say that I chickened out and never told him goodbye. Even worse, I wouldn't let him say it to me. I knew it was wrong of me—I'd read the palliative care literature. But I simply couldn't. At one point Pat said something that both infuriated me and broke my heart. Out of the blue he turned to look at me and said, "You'll get married again."

I shook my head in a fury. "No. I won't." When he asked if it was that bad, I gave him a watery smile. "No, you idiot," I said. "It was that good."

When Pat asked me to write down what he wanted for his services, I took notes without looking up so he couldn't see how much it hurt. I held myself together until he made me promise to finish the book I'd started. Working on the book would help me more than anything, he said. When I nodded, unable to speak or meet his eyes, he didn't push it. Instead he reached out to take my hand.

"We've had a good life together," he said. Then his grip on my hand tightened and he added, "I just wish it could've been longer." I lay down beside him, IV tubes and all, and stayed next to him until he fell asleep. I couldn't say what I longed to: *Please don't leave me.* I might not have been able to tell him goodbye, but the other directive in my palliative care reading I took to heart. Don't make it harder on the dying patient than it already is. Let them go.

On the fifth day of intensive care, his oncologist called the family together to say they had done all they could and were sending him home.

At the Beaufort house, my office had been transformed into a hospice room in preparation. Pat's sister Kathy, along with Maggie Schein and her husband, Jonathan, had it set up when we arrived—Pat by ambulance, me following in the car. Initially I'd balked at using my office because, strangely enough, Pat had asked me not to put him there. It was when we first returned from Emory, and he walked through the whole house as though seeing it for the last time. In my office he stood a few minutes, hands on hips, and looked around. "This is such a great room," he said, and I agreed. Then he caught me by surprise. "Don't put me here, if it comes to that. You won't be able to come back in without seeing me."

He walked out before I could ask what on earth he meant— don't put him there? He had his own writing room; why would I put him in mine? Only when hospice care was being arranged did it hit me what he'd been trying to say.

My office was where he had to be, though, even if it meant going against his wishes. It was the only room in the house where a hospital bed could be set up to look out over Battery Creek and the marshes Pat loved. For the man who wrote so powerfully of the place he'd claimed as his own, that scene had to be the last he would see. In his own words from *The Prince of Tides*, the Low-country was his anchorage. It would be his final port of call.

Friends and family arrived to help, often filling the house. They took over so all I had to do was be with Pat. I couldn't have managed without them, or the efficient and excellent Friends of Carolina hospice team. People came by and left food; some of them I only heard about later. I don't remember anything I ate during that time but will never forget the offerings left for a gathering of grieving souls. It reminded me again of the importance of reaching out to friends in need. We never forget the kindnesses offered during those times.

On our first night home, I knew who I wanted with me. Janis Owens had said to call when I needed her. I'd longed for her solid, comforting presence but didn't want to ask her to drive several hours from Virginia for what might be a vigil of several weeks (or so I foolishly thought). My son Jason came in from Birmingham and caught me with my face buried in my hands. "Mom, can I do anything for you?" he asked when he knelt beside me.

I could only think of one thing. "Janis," I said without raising my head. "I want Janis." My son left the room so abruptly I assumed that my grief had upset him, but he returned with my phone and said, "Do you need me to call her?" I shook my head and took the phone, knowing the only thing I had to say was "Come." In addition to being a strong earth-mother type, Janis is a former Pentecostal with prayers capable of soaring all the way to the heavens. After she arrived Janis rarely moved from Pat's bedside, hands folded and head bent in prayer.

Once Pat was situated in my office, I moved in with him (thankfully the daybed hadn't been taken out) and turned over the master bedroom to the girls. Pat's brother Tim arrived to stay, and other family members and friends came in and out sporadically. All of us settled in for the long haul, not knowing it'd only be a three-day vigil. In the spirit of the deathbed scenes in *Beach Music*, we read poetry to Pat. Or rather, the poets among us did: Tim and our friend Ellen Malphrus, reading from Pat's vast poetry collection of his favorites—Dickey, Auden, Millay, Wordsworth, Eliot. Pat remained unresponsive but I knew he was still with us.

Pat's former classmates Warley and Scott sang him The Citadel fight song. Jason played the guitar and all of us sang gospels, "In the Sweet Bye and Bye," "Will the Circle Be Unbroken," "Unclouded Day." My son the preacher's kid knew every hymn in the book, and I think we sang them all.

As painful as the ordeal was, the poignant camaraderie among those of us in the sickroom I can only think of as *holy*. Every dark moment seemed to be infused with a celestial light of love. On the first night, three black-robed priests appeared to perform the last rites, and the house filled with the bittersweet aroma of incense. It was an incredibly moving ceremony, a powerful ritual in a house of sorrow and death. Eyelids fluttering, Pat would be with us for a fleeting moment, then gone again, drifting in and out. Although he was barely conscious, we never doubted that he heard us.

Our vigil wasn't without its Conroyesque moments. The second night when Pat's daughters fixed dinner, they roasted almonds for a salad. The almonds scorched, and those of us in the sickroom smelled them before we heard the yelps from the girls. I stuck my head out to see what was going on, then reported back that all was well. Several minutes later, we still smelled scorched almonds—even stronger—and I left my post by Pat's side to tell the kitchen crew to turn on the exhaust. Oddly enough, outside the sickroom the scorched smell was gone. As I came back in, something caught my eye. Foolishly, I'd draped a washcloth over a small lamp to soften the light for the poetry readings earlier. I stood blinking at the smoke coming from the washcloth, unable to take in what was happening until the washcloth burst into flames. Letting out a screech, I grabbed the fiery washcloth and ran to the bathroom to extinguish it. With oxygen in use, it's a miracle that the whole house wasn't blown to kingdom come.

Pat's old buddy John Warley had a couple more mishaps. Driving in to take his place at the vigil, he found the driveway full of cars and pulled into a spot in front of the house where the ground was covered in ivy. The ivy masked the water meter, which Warley ran over. Suddenly water spewed sky-high, a geyser in our front yard. Fortunately a neighbor was nearby and came over, wrench in hand, to avert further disaster.

Warley looked shaky when he came into the sickroom. With a weary sigh, he plopped down on my daybed and told us, "Hey, y'all aren't going to believe what just happened." Before he could say another word, my bed fell in with a loud crash. None of us knew whether to laugh or cry. Warley sat on the floor with his legs sticking up, the only time I've ever seen him at a loss for words. Hearing the racket, Jason came running in and sized up the situation. He helped a stunned Warley to his feet then set about repairing the bed. I put my head in my hands and groaned.

The prevailing tragicomedy was the septic system. The mischievous gods of mishap decided that almost being blown up, having our water system wiped out, and my bed caving in weren't quite enough. Right after everyone arrived, our septic tank backed up. Trying desperately to avert more chaos, Jason and Tim attempted to fix it but to no avail. Finally we had to call in the experts. (The slogan on their truck read: YOUR NUMBER TWO IS OUR NUMBER ONE.) Watching them dig up our yard with their backhoes, Tim Conroy, with the same dark humor his brother had, turned to the sickroom to say, "Oh, God Almighty, y'all. I bet the neighbors think we're going to bury him in the backyard!"

Those of us in the sickroom stared at him in stunned silence. Then someone broke. It started with a giggle, and before any of us could stop ourselves, we were hooting and hollering, bent double with laughter. It was too much.

~~~~~

Early the morning of March fourth, Janis, Tim, Jason, and Jessica sought me out in the sickroom with a strange tale. They'd barely slept, I knew, because I'd heard them in and out of the room throughout the night. Because Tim'd taken over the job of dispensing the pain meds, he set his alarm to get up every few hours. I usually woke when he came into the room, but I would turn my head away. It was too painful to witness, one brother trying to ease the suffering of another. Sometimes the others would wander into the darkened room as well, Jason, Jessica, or Megan, to see if Pat was fitful. A labor of love, but it was taking its toll. All of them were wan and bleary-eyed, especially Tim. Hoping they'd get some rest, I'd insisted the night before on bringing in a nurse. It was the nurse they wanted to tell me about.

Jason had been appointed spokesman. Coffee cups in hand, the five of us sat around the hospital bed where Pat slept, oblivious to our whisperings. "Mom?" Jason asked. "Where'd you get the night nurse?"

"Lord, I don't know. Hospice called someone for me, seems like." The truth was, the details of the previous evening were hazy at best. Pat's old friend Father Mike Jones had come to pray with us. I couldn't even recall everyone who'd been there. After Father Mike left, I remembered lying down beside Pat and talking to him about the afterlife, and recalled that Megan sat on the floor with tears streaming down her face. It'd been late when I'd finally raised my head to focus on the others and saw how weary they looked. Had I left the room then to call the night nurse? Surely not, at that time of night. I must've asked the hospice worker earlier if she would send someone.

"Is the nurse still here?" I inquired. Her image was also hazy to me, but I pictured a slim, sweet-faced black woman dressed in a white uniform. Something else came to me: every time she came in the room to check on Pat, she was singing. I never roused enough to open my eyes, but her singing comforted me.

Jason shook his head. "We didn't see her leave, but she's gone."

"She's gone," Janis verified. "I saw her when I got here at dawn. She told me that Mr. Conroy was at the end of his journey, then she went out the door."

"Tim, Jessica, and I were up with her most of the night," Jason said. "We think her name was Sarah."

"Really?" Jessica said. "I never heard her say her name. But she sang hymns to us. And she came in here and sang to Dad, too."

My mind began to clear enough to wonder why they were telling me this, and I asked hesitantly, "So she was good, right? Y'all liked having her here?"

The three of them exchanged glances, then Jason said rather sheepishly, "Okay, Mom, you're going to think we're crazy. But we think she was an angel."

"She sang like one," I said, then nodded, pleased. "Well, good. Then no one will object to having her come back tonight. Y'all have to get some rest."

Again Jason shook his head. "No, Mom, you don't understand. I mean, we think she was an angel. For real."

When Janis voiced her agreement, I looked at Tim. He grinned his impish, Conroy grin and said, "Don't look at me like that, sistah. I swear to God, that was *not* a real woman here last night. None of us saw her arrive. She just appeared, and then she was gone. We didn't get a good look at her because we kept the lights out. But whenever one of us got up to sit with her, she sang hymns and talked to us about God."

"Have y'all been smoking pot?" I asked suspiciously.

"I wish," Tim said. "Seriously, though, there was something weird about the whole thing. That's why we were asking you where she came from."

"I'll find out today," I assured him.

"You won't, wait and see," Jason said emphatically. "Nobody will be able to tell you. She was sent by God."

Although Jay was the most spiritually minded of my sons, that was unusual even for him. I didn't argue because it was obvious that the nurse Sarah, whoever she turned out to be, had brought them comfort. "Then hopefully the Big Guy will send her back tonight," I said.

"I don't think so," Tim said. "She told us that Pat's time was here, and we wouldn't be needing her again."

My face must've revealed my fear because Jason patted my hand and said, "Tell Mom about the bridge, Tim. She'll like that."

Tim looked out the window at the early morning sunbeams dancing on the rippling waters of Battery Creek. "The nurse said that when Pat's time came, we'd know. A bridge would come down from heaven to take him."

I couldn't help but smile. "A bridge, Tim? Not a heavenly host of angels, or a flaming chariot of fire? Either one would suit Pat more than a mundane old bridge. You know he'd want to go out in a blaze of glory."

"Oh, this bridge is different," Jason said. "Sarah said it's made of gold. All of us have to cross it one day."

That was too much, even for me. "To escort us to the streets of gold? C'mon, Jay. You know I'm a firm believer in that sort of stuff, but that's a bit too hokey, don't you think?"

Their expressions told me that they didn't agree, so I let it go. If the nurse brought them that much comfort, I'd get her back that night. But to my surprise, the hospice workers didn't know who'd called her, nor did anyone else I asked. As the day wore on, Pat's breathing became more labored, and hospice sent for Dr. Laffitte. All thoughts of night nurses left my mind as I settled in by Pat's side and took hold of his hand for the last time.

Early that evening Pat left this world for the next, taking his last breath right after darkness fell. He would have appreciated the metaphor. The sunset that day had been a benediction, more spectacular than ever. And a strange thing happened before the sun, in a blaze of fiery pink, sank into the gently flowing creek. For a brief moment of gold, the sun appeared through an opening in a cloud, then a beam of light began to form a bridge directly over the creek, one that led up to our dock. Those of us in the sickroom froze in place and watched in awestruck silence. I've never seen anything quite like it before or since. It's not unusual for a bright ribbon of gold to shimmer on the water during a sunset, but I'd never seen one come directly down from the clouds like that. Finally Tim spoke. "Holy Mother of God. It's turning into a *bridge*? Are you frigging kidding me?"

He turned to stare at me wide-eyed, and I knew we were thinking the same thing: we might never know who sent Sarah, but she had brought us an undeniable message of truth.

Had I not later seen the photos that Jason had the presence of mind to take, I'd always wonder if we had imagined the bridge—if it were some kind of wistful mirage formed by our shared exhaustion and grief. Or maybe the image painted by Sarah lodged in our overwrought minds and caused us to hallucinate. The photos confirm what those of us gathered that evening witnessed, no matter how unlikely it seems. A few minutes before Pat died, a bridge appeared over his beloved creek as if to offer him a passage from this world to the next.

After a death, it's not uncommon for those in the grieving process to block out some memories while others remain etched in our consciousness. No doubt someone smarter than I am can explain the significance of the memories that are lost and the ones that can't be shaken. All I know is, it's happened to me many times. I can close my eyes and relive my sister's memorial service scene by scene, from the mournful sound of the bagpiper playing "Amazing Grace" as we entered the lovely stone church to the hushed silence when we filed out. My father's funeral I recall in minute detail, but I don't remember a thing about my mother's, not one. I'm pretty sure I wore sunglasses the whole time, even though it was an overcast, dismal day in November. My way of blocking it out, I suppose.

The days that followed Pat's death are the same. Some things are painfully burned into my brain and others a jumble of hazy images at best. I'll never forget taking Pat's burial clothes to the funeral home, and the discreet way the funeral home director returned the tote bag I'd brought them in. She didn't meet my eyes when she said gently, "Mrs. Conroy? We won't need his shoes."

What I recall most clearly about the day of the funeral are the times my knees buckled and I had to force myself to go on. One of those times was outside St. Peter's Church, where the family stood in carefully arranged order waiting for the hearse. An honor guard of young Citadel cadets, in full-dress uniforms, lined the walkway to the church for a military salute. It was a crisp, sparkling day in March, mockingly sunny and bright. When the casket was moved to the dais, I heard the sobs of grandchildren behind me but dared not look their way. Had I done so, I would've fallen apart. The whole time, I kept my eyes straight ahead.

Inside the church I followed the coffin alone, the widow's walk, with the family behind me. We were about halfway down the aisle when the organist began playing "The Water Is Wide," and I almost fell to my knees. It was an unexpected, and unexplained, gift. For whatever reason, Pat had wanted a full funeral mass, and of course I complied with the directions he'd dictated. But when I met with the powers that be of the Catholic church, I'd been dismayed by the strict protocol of the Mass. Despite Pat's wishes, I couldn't choose his favorite scripture, hymns, or other deviations to the service. So I'll never know why Pat's entrance into the church was heralded by a song so uniquely associated with him, nor how I managed to stay upright on hearing it.

The burial at St. Helena Memorial Garden is also a merciful blur. In what was a meaningful gesture for him, Pat had selected an isolated cemetery belonging to Brick Baptist Church as his final resting place. The church was built by slaves in 1855 then turned over to them during Reconstruction. It had a close association with Penn Center, one of the first schools for freed slaves, and Pat'd been thrilled to be honored by the historic center a few years back, inducted as an honorary member. Even so, it took some doing for the church brothers and sisters to allow a nonmember, not to mention a renegade Catholic, to be buried among them. I don't know for sure how that came about either. When I heard that it caused a lot of controversy in the congregation, I couldn't help but smile. It was just like Pat to be as controversial in death as he'd been in life. He's the only non–African American buried there, but that wasn't the issue. St. Helena Memorial Garden is a Baptist burial ground. But Pat had gotten it into his head that's where he wanted to be, his final homage to the rich history of his beloved Lowcountry.

I was questioned quite a bit about Pat's choice of burial sites, but as with so many other things about the man, I could never give an explanation that sounded reasonable, even to me. My standard response became, oh, that was just Pat—unpredictable to the very end.

—⁓—

The memory that haunts me most of all is the first time I went to the cemetery alone, a few weeks after the burial. I had to sneak away because there'd been a kindhearted conspiracy among friends and family not to leave me by myself. I'd been too touched by their thoughtfulness to remind them that I *was* alone now—and would be from then on. At some point everyone had to return to their lives, as I had to return to what was left of mine.

That day I had felt a desperate need to go to the cemetery unaccompanied, though I couldn't explain why. I knew Pat wasn't there, of course, but it felt as though his spirit still lingered somewhere among the lonely graves. The last time I'd been there was fraught with drama, as so many Conroy memories are. Bernie had gone with me and brought a bottle of Irish whiskey to pour around the grave. He'd wanted to leave the bottle for Pat to carry with him in the afterlife, but I convinced him that the brethren would disapprove.

I watched as Bernie sprinkled the whiskey around the grave, hoping some of it would make its way to Pat in the afterlife. Then he stood up, put his hands on his hips, and said in a voice that could've been heard halfway to Beaufort, "Goddammit, Pat. You're such a dumbass. What're you doing out here with all these good Christian people?" I grabbed his arm and pulled him to the car, beating a hasty retreat before his big mouth got us into even bigger trouble with the church.

This time, I was finally alone as I made my way to Pat's whiskey-damp plot. Now that the funeral wreaths were gone, visitors had decorated the packed-down mound of dirt with seashells, pinecones, rocks, and a scattering of flowers.

As eager as I'd been to get there, it surprised me that I couldn't do it. My eyes fell on the forlorn grave, and a dagger of pain seared my heart. Instinctively I turned my head away. The family had been right. I had no business coming by myself. I'd thought to sit quietly by the grave and converse with Pat like a properly grieving widow should do. I could tell him about the family's well-meaning conspiracy, and how I hadn't been able to visit him on my own. We'd chuckle together about Bernie's antics, then I'd tell him about the headstone I'd designed, and how I was having the first two lines from *The Prince of Tides* engraved on it.

Instead I turned away so quickly that I stumbled over a nearby tombstone. It occurred to me that I hadn't looked around at the headstones, which was unusual for me. A weird habit of mine, I've been known to pull into a completely unknown cemetery and poke around if the graves looked interesting enough. I could wander for hours, studying the headstones and imagining the stories they held.

That day I found the Memorial Garden as intriguing as any of the older, more historic places I'd visited in the past, even though it's new, an overflow from the cemetery next to the church. It's so wonderfully unpretentious, with no fancy tombstones, benches, or landscaped gardens. The plots are simple but proud and well tended. I noted that many of the stones have photos of the occupants. I studied them and wondered what their lives had been like. The mementos told me a lot: birthday cards and balloons, flags or medals, stuffed animals, a fishing pole. Then I spotted a name I knew, Arabelle Watson. Surely she was the same person Pat had told me about, a woman who'd worked for his mother when they first moved to Beaufort, and had later babysat for his children? Pat adored Mrs. Watson and paid tribute to her by basing a character on her in *The Great Santini*. In the book he called her Arabella Smalls and made her the mother of another memorable character, Toomer. I hurried back to Pat's gravesite to tell him that Mrs. Watson was one of his neighbors now, and she'd keep him company.

Sitting on the dirt by the grave, I hugged my knees close and talked to Pat about Mrs. Watson and some of his other neighbors, figuring he'd want to know who he was keeping company with. Then it hit me how foolish such a notion was. Since Pat never met a stranger, I knew that he'd already introduced himself. And he'd most likely pried their stories out too. He would know everything about his new neighbors by now. I bade him goodbye and left with a lighter heart than when I'd arrived.

As soon as I got home, I went straight to my computer and began to write the introduction to *A Lowcountry Heart*, the posthumous book Random House was bringing out in tribute to Pat, a collection of his unpublished essays. His publisher, Nan Talese, had asked me if I felt up to doing an introduction. Although I'd promised to make the deadline for a fall release, I hadn't written a single word. Whenever I tried, I'd dissolve into tears and turn away.

That afternoon I sat down dry-eyed and wrote until the introduction was finished. I wanted Pat's readers to see him among them again, chatting and stealing their stories at his notoriously lengthy book signings. I told about my trip to the cemetery, and how I imagined Pat acquainting himself with his new neighbors. I could picture him striding jovially among them as though he were running for mayor. He'd greet them like old friends, and before long, they'd be telling him about their lives, things they'd never told anyone else. He would make each of them know that they had a story to tell, just as he'd done with me and so many others. *Tell me your story*, he'd say to them.

I didn't know, nor did I particularly care at that moment, if what I wrote was an appropriate introduction for the book, or if it'd be tossed out as too fanciful. I only knew that writing it brought Pat back to me and gave me solace.

Without reading it over, I saved the document and hit send. Darkness had fallen while I worked, and I got up to turn on a lamp. Drained, emotionally exhausted, I shut down my computer, knowing I was done for the day. Before leaving the room, I stood in the doorway and looked around. *Don't put me here*, he'd said. *You won't be able to come back in without seeing me.* Bird paintings line the walls: Carolina wrens, the great blue heron, even a couple of guinea hens like my father raised. On the far side of the room hang framed posters of my book jackets, six of them now. Bookcases bulge with the books Pat gave me over the years, each of them cherished. My very own writing room, the best gift anyone's ever given me. Turns out he was right after all. Every time I come in, he's here.

AFTERWORD

The first week of October 2016, just seven months after Pat's death, Hurricane Matthew took dead aim at the South Carolina coastline, the first category 5 Atlantic hurricane in almost a decade. I hadn't turned on the TV since Pat died; after seeing the warnings in the paper, though, I kept the Weather Channel on, until a power outage plunged all of Beaufort County into darkness. Various tales circulated about how the power outage happened, with folks saying that the county cut off the power and water before we got hit to avoid live wires and contaminated water, but who knows? The outcome was the same, regardless. No power, no water. In early October, it was still miserably hot in the Lowcountry. It quickly got a whole lot hotter.

In the middle of touring for *A Lowcountry Heart*, I'd returned home between gigs for a few days of rest. The tour had started Labor Day weekend with a tribute to Pat at the Decatur Book Festival; since then I'd driven all around the Southeast visiting the bookstores he frequented. His readers waited in long lines. Many of them, weeping, told me that it wasn't possible—Pat was too big a personality to be gone. Numb, I inscribed their books "In memory of Pat Conroy."

Back home and desperate for a few days to recuperate, I had no intention of evacuating. In the past Pat and I had left whenever it was recommended, though Beaufort hadn't been hit in decades (something about the Atlantic currents and the lay of the land, we heard). The law had changed; when I first moved to South Carolina, evacuation was mandatory. Pat had a scary story he told. After his divorce, he was living alone on Fripp Island when a hurricane threatened, and the governor ordered everyone on the coast out. Pat shrugged it off. After the residents of Fripp had departed, a security officer saw a light on in Pat's house and banged on the door. "You've got to leave, Mr. Conroy," the officer said when Pat stuck his head out. "Mandatory evacuation."

"I ain't going anywhere, pal," Pat said and started to close the door.

The officer stopped him. "Then hang on a minute." He went back to his car to retrieve something, and Pat expected him to return with either a hefty fine or handcuffs. Instead the officer handed him a small object, which Pat looked at, puzzled. On a rectangular piece of plastic fixed with a sturdy string, the officer had written Pat's name and address.

"It's a body tag," the officer explained. "Please tie it around your big toe so we can identify your body. Thank you, sir, and have a good day."

Pat left the island immediately.

Unfortunately for my plans to stay put, the family had heard Pat tell that story one time too many. Everyone, especially my sons, ganged up on me and insisted I leave. Bullheaded as ever, I refused. I'm not even sure why. Forecasters predicted that the hurricane would make landfall in Beaufort early Saturday morning, October 8, most likely a category 3. Hurricane Hugo, which utterly devastated Charleston, had been a category 4, so Matthew would be only slightly less horrific. (Starting in the Caribbean, Matthew would end up leaving behind a path of death and destruction. Before it finally fizzled out in the North Atlantic seas, over six hundred people had died.)

I held out as long as I could, but late Friday afternoon I caved in and drove to Columbia, two hours inland, to stay with Tim and Terrye. Although I went reluctantly and only to keep the family from rioting, it turned out to be a good call. Most of the folks who stayed behind, including Kathy and Bobby Joe, swore later that they'd never do it again. Beaufort got hammered, and from all reports, it was utterly terrifying.

As soon as the roads reopened I drove home and almost wept at what I saw along the way. Beaufort looked like a war zone. Most streets were impassable and the downtown area was flooded. None of the traffic lights worked because power was still out, but only a few people were on the road anyhow. Due to the flooding it would be days before everyone could return. Not far from my neighborhood, I drove past a house I'd often admired for its cozy facade, a charming little cottage with a white picket fence and neat flower beds. A tall leafy tree had fallen and landed right in the middle of the roof, flattening the front porch and splitting the house squarely in two. I prayed that no one had been inside.

Although I knew from Kathy's reports that my house hadn't suffered any major damage in comparison to so many others, I approached it with dread. To prepare me, Kathy had texted some photos. The day after the hurricane hit, she walked several blocks from her house to mine to take pictures; fallen trees, downed lines, and standing waters made driving impossible. The house appeared to be okay, Kathy reported, but the yard was a wreck. She was able to drag enough debris out of the way for me to drive in. I'd have trouble getting to the front porch, she told me; several fallen branches blocked the front steps, and they were too big for Kathy to move. The backyard was even worse, she warned. There, the storm had destroyed two things that I dearly loved: our dock and a beautiful old oak tree by the water.

I thought that I'd braced myself until I drove up and got out of my car. Seeing everything so ravaged hit me like a punch in the gut. I was grateful that the house still stood, and I sent up prayers of thanksgiving as I crawled through the downed branches to get to the door. The real test waited. Inside, I fearfully approached the wall of glass overlooking the back, dread clawing at my throat. Everything from the porch was now in the living room, piled in front of the doors to the outside. After pushing my way through the pile, I stopped at the double doors and blinked in disbelief. For a long moment I just stood there stunned, unable to take it in. This couldn't possibly be the same place I'd left four days ago! Like everything else I saw that day, the storm had turned my backyard into an unrecognizable jungle of scattered debris; mangled trees with hanging, splintered limbs; strewn palm fronds; and washed-up marsh grasses.

But the creek—my beautiful creek! The sweeping, moss-draped oak that had stood so majestically on the bank—the one that had anchored one end of a tattered old hammock to a palmetto—was no longer there. That proud old oak once framed our view of the creek and the marshes, and now it was gone. All that remained was a shockingly blank expanse of sky. The poor tree had been savagely uprooted, as if a giant hand had reached down and tossed it aside like a gardener might toss a dandelion. I flinched at the sight of the oak's massive roots silhouetted against the serene blueness of the late-afternoon sky. The trunk, with its graceful, wide-sweeping limbs, lay half submerged in the water.

My mind kept trying to grasp what I was seeing—or rather, not seeing. In the blink of an eye, a landscape that was once so familiar had been swept away. All that was left of our dock were two stick-like pilings. The pilings rose from the depths of the debris-strewn creek to stand as bleak reminders of our utter helplessness against the mighty rage of nature.

I turned away from the scene so abruptly that I tripped on a clay planter and had to reach for a chair to keep from falling. Not that I would've fallen far with all the stuff in the way. Without taking time to think it through, I grasped the heavy chair with both hands and lugged it to the porch to put it back where it belonged. Oddly enough, despite the devastation of the backyard there was no litter on the porch, not a single twig or leaf. The wind and rain had swept the long, narrow porch as clean as if it had been power washed.

Mindlessly I began to put everything back in place. Although I told myself there was no hurry, and too many other things that needed doing—like throwing everything out of the fridge—I couldn't stop myself. What else can we do with chaos except try to restore order? I carried out the corner shelves, then the furniture—two metal lawn chairs and the little round table and rattan chairs where we sometimes had our evening meals. In addition to the dozen or so clay planters, heavy as tombstones, there were hanging baskets, bird feeders, and wind chimes to replace on their hooks. Any of them could've become a deadly missile in hurricane-force winds.

But on this particular day they weren't going anywhere. As if in mockery of the destruction, it was a dazzling day of blazing blue skies and white wispy clouds. Only the slightest of breezes, warm and soft, stirred the leaves and the swaying moss on the branches that had withstood the storm. Sunbeams sparkled on the rippling waters of the creek, so bright that I had to shade my eyes with my hands. Without the once-stately oak on the creek bank as part of the view, the marshes appeared to go on forever before disappearing into the horizon. The tide was coming in. Occasionally an errant tree branch or palm frond floated by, carried along by the swift current, and I wondered where the bits and pieces of our dock had landed. Had they lodged in the marsh somewhere farther down the river, or had they been carried out to sea?

I stood on the edge of the porch and tried to shake off the dizzying effect of a changed landscape. So much of the familiar was no longer where it should be, which left me disoriented and dazed. Last March my world tilted on its axis, and just as it was beginning to right itself, *this*.

The view of the creek might have been marred, forever altered; but it's still one of such heart-stopping beauty that I stood on the porch as mesmerized as I was the first time I saw it. From the start I loved the majestic oaks with their low, graceful branches, but the Carolina palmettos I regarded with a grudging admiration. It's almost impossible to bring a palm tree down, no matter how strong the wind or how heavy the rain. Palmettos are made of sturdy stuff and resistant to harsh weather conditions. They withstand the ravages of wind and rain by bending, not breaking. We can learn from them.

Just beyond the submerged trunk of the uprooted oak— almost in the dead center of the creek's wide expanse from bank to marsh—an odd movement in the water caught my eye. More debris, I imagined, snagged on something. Then I realized what it was. Once in a blue moon, the incoming tide collides with the outgoing and creates a dramatic vortex of swirling water. In the four years we had lived here I'd seen it only rarely; the first time I yelled for Pat, sure that I'd spotted a whale in Battery Creek. Pat laughed at such a fancy then explained what I was seeing. Just a tidal creek, he said, doing what tidal creeks are supposed to do—bringing in and taking out the tides. Sometimes they meet in the middle and do a little dance. As I watched it that day, the whirlpool began to scatter the sparkling sunbeams over the blue waters, and I wished for my binoculars. But I knew that the unusual convergence of ingoing and outgoing tides would be gone even in the short time it would take me to run inside. So I stayed put, and watched.

It's the way of beauty, I thought. Destruction and devastation are always there, always demanding our attention. The chaos of life makes us forget that sometimes, if we don't get too distracted by the wreckage, the losses and heartbreaks, we're offered a glimpse of something better, maybe even something we can call divine. But we'll miss it if we forget that beauty, like joy, is fleeting and never lasts more than a moment.

A sparkle of sunlight on water, then it's gone.

About the author

2 Meet Cassandra King Conroy

About the book

5 Family Photos from Cassandra

Insights,
Interviews
& More . . .

Meet Cassandra King Conroy

John Wollworth

CASSANDRA KING CONROY is an award-winning author of five novels, a book of nonfiction, numerous short stories, magazine articles, and essays. She has taught creative writing on the college level, conducted corporate writing seminars, and worked as a human-interest reporter.

King's first novel, *Making Waves,* has been through numerous printings since its release in 1995. Her second novel, *New York Times* bestseller *The Sunday Wife*, was a Booksense choice; a Literary Guild and Book of the Month club selection; a *People* Magazine Page Turner of the Week; Books-A-Million President's Pick; Utah's Salt Lake Libraries Reader's Choice Award nominee; and a South Carolina Reader's Circle selection. As one of Book Sense's top discussion selections, *The Sunday Wife* was selected by the Nestlé Corporation for a national campaign to promote reading groups.

The Same Sweet Girls was the national number one Book Sense selection on its release in January 2005; a Book of the Month club and Literary Guild selection; and spent several weeks on both the *New York Times* and *USA Today* bestseller lists.

Both *The Sunday Wife* and *The Same Sweet Girls* were nominated for the Southern Independent Booksellers Alliance's book of the year award. A fourth novel, *Queen of Broken Hearts*, set in King's home state of Alabama and released in March 2007, became a Literary Guild and Book of the Month club selection as well as a SIBA bestseller.

The fifth novel, *Moonrise*, was a SIBA Okra Pick and a Southern Booksellers bestseller, as was her book of nonfiction, released in 2013, *The Same Sweet Girls' Guide to Life.* Most recently, King has been writing for *Coastal Living* and *Southern Living,* as well as contributing ▸

Meet Cassandra King Conroy *(continued)*

essays to various anthologies. Her new book, the memoir *Tell Me a Story: My Life With Pat Conroy*, was released from William Morrow on October 29, 2019.

The widow of acclaimed author Pat Conroy, Cassandra resides in Beaufort, South Carolina, where she is honorary chair of the Pat Conroy Literary Center. ∾

Family Photos
from Cassandra

Please visit my website,
CassandraKingConroy.com,
for photos from my and Pat's life
together. They can be found by clicking
on the *Tell Me a Story* book image.

Wedding Day,
sometime in May 1998

All photos courtesy of the author unless otherwise
indicated

Family Photos from Cassandra *(continued)*

*Pat with Gregg and Mary Smith and friends
on our infamous boat ride of 1997*

When we first met Rick Bragg, at his mama's house in 1997

Megan's wedding, June 1999

*At the Lobster Pot in Maine with Anne Rivers Siddons;
her husband, Heyward; and friends from Charleston*

Family Photos from Cassandra *(continued)*

*Pat with my sister Nancy Jane sharing a
birthday celebration at the Fripp Island house*

Pat holding court with some of his grandkids

*My father decorated by the grandkids
at Christmas celebration*

Me and Pat at the beach (Photo credit: Erica Berger/Corbis)

Family Photos from Cassandra *(continued)*

Pat with siblings Kathy, Tim, Jim, and Mike

My boys with their wives; above, *Jim and Liz;* opposite,
from top to bottom; *Jason and Michelle, Jake and Brenda*

Family Photos from Cassandra *(continued)*

Elton King at one of the fish ponds on the farm

Dancing at Megan's wedding

My boys at the time they first met Pat, who loved teasing them

Family Photos from Cassandra *(continued)*

An abundance of grandkids, Christmas at the beach

Camp Fripp in full swing with a pool of grandkids

Sister Beckie at a Bama game

Pat with his longtime friend Jim Landon in Highlands, North Carolina

Family Photos from Cassandra *(continued)*

What's left of our dock after Hurricane Matthew

Discover great authors,
exclusive offers, and more
at hc.com.